David Davis is a man of God who, more than anyone else, is redigging the well of Elijah on Mount Carmel and apostolically planting ministries in the north of Israel. His vision of Jews and Arabs worshipping together as "one new man" is God's heart and strategy to release great blessing in the midst of the Earth (Isaiah 19:23-15).

— Tom Hess, Director
Jerusalem House of Prayer for All Nations
Mountof Olives, Jerusalem

The Elijah Legacy presents an excellent and thorough study of the times, life and ministry of Elijah the prophet as it relates to the situation in the world today and the ministry of the Spirit-filled church. David and Karen Davis have for decades been active in ministry to Jews and Arabs on Mount Carmel, and have also ministered extensively to Chinese-speaking churches in the Far East and US. Thus they have a keen understanding of the work of the enemy in the world today, as well as the calling upon the Church.

Elijah is a major figure in the Bible, both in the Old and New Testaments, and many books have been written and many sermons have been preached about this fascinating man. But *The Elijah Legacy,* with its revealing insight into the spiritual forces at work in the world we live in and the ministry we are called to, makes this all very real and relevant to us. I highly recommend this excellent book.

— Pastor Dennis Balcombe
Founder, Revival Chinese Ministries International (RCMI)
Hong Kong, China

I consider David Davis to be one of my closest friends. I remember the first time I heard him speak on Mount Carmel. It was as if my soul was knit to his, just as Jonathan's soul was knit to David of old. David was preaching on Elijah the prophet and the precious anointing upon his life was unmistakably evident and my heart was stirred in a very significant way. Although we don't get to see one another often, being in two very different parts of the globe, there is such a deep love and admiration in my heart for the man whom I know is after God's own heart. *The Elijah Legacy* is a book for the generation of voices being prepared right now in the wilderness, called to prepare the way of the Lord. It is a powerful word for us today.

— Rev Yang Tuck Yoong
Senior Pastor
Cornerstone Community Church, Singapore

David Davis has become a very special friend to me. In his presence you feel the love of God and the fire of God is burning when he preaches. His congregation on Mt. Carmel is not only located in this special place, but the services there are always an experience as the Holy Spirit moves in a multitude of ways.

In his book *The Elijah Legacy* David Davis has written a compelling description of the ministry of Elijah which challenges us to break out from normal Christianity and to become aware of our entrusted responsibility. Not only is Israel at the forefront of history, but it is now time for us to take a stand and pick up the mantle of Elijah.

— Pastor Daniel Mueller
Missionswerke Karlsruhe, Germany

THE
ELIJAH
LEGACY

THE LIFE AND TIMES OF ELIJAH—
THE PROPHETIC SIGNIFICANCE FOR ISRAEL,
ISLAM, AND THE CHURCH IN THE LAST DAYS

DAVID DAVIS

BRIDGE
LOGOS
FOUNDATION

Alachua, Florida 32615

Bridge-Logos
Alachua, FL 32615 USA

The Elijah Legacy
by David Davis

Edited by Beverlee J. Chadwick

Copyright ©2009 by Bridge-Logos

Printed in the United States of America.

Library of Congress Catalog Card Number: 2009939905
International Standard Book Number 978-0-88270-920-8

G163.316.N.m911.35230

Dedication

This book is dedicated to the faithful spiritual sons and daughters the Lord has given us on Mount Carmel. May they pick up the cloak of the Elijah legacy and fulfill God's highest destiny for their lives.

ACKNOWLEDGEMENTS

Special thanks to Jenny Thomson,
who went the extra mile typing the manuscript
in its various stages of development,
and to Joy Greig,
who offered insightful and helpful
editorial comments.

CONTENTS

PREFACE TO THE 2010 EDITION

We live in a world which is very different from that of 2003, when *The Elijah Legacy* was first written and published. Here in the Middle East, Ariel Sharon, Yasser Arafat, Saddam Hussein, and George W. Bush are no longer on the scene. Barak Hussein Obama and Mahmoud Ahmadinejad were unknowns six years ago. Therefore in this new edition I have updated the last two chapters, which deal specifically with Islam, Israel, and the Lord's body in these end-times.

There is now a dramatic acceleration of world events. In 1991, we had a three minute warning before Saddam Hussein's missiles hit Haifa. In 2006, Hizballah's missiles and rockets exploded on Mount Carmel sixty seconds after they were launched from Lebanon.

In April 2008, Karen and I participated in an "Israel and The End Times" conference at Times Square Church in New York City. One morning, I was watching the ice-skaters at Rockefeller Center where a young television actor was doing a TV interview outside the NBC building. People were running to see him. Then I noticed the news being flashed in neon lights right above the excited crowd: *"Iran completes 300 new centrifuges for its nuclear program."* No one in the scene below even noticed the news headline.

I believe America and much of the West are asleep. The global economic meltdown is shaking the foundations of the prosperous Western world, and the handwriting is on the wall in neon lights, warning us of future shakings yet to come.

I continue to receive numerous responses from people in different nations concerning *The Elijah Legacy*. I believe its premise and principles are even more valid today. Now more than ever we need an expanding end-time Elijah ministry of men and women who will kneel to pick up the mantle and mandate of Elijah and all that it represents. That is what this book is about.

David Davis
Mount Carmel, Israel
2010

FOREWORD

I believe with deep conviction that the Holy Spirit has inspired our brother David Davis to write this book in answer to his prayer, and the prayers of all the saints who are burdened by the desperate need for Jesus to release the Elijah legacy now. IT'S TIME! David writes by revelation through the intense and deep dealings of God in his life in the very place on Mount Carmel where Elijah the prophet once stood and cried out from the very depth of his being by the anointing of God that must have burned like an intense fire within him: "Lord God of Abraham, Isaac and Israel, let it be known this day that you are God in Israel.... Hear me, O Lord, hear me, that this people may know that you are the Lord God, and that you have turned their hearts back to you again." O may this cry be heard once again throughout the nation of Israel and all the nations-even to the ends of the Earth. May the God of Elijah answer by fire.

NOEL MANN
Senior Pastor,
Zion Christian Ministries
Brisbane, Australia

VISITATION ON
MOUNT CARMEL

I stood on the northernmost promontory of Mount Carmel and looked out over the Mediterranean Sea. My two weeks in Israel were almost over. One quick stop at Caesarea and then I would fly back to the States. My heart was full of the deep things the Lord had been speaking to me.

As I looked across beautiful Haifa Bay and up the Mediterranean coast to Lebanon, I thought of how Elijah, Jesus and Paul had come this way taking the message of salvation from Israel to the nations. I had been reading about Elijah and what had happened on this mountain, and I asked the Lord to speak to me again.

After a while I went back to my rented car. For two weeks I hadn't heard or seen any news reports. So, as I started to drive I turned on the car radio to see if I could find some English language news. Suddenly a deep, rich baritone voice came booming through the radio singing, "It is finished." A full choir joined in singing, "It is finished!" "It is finished!" The presence of God filled the car as I began to experience a visitation of the Holy Spirit. I couldn't drive and had to pull over to the side of the road. There on Mount Carmel I began to weep uncontrollably. It was as if a heavenly choir was in the car singing, "It is finished!" I wept and wept. I kept thanking Jesus for what He had done for me. Old things deep inside the core of my being were breaking up and being removed by the Spirit of God. He kept coming in waves. When I didn't think I could take anymore, He would wait. Then His love would wash over me again. I was afraid to move. Great sobs welled up from within me, as if a deep purging was taking place. All He said was, "It is finished!" He had answered my prayer and was speaking to me.

After a time the song faded and only static came from the radio. I turned it off and sat in His silence. The weeping subsided, then began to rise up again. Time appeared to have stopped. I seemed to be having some kind of heart transplant. I looked around at Mount Carmel. Israel and Carmel were being implanted into my spirit. "He will tell you things to come." I didn't know the specifics—all I knew was the old life was "finished."

As I began to recover I realized that I felt at home there. I did not know that one day I would live in an old villa only a few hundred meters down the mountain from where God had just invaded my car and me. The building He would give us on Carmel would be filled with Jewish and Arab drug addicts. A congregation of Arabs and Jews would be born there. Only God knew that I would soon marry a Jewish woman and together we would immigrate to Israel—that we would live on Mount Carmel and witness biblical prophecy being fulfilled as we watched thousands of Russian Jews sail into Haifa. I did not know then that Patriot missiles would be fired at Iraqi scuds a few meters from where I was now parked while Karen and I would be running for our bomb shelter. One day the Lord would bless us with two foster sons who would attend school directly across the street from where I now sat in a rental car.

The visitation ended, but I was undone. The Holy One of Israel had met me on Mount Carmel, and I knew that I would be back.

THE ELIJAH AND ELISHA MODELS

After serving the Lord for over twelve years on Mount Carmel, I have come to understand the ministries of Elijah and Elisha as models for an end-time, trans-generational company of Jews and Gentiles.

I believe they prophetically represent the "one new man" forerunner ministry the Lord is now raising up in Israel and the nations at the end of the age. The Old Testament canon concludes with a prophecy about our day: "Behold, I will send you Elijah the prophet before the coming of the great and dreadful day of the LORD" (Malachi 4:5). This is a last days prophecy pointing toward an Elijah company who will "turn the hearts of the children to their fathers" (v. 6). The "children" can also refer to the Church turning their hearts and understanding to "their fathers"—restored Israel, and the Jewish heritage of our faith.

The purpose of this book is to testify to what God is doing now, and is about to do, on Mount Carmel and in Israel. The book is also an examination of the life and legacy of Elijah, the man, the ministry. The price he paid, and his commitment and courage continue to challenge me and cause me to long to walk like him. It is my hope that you, too, will be provoked by the examples of Elijah and Elisha, and to cry out for the fire of God to fall upon your heart, your community and nation. Jesus paid a terrible price to make the Elijah legacy available to us. Will we pay the price to receive this mantle of our inheritance?

THIS IS THE CALL FROM CARMEL.

PROPHETIC REVELATION

I spent a quarter of a century in the American university system. At one time or another I was a student, graduate student, graduate assistant, assistant professor, associate professor, tenured full professor, and chairman. I received a bachelor's degree, a Master of Arts, and finally became a Doctor of Philosophy. The chief god in the pantheon of the twentieth century American university system was secular humanism—"man is the measure of all things."

The century of humanism produced many of the world's greatest technological and scientific advances. Automobiles, airplanes, astronauts, atomic bombs, medical breakthroughs, radio, film, television, and personal computers radically changed our world. The twentieth century also produced two world wars and the Holocaust. Many more millions died in wars in the century of enlightened humanism than in any other. The worship of the creature rather than the Creator also ushered in an unprecedented moral landslide. Pillars of western Judeo-Christian society—such as marriage and family—were shattered by seismic shock effects from the onslaught of humanism in the second half of the twentieth century. Europe and Scandinavia today have entered what has been termed the "post-Christian" era, with brash young America not far behind.

FROM INFORMATION TO REVELATION

My historian father collected newspapers and magazines until the day he died. With a pencil he made marks, like underscoring and exclamation points, in many articles which he read and kept. He refused to let us throw out the growing piles of newspapers. To no avail, I tried quoting Mark Twain to him: "There is nothing more useless than yesterday's newspaper." My father had become obsessive about acquiring more information. Today, through computers and the information super-highway, information can be stored and studied as in no previous generation. After being an academic scribe for so many years I have come to realize that we don't need more information, rather we need revelation. I have become almost obsessive about not keeping old newspapers.

PROPHETIC VISION

"Where there is no revelation the people cast off restraint" (Proverb 29:18). Revelation means "prophetic vision." (See margin of NKJV.) Revelation only results from a consistent intimate fellowship with God. Paul prayed for the Church that we would receive revelation, or "all wisdom and spiritual understanding" (Colossians 1:9). The difference between gathering information and receiving divine revelation is of the utmost importance. Without prophetic vision we will be lost in a spiritual wilderness or "perish" (KJV). To be "prophetic" simply means to understand what is in God's heart now-the hour in which we live.

Our vision needs to be continually updated with God's purposes. What is God saying now? The New Testament consistently teaches that the fundamental nature of life in the Spirit involves a disclosure of spiritual "mysteries" that cannot be fully comprehended by the human intellect. Prophetic revelation is the antithesis of humanism. God's mysteries can only be spiritually discerned, or revealed by the Spirit. For instance, Jesus called the Kingdom of God "the mystery" (Mark 4:11). His Kingdom was being revealed to His disciples. A biblical mystery is a secret or hidden truth that can only be known by revelation. Paul wrote of the "mystery of God" (Colossians 2:2), as well as the mystery of the Church (Ephesians 3:3), and the mystery of Israel (Romans 11:25).

It has been said that the longest distance between two points is the distance between the head and the heart. In these last days we desperately need to move from information to revelation—or from the preconceived to the prophetic.

PROPHECY BEING FULFILLED

Here are some recently fulfilled prophetic promises to Israel. God prophesied that He would bring His people back to Israel from the "north country" in a "great throng" (Jeremiah 31:8). He said He was going to gather them so that they would enter into the New Covenant with Him (v. 31-34). In other words, they have an appointment with Jesus on the mountains of Israel.

Since the collapse of the former Soviet Union, when Jews were finally allowed to emigrate, almost one million Russian-speaking immigrants have joined a nation of five million Jews. Thousands have arrived by boat at the Haifa port here on Mount Carmel. Downtown Haifa sounds like Moscow or Kiev. These new immigrants are turning to Jesus in unprecedented numbers, fulfilling unknowingly what was prophesied thousands of years ago. Now almost half the body of Messiah in Israel (42% in the only study available) are Russian-speaking immigrants. Two congregations in the land almost closed their doors in the early 90s. Today over 80% or more of their members are from the former Soviet Union.

The number of Messianic groups in Israel has more than tripled in the decade since mass Soviet immigration began. At the end of the 1980s, twenty-four Messianic groups existed.

By the turn of the new millennium there were more than eighty Messianic groups, including formal congregations and less formal "house groups."

It doesn't take a prophet to see that God's handwriting was on that symbol of communism the Berlin Wall. He simply knocked the wall down, and began sending His people home. At the same time He has opened the former Soviet Union to the gospel and a massive revival. In a nation where God was declared dead, He is very much alive.

THE LAST EXODUS WILL SURPASS THE FIRST

This isn't all of the prophetic picture by any means. This last exodus will exceed the first one, the national deliverance of the Jewish people from Egypt. Jeremiah prophesied about the approaching moment in which we are living: "Therefore, behold, the days are coming," says the LORD, "that they shall no longer say, 'As the LORD lives who brought up the children of Israel from the land of Egypt,' but, 'As the LORD lives who brought up the descendants of the house of Israel from the north country and all countries where I have driven them. And they shall dwell in their own land'" (Jeremiah 23:7-8). The people of Israel will no longer look on the first exodus as their greatest national miracle. They will see that this final ingathering far surpasses it! Why? Because millions have an appointment with their Messiah in the land of their inheritance. He said it, and it is happening now.

For those of us who are laboring in His vineyard on Mount Carmel, we have very specific assurances of what the Lord is doing and is going to do here. Micah prophesied it clearly: "Shepherd Your people with Your staff, the flock of Your heritage, who dwell alone in a woodland in the midst of Carmel.... As in the days when you came out of Egypt, I will show them wonders. The nations shall see and be ashamed of all their might" (Micah 7:14-16). This is happening now. And so much more awaits us regarding the prophetic Word of God.

DRY BONES

Of course Satan knows all this as well. That is why, here in Israel, we are in the midst of such an unrelenting onslaught of physical and spiritual warfare. On Mount Carmel we not only contend with the religious spirits of Rabbinic Judaism, nominal Christianity, and Islam, but there are also New Age cults all over God's mountain, as in the days of Elijah. The most famous landmark of Haifa is the golden domed temple of the Baha'i, which overlooks the Haifa port and faces the tomb of their dead false prophet.

The lost sheep of the house of Israel need to be confronted with the power of God as in the days of Elijah. As the Lord pours out His Spirit here, as has been prophesied, we will see "life from the dead." This time it won't be a single boy like the ones Elijah or Elisha raised from the dead. This revival will include a whole valley full of dry bones. "For if their [the Jews] being cast away is the reconciling of the world, what will their acceptance be but life from the dead?" (Romans. 11:15).

In 2001-2002, we saw over two hundred (mostly Jewish people) pray to receive the Lord mainly through the "Jesus" film project. Another one hundred Lebanese, who fled their homes when Israeli troops pulled out of Lebanon in May 2000, have also accepted Jesus, leading us to plant a Lebanese congregation.

There have been several dramatic healings among two Galilee Arab congregations, drawing another three hundred to accept Jesus. Some of them are Muslims.

We have witnessed Arab and Jewish drug addicts and alcoholics set free by the power of God. But we desperately need more of His power and His love in order to reach our people. We know it is going to happen. Why? Because God said it.

THE METHODOLOGY OF "MIDRASH"

There is an ancient Jewish concept of understanding biblical prophecy which is called *midrash*. The word comes from a root which means "to search." Hebrew writers and commentators understood and applied four basic modes of interpretation to Scripture and biblical prophecy. These include:

(1) "Simple"—plain, literal sense of the text. Many modern humanistic scholars consider this grammatical-historical exegesis as the only valid interpretation of Scripture.

(2) "Hint"—a word, phrase, or some other element in the text that hints at things of which the Bible writer was not aware,

which are not obviously conveyed by the "simple" meaning.

(3) "Search"—an allegorical application of the text.

(4) "Secret"—a hidden meaning.

In Hebrew exegesis, these four methods of examining a portion of Scripture are called *pardes*, which is an acronym formed from the Hebrew letters for the word "orchard." In other words, there can be an "orchard" or "trees" of multiple meanings in a particular passage of Scripture.

Midrash is a Hebrew methodology of understanding prophecy as a pattern which is in a process of recapitulation moving toward an ultimate fulfillment. Prophecy is not only specific ("simple") prediction, but also contains "hints" and a "search" for deeper meaning. Therefore, there are often multiple fulfillments of a single prophecy. Initial and intermediate fulfillments can be a type of foreshadowing revealing something about a final fulfillment.

Here is a specific example of a biblical prophecy with more than one meaning. Hosea 11:1 says: "When Israel was a child, I loved him, and out of Egypt I called My son." The prophecy is obviously about God's fatherly love for the people of Israel, and refers to their deliverance from Egypt. However, in Matthew chapter 2, the Spirit-inspired text records how Joseph and Mary took the young Jesus and fled from King Herod into Egypt. Matthew then applied the Hebrew methodology of *midrash*. He wrote that Jesus stayed in Egypt "until the death of Herod, that it might be fulfilled which was spoken by the Lord through the prophet, saying, 'Out of Egypt I called My Son'" (Matthew 2:15). The prophecy was first fulfilled when God literally brought His people out of Egypt. There was a second fulfillment of the same prophecy when the young Jesus left Egypt and returned to Israel. Hosea's prophecy is an historical reference to Israel's physical redemption from Egypt. It is also a prophecy referring to the Messiah Jesus, who provides spiritual redemption from the bondage of sin and death. The authors of the New Testament and Jesus himself often employed the methodology of *midrash* in their teachings. (For a more in-depth description of the principles of midrashic interpretation of Scripture, see David H. Stern, *Jewish New Testament*, p.11-14.)

"ELIJAH IS COMING FIRST"

In our present circumstances, in northern Israel, we are witnesses of a wonderful prophecy for Galilee which is being progressively fulfilled today. Isaiah 9:1-4 is a specific prophecy about "Galilee of the Gentiles." Matthew also wrote about Galilee. After Herod put John the Baptist in prison, Jesus "departed to Galilee ... that it might be fulfilled which was spoken by Isaiah the prophet: 'The people who sit in darkness have seen a great light, and upon those who sat in the region and shadow of death light has dawned'" (Matthew 4:12-16).

This was the initial fulfillment of Isaiah's prophecy. However, in the years 2000 and 2001 alone, over five hundred Jews and Arabs accepted Jesus in Galilee. The light of Jesus has indeed dawned, but is continuing to get brighter. The prophecy is continuing to be fulfilled.

The next verse of the Isaiah prophecy proclaims that God "multiplied the nation and increased its joy; they rejoice before You according to the joy of harvest" (Isaiah 9:3). This verse is also being fulfilled today. God has "multiplied" the people of northern Israel with thousands of Russian-speaking immigrants and Lebanese refugees together with native-born Jews, Arab Christians, and Muslims. Simply put, now is a *kairos* ("set time") moment of harvest in Galilee and on Carmel. And there will be an even greater fulfillment, as we shall see in Chapter 15.

PURPOSE

This book is in part an attempt to apply this multiple level of midrashic understanding to the prophecies, events, and characters of Elijah's ministry. What happened then was a foreshadowing of what God is doing, and is about to do, here in Galilee and on Mount Carmel. Elisha and "the sons of the prophets," and Ahab and Jezebel carry deep meaning for us to glean today. By examining, understanding, and embracing the Elijah legacy, we may be personally challenged and changed. We may also discover layers of hidden meaning concerning the significance of Israel, and the Church in the last days. I believe the legacy of Elijah points to a restoration of Israel and the Church which is yet to be fulfilled.

The last appearance of the prophet Elijah was on a mountaintop in Galilee at the Transfiguration of Jesus. This took place after the death of John the Baptist who had come "in the spirit and power of Elijah." It was then that the greatest Prophet said these remarkable words: "Indeed, Elijah is coming first and will restore all things" (Matthew 17:11).

THE LIFE AND LEGACY OF ELIJAH POINTS TO AN END-TIME RESTORATION WHOSE TIME HAS COME.

A ONE MAN STAND

It was the darkest of times in northern Israel. For half a century six wicked kings had fought for power. Solomon, David's son, had started out with such great promise. His kingdom was unsurpassed in glory and fame. But as an old man Solomon "loved many foreign women." The worm of compromise that had eaten into his character and commitment to the God of his father finally emerged for all to see. He had never dealt with his sensuality and lust for young women. A harem of a thousand wives and concubines had stolen his heart from his God. He did not fully follow the Lord, as had his father David, and the divided heart of the king led to division in his kingdom. The result of Solomon's apostasy was bloody civil war in Israel.

GOLDEN CALVES

Jeroboam led the ten northern tribes out of the confederacy and covenant with Judah and Benjamin. He replaced the temple worship in Jerusalem with a counterfeit. At Bethel and Dan in northern Israel he built two golden calves. The northern tribe exchanged their God for heathen idolatry. Jeroboam cried: "Here are your gods, O Israel!" (1 Kings 12:28). The usurping king installed a corrupt leadership. Whoever wished to be a priest presided over false worship on the high places of Samaria, Galilee and Mount Carmel. Israel was plunged into unparalleled degradation and degeneracy. "The sin of Jeroboam" ushered in an era of immorality, perversity, and bloodshed. The pages of the history of this time are stained with the blood of brothers, drunkenness, debauchery and murder.

JEZEBEL'S REIGN OF TERROR

The tide of evil continued to rise through the ungodly reigns of five kings and reached its crest in the twenty-two-year reign of another usurper named Omri. This king "did worse than all who were before him" (1 Kings 16:30). He had a son who was to outdo even his father in wickedness—his son's name was Ahab. The Bible records that the sins of Jeroboam were trivial compared to what Ahab would do. He went to Sidon (Lebanon today), the occult center of the Middle East at the time. There he married the daughter of Ethbaal ("man of Baal"), the king-priest who presided over a demonic religion. The daughter's name was Jezebel. Ahab brought his princess-bride and her pagan religion into his court in Israel. Together they built a temple to Baal ("owner") where they worshipped and served the Canaanite demon-god of nature, fertility (sex), and reproduction. They ushered into northern Israel a flood of falsehood and filth which surpassed all previous idolatry.

Metal images of Baal were forged and set up on Mount Carmel and on all the mountains of Israel. Fires would be stoked in the open bellies of the metal idols. The priests of Baal would then take the first-born sons from Israelite women and throw the infants into the fire in the stomach of the idol. As the mother screamed in horror, the false prophets of Baal would dance, shriek, bang on musical instruments, cut themselves with knives and cry out to their god. These altars to Baal were built on the high places of Galilee. Alongside child sacrifice, organized ritual prostitution and homosexuality were sanctioned and encouraged. "Asherim," fertility poles, were set up in homage to Asherah, the wife of Baal in Canaanite mythology. The men of Israel consorted with prostitutes and homosexuals in acts of consecration to Baal in drunken orgies on the mountains of Israel.

Jezebel instituted a reign of terror as she began to systematically murder the true prophets of God. The wave of evil begun by Solomon fifty years earlier had reached its crest. A weak king seduced by an ambitious harlot reigned in Israel. "Ahab did more to provoke the Lord God of Israel to anger than all the kings of Israel who were before him" (1 Kings 16:30). The seventh (seven is the number of completion) king was the worst. Governmental establishment, endorsement and participation in gross sin are always a flash point for God's judgment. God had seen enough. The Holy One of Israel will only endure so much persistent unfaithfulness before He acts. The darkest hour of the night is just before the dawn. Israel had reached such an hour. There was a faint glimmer on the horizon. Jehovah had found a man to stand with Him.

A MAN ON A MISSION

What a scene we have before us! King Ahab, the resplendent image of materialism and prosperity, representing civil and religious power, is sitting on his throne in his ivory palace surrounded by his sycophants. Into this gaudy scene a lone figure suddenly appears. He is a rugged man from the wild mountains of Gilead ("rough stone witness"). This mountain man from the edge of the desert wears a leather belt and a rough short cloak is thrown over his shoulders. It is the mantle of a prophet. His name is Elijah ("Jehovah is my God"). He seems to explode into the world of Ahab. What a power encounter of opposing forces! Elijah has a word for a decadent nation from the Lord God of Israel. This prophet was a man on a mission with the power of a word not his own.

And what was God's word to the backslidden king and nation? "Drought!" A dreaded word to a people perched precariously on a narrow strip of dry land between the Mediterranean Sea and the desert. The curse of an "iron heaven and bronze earth" was promised in the Torah for those who persistently break God's holy covenant. (See Leviticus 26:19 and Deuteronomy 28:23.) God's man looks Ahab in the face and pronounces God's word: "As the LORD God of Israel lives, before whom I stand, there shall be no dew nor rain these years, except at my word" (1 Kings 17:1).

We learn much about this startling man from his first words. First, he has a living relationship with the living God. He knows the Lord God of Israel. He has been with Him. The nation has changed its gods, but not this man. "The LORD God of Israel lives," even in the midst of a people walking in deep darkness. Next, this man can publicly proclaim that he stands before Jehovah. He is in right standing with the Creator of the universe. The Hebrew word that he uses here for "stand" means that he "dwells, abides, continues and is sustained, nourished and established," by his God. He means that he is employed by the God of Israel. He is His servant and spokesman. Elijah is blameless before the Holy One of Israel, a vessel fit for the Master's use. Oh, the example of Elijah! The courage! The commitment! A heart as God's own heart. God had found His man.

THE DAYS OF ELIJAH

Are the days of Elijah so much different from our own? We shudder at child sacrifice. Is a saline abortion any different? The infant is injected with a salt solution that causes the tiny victim to explode. The abortion doctor then has to fish all the pieces from the mother's womb. Can God bless a government or nation that legitimizes and condones partial birth abortion? Is murdering a baby by crushing its skull as it is being born worse than pagan child sacrifice to Baal? Today nations harvest and sell aborted baby parts, like brains and skin, to make cosmetics.

That is why our congregation sponsored the first Pro-Life work in northern Israel, helping to expose women to the truth about abortion and assisting them in the option to keep their babies. Israel has one of the highest abortion rates in the world. In fact, many nations are participating in an abortion holocaust.

Our new worship center is on the highest point of Mount Carmel, where it is believed that child sacrifices were once performed. Now we celebrate the Lord's Supper there and have dedicated the area to Jesus. Also now on this property is our Or HaCarmel ("Light of Carmel") women's shelter, where Jewish and Arab women in crisis, as well as refugee mothers and children from Africa are taken in.

Perhaps we shake our heads at the rampant sexual immorality in Ahab's world. But aren't we much worse? MTV pronounces that their goal is to "steal your children." Then they proceed to poison a generation of young people all over the world with ungodly filth, profanity, violence and blasphemy. "There is a generation that curses its father, and does not bless its mother" (Proverbs 30:11). Eight-year-olds daily imbibe hours of trash that would horrify our parents. We inhabit a world of moral madness where one out of three American children are born out of wedlock. We are a fatherless generation where half the world's children know no father. The holy covenant of marriage and the family are under savage attack. Alternate lifestyles are given equal moral value. This is the era of pornography, as our world is inundated with everything from TV porn, to Internet porn, to international kiddie porn. Sex, materialism, self, and the occult were the idols of the Jezebel invasion. They are still ours today. There are new-age cults all over the high places of Galilee.

We wonder how Ahab could import satanic, occult practices into Israel, yet Hollywood's six biggest box office film hits of 1999 all shared satanic themes. In 1995, there was an uproar in America over one lesbian character on prime time TV. Four years later there were more than thirty homosexual characters on prime time "family hour" TV. The "Fashion Channel" is overtly pornographic, and now there will be a "Gay Channel." One recent prime-time TV series began with a high school girl performing oral sex on a fellow student in order to get his vote in a student election. We hope that President and Mrs. Bush (born-again believers) cleansed the White House with prayer before they moved in.

Yes, we are still living in the days of Elijah. The prophet had a word for Israel in one of its darkest hours. In these last days we certainly need a sure prophetic word. Do we see the signs of the times?

When Karen and I were in the States in August 2000, we were shocked at the rampant growth of gross materialism at the end of the age of the Clintons. Every airplane and coffee shop digitally displayed the up-to-the-second stock reports. You could not avoid it. It was the overt worship of the god of mammon. We cannot serve God and mammon. I asked, "How long will God put up with this?"

As the world watched the horrifying events of September 11 unfold in real time, there were no digital displays of stock reports on TV sets that day. The symbols of American prosperity were being destroyed before the eyes of the world. Even after the devastation of September 11, prophetic voices are still muddled, unclear, and double minded. Three weeks later, we were ministering in a shaken Singapore. A young lady told me she had just returned from a prophetic conference in the States. I asked her what was the word of the Lord from the prophets? She said it was unclear—either revival or judgment. The true prophetic voice is never unclear. "For if the trumpet makes an uncertain sound, who will prepare for battle?" (1 Corinthians 14:8).

SCORPIONS AND LOCUSTS

On September 8, 2001, I warned our congregation that the "bottomless pit" of lies and destruction described in Revelation 9:1-11 had been opened. The scorpions of satanic anti-Semitism were being released in unparalleled measure through the BBC, CNN, world media, and the European Union. The UN Conference on Racism in South Africa was just ending. The conference became an international anti-Semitic "Israel-bashing" event. It was a frightening flashback to Germany of the 1930s. All the old lies about the Jews were publicly rehearsed. The next day we experienced "Bloody Sunday" in Israel—three terrorist attacks in one day. An Israeli Muslim from Galilee who had two wives and two families blew himself up at a train station north of Haifa. Three dead, twenty-six maimed and wounded was the murderous toll in lives. But the horror of "Bloody Sunday" was about to be eclipsed less than forty-eight hours later by the mass murder of thousands in New York City and Washington on "Black Tuesday" by Islamic "locusts." Those who support barbaric mass murder of innocent people danced and cheered in the streets of Baghdad, Beirut, Gaza, and East Jerusalem.

On November 30, 2001, I taught on the demonic roots and history of Islam, in our Mount Carmel School of Ministry. The message was entitled: "The Rise and Fall of Islam." (See Chapter 14.) That night a young Indonesian pastor attending our school received an e-mail from home. Muslim *jihad* (holy war against non-Muslims, especially Christians and Jews) terrorists were burning the villages near the pastor's hometown, where 63,000 Christians had fled for refuge. The Muslims were coming with armored personnel carriers and automatic weapons against the defenseless Christians. Muslims had declared a "Bloody Christmas" in Indonesia.

The next evening three Muslim terrorist bombs ripped through the main pedestrian mall and coffee shops of central Jerusalem killing ten teenagers and wounding 180. Twelve hours later in Haifa on Mount Carmel, a Muslim blew himself up in a crowded bus. Fifteen more Israelis were murdered and 30 more were in the hospital.

A DEFINING HOUR

This is a defining hour for the Church of Jesus Christ. I am sure there are many unheralded prophets or pastors who realize that we are in a Revelation 9 season of end-time lies and deception, and that a murderous blood lust has been unleashed against the people and purposes of God. The Laodicean church needs to wake up before it is too late. "Anoint your eyes with eye salve, that you may see" (Revelation 3:18). We need prophetic vision. We have received a wake-up call. Have we simply pressed the snooze button and rolled over again?

Our atmosphere is darkened with the smoke of deception, as the poisonous lies of scorpions spread across the land. The locusts of destruction have been loosed from the bottomless pit. The hell of Muslim terrorism litters the streets of Tel Aviv, Jerusalem, Haifa and New York with human body parts for the world to witness. "One woe is past. Behold, still two more woes are coming after these" (Revelation 9:12). The handwriting is on the wall. Can we read it? It is going to get much worse.

I am told that if you put a frog into a pan of water and gradually turn up the heat, the frog will die without noticing. We have become so accustomed to filth we hardly notice the stench. Yes, the days of Elijah are still with us, only worse. That is why we need "Elijah companies" to take a stand with Jesus at this defining hour. "He chose us in Him before the foundation of the world, that we should be holy and blameless before Him in love" (Ephesians 1:4). Elijah was in right standing with the Holy One of Israel. This is the beginning of the Elijah legacy.

HIDE YOURSELF

After the dramatic encounter with King Ahab, the word was out about the prophet Elijah. He was famous overnight because his prophecy came true. There was no rain, not even dew, and severe famine gripped the land. Suddenly prosperity and plenty had turned to thirst and hunger.

And what of the newly-renowned prophet whose name was upon everyone's lips? Was he busy somewhere using his newfound fame to build a worldwide ministry on the Internet with a fancy website? God had radically different plans for His servant: "Get away from here and turn eastward, and hide by the Brook Cherith, which flows into the Jordan" (1 Kings 17:3). The Lord told Elijah to leave the place of prominence, publicity, and exposure, and to return to his place of seclusion. There he was to hide himself from the world of Ahab.

The Lord used a word here that means "to hide in the secret place of repair." The prophet had fulfilled his first divine commission, and now he was to shut in with God. He was given very specific orders. The Brook Cherith was to be his home. "Cherith" is a covenant word which means to "cut off," be separated from the world system and consecrated, or set apart for God. The word for "brook" in Hebrew is *nachal*. It is a wadi, or small narrow valley which is to be occupied as an inheritance. A nachal is a little stream or trickling brook in the dry summer months, but suddenly becomes a torrent bursting its banks in the rainy winter months.

Elijah was to "fill up" at the brook before he would be released again. The prophet was being told to go on an extended retreat with his Lord in preparation for his next assignment. He was to cut himself off from distractions and temptation, and rest in sweet communion with his God. The prophet obeyed and returned to his secret place.

BY THE BROOK

Rivers in the Bible often represent the moving of the Holy Spirit. This brook was moving, not static. It was a clear and refreshing mountain stream that flowed into the Jordan River. "Jordan" means "to go down." The Jordan is the place of humility and dependence on God, which represents death to the self-life. The Lord is always telling us to get to the place of cutting off, of separation from self and ego. This is the word of the Lord to all His servants, "Hide yourself in Me."

How was the Lord to sustain His prophet? "You shall drink from the brook, and I have commanded the ravens to feed you there" (1 Kings 17:4). If we had just publicly pronounced to a king a national prophecy which then came to pass, and afterwards we were told to go live in the woods—would we go? Further, if we were told we would drink from a mountain stream after we had prophesied a drought—would we go? And further still, if we were told that survival food would be brought to us by birds—would we go? Or would we ask for a second opinion, or three witnesses, or call a committee meeting? What did Elijah do? He obeyed God. "He went and did all according to the word of the LORD" (1 Kings 17:5).

The spirit of Elijah responds with immediate obedience. Obedience that is not immediate is not obedience—it is procrastination. The prophet chose the hidden life with God. He knew better than many New Covenant believers that, "You died, and your life is hidden with Christ in God" (Colossians 3:3). Elijah was learning what John the Baptist would learn, that for God to increase, he must decrease.

THE PROPHET'S SECRET LIFE

Every person has a secret history with God. No one really knows this secret life but God and that person. I believe that Elijah had been given such divine authority because of his secret, intimate life with God. He was a man of prayer, communion and dialogue with God. Every prophet is first of all an intercessor, otherwise he or she will be a false prophet. Our public ministry will only be as powerful as our private prayer life. The divine principle and standard has always been "purity before power." Character comes before commission. Many are powerless because they are prayerless.

Elijah prayed "earnestly." (See James 5:17.) He "pressed in" with burning, zealous prayer. He would not let go until he received the answer. This was the key to his divine authority and power. "We have not because we ask not," Jesus said. We are to "earnestly desire the best gifts," and to "pursue love, and desire spiritual gifts, especially that you may prophesy" (1 Corinthians 14:1). We are to be zealots in prayer. The deluded Muslims who blow themselves up along with innocent people in our buses and restaurants are zealots for their demonic cause. The end-time Elijah company will be zealots for the cause of Jesus—salvation, not destruction—love, not hate.

Elijah lived in "the secret place." Jesus commanded us: "But you, when you pray go into your room, and when you have shut the door, pray to your Father who is in the secret place; and your Father who sees in the secret place will reward you openly" (Matthew 6:6). The authority and anointing on Elijah was being produced in the place of sweet communion with his heavenly Father. It is the place of stripping and equipping, and the place of prophetic preparation.

I have been blessed to have a "secret place" on a promontory on Mount Carmel overlooking the sea. It is just down a path from where the Lord so powerfully visited me in the rental car in the mid-1980's. God often speaks to me there. I highly recommend finding your own "secret place."

"He who dwells in the secret place of the Most High, shall abide under the shadow of the Almighty" (Psalm 91:1). "Come away with Me," says El Shaddai, God Almighty, "and dwell with Me in My shadow." You can't be in someone's shadow unless you are very close to Him. Elijah accepted the divine invitation. He went and lived at the place of separation and preparation, and the Lord was faithful to His promise. Ravens brought him two meals a day for a year. His daily bread was the Word of God, as he fed on God's faithfulness and drank from the ever-flowing stream of the River of Life, the Spirit of God.

OUR SECRET HISTORY WITH GOD

What about our secret history with God? How would it read? Would we want it read publicly? Our private life with Him is far more important to God than our public ministry. Our lives are open books to Him. King David could cry out with an undivided heart: "I will behave wisely in a perfect [blameless] way. Oh, when will You come to me? I will walk within my house with a perfect heart. I will set nothing wicked before my eyes" (Psalm 101:2). Elijah wasn't tempted by a TV set or the Internet.

I will never forget what I read about Hudson Taylor's wife when she was dying in China. Taylor asked her if there was anything she wanted to confess. She was able to look at her husband and say, "There hasn't been a cloud between me and my Jesus these fifteen years." She had practiced His presence. Oh, to live like that with a spotless private life washed in the blood of the Lamb! I long for a secret history with God like that.

A DRIED-UP BROOK

One morning the prophet arose and went to drink from the fresh mountain stream. He stopped and stared. The brook had dried up. He had prophesied the drought, the rain had stopped, and now his precious little brook had stopped flowing. What should he do? The Lord had said, "Drink from the brook." I have been at the place of the dried-up brook, when the blessing has stopped flowing. And I know many others who have been there and some who are there even now. What should we do at these times? We need to expectantly wait for the Lord: "Trust in the LORD with all your heart, and lean not on your own understanding. In all your ways acknowledge Him, and He shall direct your paths" (Proverbs 3:5-6). I've found that it's much easier to memorize His Word than to truly trust and obey Him.

As the prophet waited at the dried-up streambed, he must have realized a season was ending. We also need to discern the Lord's seasons. In August of 2001, Karen and I spent two glorious weeks in a cabin in the Swiss Alps. We marveled at the beauty of God's creation. It was one of the sweetest times we've ever had with Jesus, His Word, and each other. As our season of refreshing drew to a close, we knew He was sending us back to the war in Israel. We sensed ominous times were on the horizon. We prayed, "Lord help us carry this rest and new anointing with us as we come down from the mountain. We want your divine authority in our lives." Two weeks later came September 11, 2001.

"GO TO ZAREPHATH"

God spoke to His waiting prophet. He told him to "Arise, and go to Zarephath which belongs to Sidon" (1 Kings 17:9). "Zarephath" means "refining." Purified metal is heated and melted until it is separated by fusion from foreign earthy ingredients (dirt). Sidon was Jezebel's hometown. Elijah was told to go to the last place on Earth he wanted to visit. The Jewish prophet was told to go to a pagan town where a heathen widow would provide for him. This was worse than ravens! Many of us would have complained to the Lord, "I've had enough refining. I've been sitting in this gulch for a year! What about my ministry?" What did Elijah do? "He arose and went" (1 Kings 17:10). Instant obedience—that is the spirit of Elijah. It was a dangerous mission because he had to walk across Galilee from the Jordan to the Mediterranean. Ahab's army was looking for him to kill him. But he went. Now the solitary prophet was about to become one of the world's first cross-cultural evangelists. The famous man of God was on a journey to much more than a heathen widow and her fatherless boy.

HOUSE OF VICTORY

Some years ago a young man named Eric Benson heard us speak in New York City about "the one new man" ministries to Arabs and Jews on Mount Carmel. He is a Gentile with a burden for the Jewish people. In Bible school they had called him "Rabbi Benson." He volunteered to come out and live at House of Victory (*Beit Nitzachon*) and work with addicts and alcoholics. Eric came to Israel with not much more than a bicycle and a backpack. He lived and served faithfully at House of Victory. (Working with drug addicts for several years is definitely a "Zarephath" experience.) The sister of an Arab drug addict came to the Lord at one of our meetings. Eric and Sofia fell in love. I had the privilege of marrying them on the top of Mount Carmel. Jews and Arabs rejoiced in the Lord together, and we called the celebration "the dance of the two camps." What if Eric had not obeyed the Lord's call and stayed in New York where his brook was drying up? Today Eric is the director of House of Victory and Sofia is the business manager. They have two beautiful daughters, Sharon and Lily.

Recently Karen and I celebrated Eric's birthday with him and his family in the salon of his apartment on the top floor of House of Victory. Karen and I lived there during the Gulf War, when the Lord released the building to us. Carmel Assembly (*Kehilat HaCarmel*) was birthed in Bible studies in that room. (See my book, *The Road to Carmel*, for history of these ministries.) Eric's "family" at his party included a dozen drug addicts and ex-addicts—Arabs and Jews, some of whom were Russian immigrants. There were four languages going at once. One Arab who had come off heroin in our program, had recently visited his hometown in Galilee while on an excursion with the students at House of Victory. When this young man's mother saw him in his transformed state, she called village friends together, Muslims and Christians, to see her "new son." They celebrated with a feast. Eric had gone to Zarephath where the blessing of family awaited him.

FISHERS OF MEN

The Lord spoke to Dani Sayag, our young Israeli pastor, to move with his wife LuAnne and their three daughters to the Haifa neighborhood of Bat Galim where there had been virtually no testimony of Yeshua. It is right next to the Mediterranean and Dani likes to fish. The Lord told him it would also be a place for fishing men. Shortly after moving there, Dani went fishing one night. He met a homeless alcoholic addict who was an immigrant from Russia. The man had lived on the streets of Tel Aviv and Haifa for three years. Igor's skin was cracked with layers of dirt. Dani brought Igor to House of Victory where he became a "new creation in Christ."

Another of the many men "fished" into House of Victory was a young Jewish immigrant from Uzbekistan. He had become a heroin addict living on the streets of Haifa. After finding salvation in Yeshua at House of Victory, he went through our Dor Elisha ("Elisha Generation") internship program and is now serving as our youth pastor. Eliel was recently married in our worship center to a strong believer from Germany. Together they have become a powerful example of the "one new man" in Messiah.

Eric and Dani went to Zarephath. When the brook dries up, those who are fully surrendered to the Lord will always go to Zarephath. The Elijah company chooses to go through God's refining fire in order to become vessels of honor fit for the Master's use.

As Elijah walked to Zarephath he was about to discover that prophets are also purified by people.

-3-

LIFE FROM THE DEAD

An exhausted and hungry fugitive entered the gates of Zarephath and "indeed a widow was there" (1 Kings 17:10). It was no coincidence-God is always working both sides of the street. The thirsty Jewish prophet asked the Gentile widow for a drink of water. Eight hundred years later, the greatest of Jewish prophets, Jesus, would ask another non-Jewish woman for a drink of water in Samaria. Both encounters resulted in life from the dead.

The emaciated widow and her son were starving to death. She only had a bit of flour and a few drops of oil for their last meal. I suppose she thought that after their last bit of bread she and her son would lay down and die the horrible death of starvation. However, the Lord had told Elijah that this dying widow would provide for him and sustain him. I think once again most of us would have disbelieved God, or at least argued with Him. Perhaps our reasoning would be that we should sustain her, rather than become a burden to her. How could she provide for us anyway?

But our prophet simply obeyed God. Like Abraham, "He did not waiver at the promise through unbelief, but was strengthened in faith" (Romans 4:20). Elijah was fully convinced that whatever God had promised, He was able and willing to perform.

A LITTLE FLOUR AND OIL

The prophet gave the widow some strange orders. First, he told a woman who was starving to death not to worry! Then he told her to cook him a cake with her last meal. When he finished eating and there was nothing left that she and her starving son could eat. How could he make such outrageous demands on the poor woman? There is only one reason. He had received and embraced the prophetic word of God, "The bin of flour shall not be used up, nor shall the jar of oil run dry, until the day the Lord sends rain on the earth" (1 Kings 17:14).

This word has brought courage, faith, and provision to countless saints over the centuries. It is what sustained us through the early years at House of Victory and still does today. For eleven years there has always been food on the table for afflicted Arabs and Jews starving for love, acceptance, and a new life.

Carmel Assembly and House of Victory have never been in debt. God has met every need and paid every bill. There has always been enough. Sometimes, barely enough—but enough. The "flour and oil" have never failed as we expectantly wait for the rain of heaven-sent revival and a great harvest of Arab and Jewish souls. It is written. The Lord has spoken it. He will do it and we believe it.

How did the widow respond to this stranger's demands? Many women might have rebuked this foreigner for trying to take the last bite from her and her dying son. But not this woman. She obeyed him! They went to her house and she cooked him a little cake with her last breadcrumbs and a few drops of oil. Did she and her son watch the stranger eat their last meal? She had used up her flour and oil. When the bowl was empty the miracle began. She looked at the bowl again and there was flour in it. It had been empty. She looked at the jar, and there was fresh oil where there had been none. God was multiplying the food! What a lunch this trio must have had! It was the first of many such meals for the next two years. For Elijah the daily miracle of provision had begun again. First, it was through a raven, now a bowl of flour and a jar of olive oil in a heathen lady's home in a pagan city. The widow had given her all and God met her need.

PROPHETS ARE FATHERS

Elijah now had a family. All true prophets are fathers. What did God say about Abraham, one of His first prophets?

> For I have known him, in order that he may command his children and his household after him, that they keep the way of the LORD, to do righteousness and justice, that the LORD may bring Abraham what was spoken to him. (Genesis 18:19)

Paul told the Corinthian congregation which he had planted that they "might have ten thousand instructors in Christ, yet you do not have many fathers" (1 Corinthians 4:15). The Sidonian widow and her son were beginning to realize that "God is a father to the fatherless, a defender of widows" (Psalm 68:5). God had set a solitary man in a family.

I like to think that one of the great joys of Elijah's life at Zarephath was his relationship with the fatherless boy. I see the rough mountain man wrapped in his hairy cloak with the inquisitive little boy on his lap asking questions. The prophet recounts the thrilling stories of other boys, like Moses, Joseph, Samuel and David. Did he also tell the boy's mother the story of how the God of Israel provided for Ruth and Naomi, Gentile and Jewish widows living together in Bethlehem? (There is an ancient unsubstantiated Jewish tradition that the boy grew up to be the prophet Jonah.) I have always been moved when reading the biographies of other "prophets of fire," like

John Knox, General William Booth, Charles Spurgeon or D.L. Moody, to discover how delighted these men were with children.

Imagine what the boy and his mother learned just by listening to Elijah pray. Jesus said, "He who receives a prophet in the name of a prophet shall receive a prophet's reward" (Matthew 10:41). Because the widow received the prophet she and her son received an eternal reward. They entered into a relationship with the living God. Their home became a sanctuary, a house of prayer. And a lonely prophet received a son and a sister—a family.

"MORE THAN A PROPHET"

A number of years ago the Lord spoke to me that He desires "more than a prophet." This is how Jesus described John the Baptist, the prophet who came in "the spirit and power of Elijah." John, Paul, Elijah, and Jesus had no children, yet they were all great fathers. They reproduced their character in the next generation. Their followers wanted to be like them.

Karen and I have no biological children. We were married later than many people, and God never gave us children. In the spring of 1994, we decided to bring two young brothers, one thirteen and the other eleven, into House of Victory. Some did not understand, but the Lord told us to do it. Their father was an alcoholic and their mother had other serious problems. (Both have since died.) The boys were at a critical moment in their young lives. Then the Lord told Karen and me to take them into our house and become their foster parents. Overnight we became a family. Karen was now a mother, and I was trying to become a father.

It wasn't easy for any of us. I think we learned more about ministry by building our family with Ron and David than in any other work we've done with the Lord. "Father" in Hebrew is

Av or *Abba*. It means much more than a physical father. It can mean architect, creator, builder or one who causes something to be. *Av* is a producer, provider, and protector. *Avi-Ad* is our "Everlasting Father." The Lord told me that if I couldn't minister to Ron (his full name in Hebrew is *Yeshurun*), I wouldn't reach Jewish people. Ron was wounded like they are. *Yeshurun* is a name for Israel. (See Deuteronomy 32:15; 33:26.) It means "straight" and "blessed." Ron was dramatically saved and filled with the Holy Spirit. He became a transformed young man. I was blessed to marry my oldest son in our new building on Mount Carmel. He and his wife, Johanna, are on fire for the Lord, have gone to Bible school and are called to ministry. Our younger son David, after completing his Israeli army service, began working at GodTV in Jerusalem.

ELIJAH BECOMES A FATHER

Hidden away in a foreign city with a mother and son, Elijah was beginning to learn that God wants men who are "more than a prophet." For two more years Elijah was being molded by the hand of the Lord, as God fashioned him for the most important work of his life—his future relationship and ministry with another son, named Elisha. "For we are His workmanship, created in Christ Jesus for good works, which God prepared beforehand that we should walk in them" (Ephesians 2:10).

At this point in his ministry, Elijah had delivered one very brief message of about twenty-five words. Preachers were straight and to the point in those days. He had developed his devotional life at the brook, but God was continuing to purify his prophet in private through other people. What were his day-to-day interactions in his new home with the widow and his new "son"? They certainly couldn't argue about the menu because it was the same thing every day.

ELIJAH, THE FORERUNNER

The precious domestic scene in Zarephath is also a prophetic picture of the gospel going forth from Israel to the rest of the world. Elijah had a "forerunner ministry," preparing the way for the coming "one new man in Christ" of Jew and Gentile "reconciled in one body through the cross" (Ephesians 2:14-16). In fact, this interlude in Elijah's life was so significant to Jesus that it was the first example He used in His first recorded message in the synagogue in Nazareth. (See Luke 4:24-26.) The religious Jews in the synagogue were so furious at Him for using a heathen example, they tried to throw Him off a cliff. To me, some of the saddest words in the Bible are: "Then passing through the midst of them, He went on His way" (v.30). His own people missed Him because of exclusiveness and pride. Each time I preach in Nazareth I warn my Arab brothers not to commit the same sin that cursed their city two thousand years ago. I urge them to love the Jews and receive their Jewish brothers.

"GIVE ME YOUR SON"

As Elijah's time in Zarephath was drawing to a close, the son he had come to love became very sick. Then to the prophet's shock the boy died. The widow was distraught. She accused the man of God, "Have you come here to bring my sin to remembrance, and to kill my son?" (1 Kings 17:18). The prophet let her words fall to the ground. As the bereaved widow clutched her son to her bosom in her anguish, he saw and felt her broken heart.

Then he said to her, "Give me your son" (v.19). He gently took the dead boy from her arms and carried him up to his prophet's chamber in an upper room. Elijah laid the beloved boy on his own bed and began to cry out to the Lord. There was no answer.

pr.

I believe the Lord was taking Elij
intercession he had never been before. It
empathy with the widow and her loss. In
down on the dead child and stretched himself out ...
"O LORD my God, I pray, let this child's soul come back to
him" (v.21). Again there was no answer. The prophet got up.
We don't know how much time passed. The devastated widow
was downstairs hoping against hope. Elijah stretched himself
out on the boy on his bed again and prayed the same prayer.
The words he used in Hebrew meant, "Please, I beseech you, I
beg you for this boy's soul." Elijah waited. The mother waited.
There was no response from the boy or God.

As Elijah ended his prayer for the second time, what was
he thinking? Should he go downstairs and try to comfort the
widow? He refused to give up. A third time he covered the
small cold body with his large frame. Again, he begged God
to raise the boy from the dead. The text says that the Lord
listened to the voice of Elijah. God heard his words and felt a
father's pain for a dead son. In the holy stillness of that upper
room something started to happen. Was that a breath from the
child's nostrils the prophet felt on his face? Yes! He started to
breathe again! His eyes slowly opened. He was looking at the
face of his father. Elijah hugged his son and kissed his cheeks
over and over. He was alive! He who had been dead was alive
again! Elijah gathered the little boy into his strong arms.
Downstairs the widow waited and wept. Hearing a creak in
the stair, she looked up. The prophet was coming down the
steps. In his arms was her only son. Slowly, Elijah crossed over
to the mother and put the boy in her arms. The child looked up
and smiled at his mother. Elijah said, "See, your son lives!"

ONE ON ONE

Elijah had been stretched into a dimension of prayer
few of us know much about. The lives of the great men of

yer that I have studied have several things in common. First, they all began by going "one on one." By that I mean they received the Lord's burden for a particular person who seemed hopeless, and about whom no one else cared. For Rees Howells it was the town alcoholic. The Lord arrested the heart of D.L. Moody by the eyes of an orphan boy in the streets of Chicago. For Amy Carmichael, it was a child prostitute in India. George Mueller, William Booth, Jackie Pullinger all have the same story. For David Wilkerson it was Nicky Cruz. Each one seemed impossible. But these prophets of prayer received God's burden, saw what others did not see, and would not let go of God until the answer came—*life from the dead!* All of these modern-day prophets seem stern to some because of their uncompromising message of the transforming power of the Cross. But they all have another thing in common— underneath is a tender spirit full of sensitivity for others.

I have seen the look in the eyes of a mother when her son who was a hopeless drug addict had been restored to her. One Arab mother said to me, "My son used to steal from me, now he prays for me." I have seen children climbing onto the lap of a father who had been lost to them for years because of the curse of drugs or alcohol. I watch wives whose husbands were dead to them enter into a new life of health and hope. We are so blessed to be able to say with Elijah to these loved ones, "See, your son lives!"

YOU AND YOUR HOUSEHOLD

A young Israeli believer who was a cosmetician brought her girlfriend, another Jewish cosmetician, to a meeting at House of Victory. The message that night was on sexual purity. I thought to myself, "This young lady will probably walk out of here when she hears the subject." To my surprise, she began to weep, and she accepted the Lord at her first meeting. Both young women have been running hard after Jesus ever since.

A few years later I had the privilege of marrying this beautiful young woman to an American volunteer who had been serving at House of Victory. The wedding was held outdoors on a lovely spring evening at a kibbutz adjacent to the Mediterranean Sea at the foot of Mount Carmel. The decorated grounds were packed with perhaps two hundred Israelis, mostly friends and relatives of the bride. During my message I felt led to go right into the story of Jesus and Nicodemus and the new birth. "Most assuredly, I say to you, unless one is born again, he cannot see the kingdom of God" (John 3:3). I explained how the bride had become born-again as a fulfilled Jew. I then looked over at Mount Carmel and told the audience that what was taking place was a living fulfillment of biblical prophecy. God had brought them back to the mountains of Israel, where He will sprinkle clean water on them, give them a new heart and put His Spirit in them when they enter into His New Covenant. At the wedding feast, the music was praise and worship in Hebrew led by Karen and our worship team. Customarily at Jewish weddings, the father of the bride offers the traditional toast to the newly married couple by proclaiming, *"L'chaim!"*—"To Life!" As everyone held up their glasses for the toast the bride's father shouted, *"L'chaim,* and Hallelujah!" The bridal couple spent their honeymoon doing two weeks of "follow-up," visiting many of their Israeli friends and sharing their faith with them.

Some years later the bride (who is now a mother) called me and said that her father, a former tax collector, was coming to our Shabbat meeting because he wanted to get saved. The following Shabbat he walked into my office before the meeting and said, "I believe in Jesus." I said, "Good. We'll pray with you at the end of the meeting." He responded, "No. I want to do it now." He prayed to ask Jesus into his heart and started crying. Later, he also came to the altar call. He has hardly missed a meeting since and usually sits in the front row so he won't miss anything. His wife has also come to the Lord, and now his son, a musician, is coming to meetings. He told me he had watched the video of his sister's wedding over and over, and he wanted to know about Jesus also.

Elijah learned about family in Zarephath. His father's heart had turned to the widow's son. He had seen the resurrection power of God in a foreign land. Now he was ready for his next assignment.

THE ELIJAH LEGACY IS MUCH "MORE THAN A PROPHET."

4

CONFRONTING AHAB

After "many more days" of secluded family life, God was about to speak to His messenger again. These must have been golden days of celebrating God's miraculous provision with a boy who had been dead. But Elijah's self-emptying process of preparation was to continue. The necessity of death to the self-life is evident from the lives of all the prophets. God won't fill a vessel that isn't empty. Consider the desert preparations of Moses, John the Baptist, Paul or Jesus. A person's ministry is his life—that which he is—not just his teaching or preaching. His ministry is the message worked into the character of God's spokesman.

After two years of waiting, Elijah received his fourth word from the Lord. He had been told to prophesy a drought, hide himself, and go to Zarephath. Now God told him, "Go, present yourself to Ahab, and I will send rain on the earth" (1 Kings 18:1). Was he on his knees in his prophet's chamber when the Lord spoke to him? How would he be able to tell the widow and the boy he loved so dearly that he had to go? Could it be he took the boy with him? Who was his servant on Mount Carmel who seven times would look for the promised rain clouds? And, what was awaiting him in Israel?

Back in Israel there was severe famine and drought as even the animals were dying. The people blamed Elijah, and he had been branded "the troubler of Israel." Jezebel was on a witch-hunt massacring the true believers, and one hundred of the remnant were hiding in caves. The queen had installed her own false prophets, while she and the state lavishly supported these hirelings, who flattered her and told her what she wanted to hear. Ahab's soldiers were searching for Elijah to kill him. It appeared that the darkness had snuffed out the last flickering light of testimony to the true God.

FAREWELL TO ZAREPHATH

Elijah must go and fulfill his destiny. The call was clear, "Go, and confront Ahab and his world." There was a farewell scene where many tears must have been shed. Mountain men cry, too. I see the trio walking slowly to the gate of the city together. Then there was a last embrace, before Elijah went on his way, and mother and son waved farewell. Before him stretched not only the rugged mountains, but a mission that in human terms was impossible. All the Lord's servant had was a word from his God.

Obedience is part of the prophetic character. From Abraham to Jesus "one man's obedience" has changed the world. As he was about to disappear from the widow's view, a chapter of their lives was ending, and a new one was about to begin. What was Elijah thinking as he turned his thoughts back to Israel? Was he praying, "Lord, show me what to do? How am I to confront Ahab?"

"ABUNDANCE OF RAIN"

In 1996, I was invited to Britain to minister at a Prayer for Israel Conference at Westminster Chapel in London. I was asked to speak on "The Sound of the Abundance of Rain" (1 Kings 18:41), and the great harvest I see coming to Galilee, Mount Carmel, and Lebanon. After the conference I began a ministry tour of northern England. One night in York, I awoke and sensed the presence of the Lord. As I lay there praying the

Lord spoke to me. In the stillness of the night I heard Him say, "Confront Ahab, and I will send the rain." The voice was almost audible.

"I AM GOING BEFORE YOU INTO GALILEE"

It was very similar to the way the Lord spoke to me in 1989 shortly after we had moved to Israel. Then He said, "I am going before you into Galilee; there you will see Me. Tell the disciples." So, we knew that the Lord's work for us with drug addicts would be in northern Israel, even though we were still living in Jerusalem. At that time we received another very strong rhema word, "Then Jesus returned in the power of the Spirit to Galilee, and news of Him went out through all the surrounding region" (Luke 4:14).

As we waited in Jerusalem, a call came from an Arab pastor inviting us to minister in a Muslim town in Galilee. In that meeting, the Lord broke my Jewish wife's heart for the Arab people. I shared that God was going to raise up a "one new man" rehabilitation center for Arabs and Jews in northern Israel, and that Jesus was going to return to Galilee in the power of the Spirit. Most leaders in Israel told us we could only work with Arabs or Jews, not both groups together. But the Lord had told us "both." We obeyed His vision, and right after the Gulf War the Lord birthed House of Victory and Carmel Assembly, ministries to Jews and Arabs.

A CONDITION FOR THE RAIN

Now, in England, God was speaking to me to "confront Ahab." It was a condition for "the abundance of rain"—the move of His Spirit on Carmel. What did He mean? "Ahab" in Hebrew is *Achav*. *Ach* means "brother," and *av* is "father." In the Lord's body we are called to be brothers, a brotherhood, "yoke fellows," in covenant relationship with each other. We are also called to grow in maturity and become spiritual fathers, to make disciples. I began to realize the Lord was speaking to me about myself, as well as His body in northern Israel and our congregation on Mount Carmel.

THE AHAB PLAGUE

There in Britain I began to study everything the Bible said about Ahab, who had brought such devastation upon his people and land. As I read his words and studied his actions, what began to emerge was a composite of a very weak male believer. Ahab was a poor husband, father, and leader. In fact, he was the opposite of Elijah, and represented everything a man of God should not be. I saw that he was the epitome of carnality, compromise, covetousness, and cowardice.

In every way the "spirit of Ahab" is opposed to the "spirit of Elijah." They are always on collision course. Ahab was carnal, while Elijah was a man of deep communion and single-minded commitment to God. Ahab's life was compromised, but Elijah's whole life was consecrated. Ahab coveted what belonged to others, and Elijah was a man of great compassion. Ahab was to die in disgrace, in disguise as a coward. Elijah is one of our great examples of courage and would have a glorious departure.

The confrontation on Carmel (which means "God's fruitfulness") was an engagement, a battle to the death, in a war between the "soul man" and the "spirit man." Ahab looked impressive with his crown, armor, robes, soldiers, and seductive wife at his side. But he was an emasculated man, rotting on the inside from the cancer of lust, self-will and self-promotion. In classical Greek tragedy there is always a dramatic showdown between the protagonist ("the good guy") and the antagonist ("the bad guy"). The scene is called an *agon* ("agony") and is always a battle to the death. When the scene is over and the dust has settled, the truth was always revealed. An *agon* was about to be enacted on Mount Carmel for all Israel to witness.

"MIXTURE-MAN"

In the fatherless generation we live in, we desperately need men who are godly role models. "Ahabs" abdicate their God-given commission and authority as husbands, fathers and brothers. Ahab is "mixture-man," who fears man more than God. He is fleshly, earthly, soulish, and "the carnal mind is enmity to God" (Romans 8:7). He is motivated by his own lusts, and "the natural [soulish] man does not receive the things of the Spirit of God" (1 Corinthians 2:14). A person who operates in the soul realm of his natural desires, thoughts and will, cannot and will not receive the things of the Spirit of God.

The soul is the seat, or throne, of the human ego. The spirit of a regenerated believer is the sanctuary of the exalted Christ. Men of God long for the Spirit to sanctify and reign in their souls. God is not soul, He is Spirit. Ahab set up an idol of self in his own heart, while Elijah allowed the Lord to crucify his old self at Cherith and Zarephath. Ahab carried the foul odor of envy and selfish ambition, "the devil's twins." "Where envy and self-seeking exist, confusion and every evil thing are there" (James 3:16)—a fair description of the Ahab-Jezebel kingdom.

"Ahabs" not only operate in the unregenerate world, but, sad to say, they can also be found in the Body of Christ. Legions of husbands and fathers are not priests in their homes. They are bound in soulishness and are too busy with other priorities to allow the Lord to set them free. The flame of their family prayer altar has died out, if it was ever lit. "Ahabs" are not deep men of the Word. They may memorize it, or quote it, but because they don't live it, they never mature. They may go to many church meetings, but are "sermon-proof." They don't change and never really grow up. King Ahab actually became infantile as he grew older. These men are not teachable or correctable, are always defensive, excusing themselves rather than confessing. As a result they remain stunted in their spiritual growth. "Ahabs" are the plague of godly wives who long for their men to grow up.

Some "Ahabs" I have known major in minors. For example, here in Israel the "end-times" (or what some call "millennium fever") is a topic for endless debate. "Majoring in minors" can be a form of escapism which precludes its practitioners from paying the price of steady formation of Christ-like character. The foundations of those who are like Ahab are weak, shaky and not grounded in the transforming power of the Cross. Some are reeds blowing in every wind of the latest doctrine.

SUMMITS AND DISCIPLES

Some years ago, at a meeting of two congregations on the shore of the Sea of Galilee, I shared on this subject of Ahab. When I gave the altar call, almost every man in the meeting came forward. Men want to change! It is the job of leaders to help them. As an attempt to meet this desperate need to confront the Ahab spirit in our midst we began to have summit meetings on Mount Carmel with most of the male ministry leaders in northern Israel—with Jews, Arabs, and Gentiles. As men sat at the feet of Jesus for three days, the Lord began doing very deep things in the relationships between all of us Galileans. The fruit remains today. There are now two national summit meetings every year in the desert, as well as summits for women.

Reuven and Yanit Ross, formerly on our leadership team, developed some in-depth, disciple-making material which we began using in small, weekly discipleship groups. In these intimate gatherings we were learning to confess our sins to one another and to be accountable for our behavior. "If we walk in the light as He is in the light, we have fellowship with one another, and the blood of Jesus Christ His Son cleanses us from all sin" (1 John 1:7). The result has been a new measure of maturity in many of our people, beginning with the leaders. Two men in their fifties once thanked me for our little group, saying that no one had ever taken the time to mentor them.

Disciple-making was the lasting, world changing ministry of Jesus. He poured himself into a dozen tough Galileans. Disciples were His plan, and still are. In our congregation we usually have several groups running at once. Four other congregations in Israel are now embracing and using this material. The Rosses not only have imparted the vision of disciple-making in Israel, but also in England, Europe, South Africa, the Far East, and the U.S. Jesus' command, "Go, and make disciples," was given on a mountain in Galilee. (See Matthew 28:16-20.)

Summits and disciple-making groups are just two of the ways we are attempting to confront the "Ahab spirit" in our midst so the Lord will send a downpour of the rain of His Holy Spirit to our dry and thirsty land.

"FEEDING OUR HORSES"

And what was Ahab doing as Elijah returned to Israel? Had he repented for being the slave of a heathen witch who hated the God of Abraham, Isaac, and Israel? Had God's righteous judgment of drought softened his heart? Hardly. The king was actually sending out search parties to look for grass for his horses and mules. The animals that propped up his dignity were more important to him than the lives of his subjects. His heart was harder than ever.

How much of the same sort of thing can be found in God's Church today? In the affluent Western Church preachers of prosperity proclaim that if we are not rich, our faith is weak. Tell that to starving villagers in Africa, China, North Korea, or Afghanistan. Are our luxury cars "Ahab's horses?" Are we becoming like the "rich man who was clothed in purple and fine linen and fared sumptuously every day. But there was a certain beggar named Lazarus, full of sores, who was laid at his gate," (Luke 16: 19-20) and we fail to notice?

Some years ago, a Jewish Russian immigrant was taken off the streets by the House of Victory staff. This man had open running sores on his legs. His heart actually stopped for twenty seconds in a Haifa hospital. He had been a hard-core heroin addict for years. While he was at House of Victory his mother died suddenly. Jesus healed him and set him free from deep depression. Now this man who looked like a skeleton several years ago is healthy. He told me, "God loves me. It's the grace of God. I have family. Thank you, Jesus." Will the Church of Jesus Christ care for such people, or are we too busy "feeding our horses," acquiring more things we don't need, doing things we don't need to be doing?

STRANGERS, WIDOWS, AND ORPHANS

In the Torah, the children of Israel had been clearly and consistently commanded by God to care for the stranger, the widow, and the fatherless. Grain, grapes, and olives, the blessing and sustenance of the land, was to be given to these three groups of outcasts. The foreigner was even to be treated as a member of the family. If the Israelites obeyed the Lord in this matter, blessing would be the result. "The stranger, and the fatherless and the widow who are within your gates, may come and eat and be satisfied, that the Lord Your God may bless you in all the work of your hand which you do" (Deuteronomy 14:29).

If the people disobeyed God and broke His Law and mistreated widows and orphans, the people would forfeit the blessing of God and come under His righteous curse.

"Cursed is the one who perverts the justice due the stranger, the fatherless, and widow" (Deuteronomy 27:19).

We must follow Elijah's example. For two years he had selflessly given of himself to a widow and a fatherless boy, both of whom were strangers and foreigners to the covenants of Israel. He had brought righteousness and mercy to their home and land. "Widow" means those who are discarded, desolate, and forsaken. We have friends who started a work in Hong Kong for Chinese widows left on the streets to die.

An Arab pastor friend of ours has run an orphanage in Galilee for years. The Israeli government recently gave him an award for his work. In the fall of 2001, a number of Muslims and nominal Christians were supernaturally healed through his ministry. As a result two hundred and fifty Arabs have come into a personal relationship with the Lord in his area.

The outcasts have a special place in the Lord's heart. "Blessed is he who considers the poor, the LORD will deliver him in time of trouble. The LORD will preserve him and keep him alive, and he will be blessed on the earth" (Psalm 41:1-2).

Elijah was a forerunner of the Good Samaritan, ministering and caring for those unlike himself. The prophet had a great passion for his God which released in him a compassion for the hurting and needy. He took the word of salvation to the lost. Ahab did exactly the opposite. He imported, practiced, and promoted paganism and was instrumental in unleashing the filth of the world among the people of God. Whenever the Church begins to embrace the systems of the world the righteous judgment of God will surely follow. The land that should have been flowing with the abundance of God's blessing was languishing under the curse of drought and famine, while the leader was trying to feed his horses.

THE "TROUBLER OF ISRAEL"

Yes, Ahab and Elijah are always on collision course. Once again, the king and the prophet were face to face. Ahab immediately blamed Elijah for Israel's troubles. Ahabs are experts at blame-shifting. He called Elijah the "troubler of Israel." This is ever the charge of the apostate or backslider toward God's servants. Elijah was among the select company of prophets like righteous Amos who was told by a false priest, "The land is not able to bear all his words" (Amos 7:10). Paul and Silas were charged with "bringing exceeding trouble" (Acts 16:20) to Philippi. Of them it was said, "These who have turned the world upside down have come here too" (Acts 17:6).

One of the accusations against Jesus was: "He stirs up the people" (Luke 23:5). The reason for this hatred toward God's messengers was made chillingly clear by the Lord Jesus when He said that He is hated by the world "because I testify of it that its works are evil" (John 7:7).

God's "troublemakers" always warn men of their danger, confront them to turn from their idols, and expose hypocrites. Such a ministry does not breed popularity with the unrepentant. But those who are faithful receive the prophet's reward:

> Blessed are you when men hate you, and when they exclude you, and revile you, and cast out your name as evil, for the Son of Man's sake. Rejoice in that day and leap for joy! For indeed your reward is great in heaven, for in like manner their fathers did to the prophets. (Luke 6:22-23)

HAS A NATION CHANGED ITS GODS?

How did Elijah respond to Ahab's false charge? He immediately identified the source of Israel's afflictions. It was Ahab and his father and the kings who preceded him who were the cause of Israel's miserable state. He told the king to his face: "You have forsaken the commandments of the LORD and have followed the Baals" (1 Kings 18:18). At a later date, referring to the apostasy of Judea and Jerusalem, the Lord himself expressed His anguished heart over the condition of His people speaking through the prophet Jeremiah:

> "Has a nation changed its gods, which are not gods? But My people have changed their Glory for what does not profit. Be astonished, O heavens, at this, and be horribly afraid; be very desolate," says the LORD. "For My people have committed two evils: they have forsaken Me, the fountain of living waters, and hewn for themselves cisterns—broken cisterns that can hold no water." (Jeremiah 2:11-13)

Both Elijah and Jeremiah described accurately the hardened heart of the apostate nation. Ahab had forsaken Jehovah and His commands, and led the people to worship other gods. The nation had actually changed gods! They had exchanged the living waters of the Spirit of God for the filthy sewer water oozing from broken cisterns—a false religious system of their own making.

THE DEPLORABLE STATE OF STATE RELIGION

Isn't this the condition of much of the world today? Only a century and a half after apostles like Paul laid the foundation of the true church of Jesus Christ upon the European continent, the gospel was Romanized and secularized into a false state religion. The biblical Jewish roots of our faith were dismembered and replaced with pagan holidays, rituals, and a nominal state church. Even the Reformation stopped short of full restoration and more state churches arose. Nominal

Christianity became the norm. Division and dead churches have littered the landscape ever since.

America began with a handful of Bible-believing pilgrims who were no longer welcome in Europe or Britain. Has America too changed its gods for the gods of materialism and secular humanism? Children aren't allowed to pray in schools, and it is now illegal to display the Ten Commandments in public buildings. For seventy years, the former Soviet Union attempted to remove God from its communist empire. Since its collapse a decade ago there has been a great ingathering of souls with hundreds of Bible-based churches sprouting up across eleven time zones from St Petersburg to Vladivostock. Nations may change their gods, but God will have the final word.

GETTING GOD'S PLAN

The "troubler of Israel" had been identified. Elijah proposed a dramatic *agon* or public power encounter between Jehovah and Baal. He told Ahab to gather the nation together on Mount Carmel, and to bring the 850 prophets of Baal and Asherah. I've often wondered where or when the Lord gave His servant this strategic plan. In Zarephath he had only been told to confront the king, and rain would return. Now he had been given specifics about the place and the people to be invited. I believe Elijah had a long prayer walk of about thirty miles from Sidon (Lebanon) back to Israel. Since there was no food, he was probably fasting. Much of his journey was along the Mediterranean shore. As he looked out to sea searching for rain clouds, he must have been asking, "Lord, how, where, when do I confront Ahab?"

When God sends a man on a mission He doesn't give him all the specifics up front. He just says, "Go!" If we obey, He then begins to show us His plan step-by-step. This is one of His ways of keeping us humble, and dependent upon Him.

Ahab took up the prophet's challenge. Messengers were sent from Dan to Bethel proclaiming, "Gather all Israel to Mount Carmel."

THE LEGACY OF ELIJAH WAS ABOUT TO ENTER A NEW DIMENSION.

5

"The God Who Answers
by Fire"

The Lord of Hosts chose Mount Carmel for His historic
show-down with idolatry. The place is known as *El
Muhrakah*, "the sacrifice," or "the place of burning." For over
two millennia, travelers and pilgrims have made their way up
to this large, flat, rocky promontory on the southeastern end
of "Carmel by the Sea" (Jeremiah 46:18). Jews, Christians,
Muslims, Druze, and Bedouins all revere the location.

One of my particular passions is to study God's Word
at the places where these events happened. My father was
an historian with the federal government in Washington,
D.C. When I was a child, our holidays often centered on
important places in American history. I fondly recall our visits
to Monticello, Thomas Jefferson's home in Virginia. At the
Gettysburg battlefield, the American Civil War came vividly
alive to my young imagination. Later, I would direct or act
in large outdoor historical dramas in Virginia, Maryland,
Kentucky, and Texas.

"A Box Seat for Armageddon"

Today, from the high ridge of Muhrakah a visual feast
awaits the visitor. To the west is the majestic Mediterranean.
Not far down the coastline lies Caesarea, where the gospel

went forth to the Gentiles. The Roman theatre where Herod died is still there and is used for occasional concerts. To the east through the olive and oak trees, rocks and shrubs below, one can make out the narrow stream of the Kishon River at the foot of Carmel, as it winds its way north to empty into Haifa Bay. But what dominates the landscape is the magnificent expanse of the Jezreel Valley, which is spread out before us like a huge multi-colored quilt. The plain is thirty miles long and fifteen miles across at its widest point.

Many biblical scholars believe that we are gazing upon the battlefield of Armageddon (*Har Megiddo*, or "mountain of Megiddo"). The ruins of the Canaanite city of Megiddo, which was later rebuilt by King Solomon and where he maintained his famous horse stables, is located at the southeastern entrance to the valley. "And they gathered them together to the place in Hebrew called Armageddon" (Revelation 16:16). When a pastor friend from the States once visited us and saw where we were building the new worship center on the top of Carmel, he quipped, "Save me a box-seat for Armageddon!" Tourist groups flock to Muhrakah. I have heard Israeli tour guides explain to visitors that this is where Christians believe the battle of Armageddon will be fought.

As we look across the huge fertile plain it is difficult to imagine that a century ago most of it was uninhabited marshland infested with mosquitoes and malaria. A number of well-known writers have described the deplorable condition of the area in the nineteenth century. Mark Twain's description of northern Israel certainly wouldn't have encouraged tourism: "The Galilee is a pile of musty mounds of barrenness— I never saw a human being on the way." (See *Innocents Abroad*, 1867.)

At the turn of the twentieth century many Jewish immigrants, who were fleeing persecution and pogroms in Eastern Europe and Russia, made their way to Galilee. The grandparents of a Messianic Jewish friend of ours walked from Russia. These returning pioneers purchased land from the Turkish Ottoman Empire before its defeat in World War I. Others came and bought land in the area from wealthy absentee landlords in Beirut, Damascus and Istanbul. These immigrants were the pioneers who helped drain the swamps of Galilee and create agriculture and industry. The first modern Israeli industry here was the Nesher ("Eagle") Concrete Company, located on the Kishon River at the foot of Carmel. We purchased cement from them for the construction of our new building. Before World War I the absentee Ottoman landlords had taxed those who lived here according to the number of trees on their property. So to avoid taxation tenants actually stripped much of the land of its trees, destroying the ecology.

A VALLEY DRENCHED IN BLOOD

The magnificent Jezreel Valley we see today also has an amazing historic and prophetic story to tell. For over three millennia this plain has been drenched with the blood of many armies. Joshua conquered the Canaanite king of Megiddo and the king of Jokneam in Carmel here. (See Joshua 12:21-22.) Our youngest son, David, was stationed at an army base near Jokneam (*Yoqneam* in Hebrew). On March 21, 2002, a Muslim homicide bomber blew himself up on a bus near here. Seven died, four of whom were Israeli soldiers, while the wounded included Israeli Arabs. Six weeks later, seventeen Israelis died in a burning bus blown up by another Muslim homicide bomber at Megiddo.

Near the foot of Carmel on the banks of the Kishon, Deborah and Barak's forces routed Sisera and the Canaanites. It was also here that Gideon's three hundred defeated the Midianites, Amalekites, and "the people of the East." Saul and Jonathan retreated from the Philistines across this plain and died on Mount Gilboa, which is visible in the distance. The false prophets and priests of Baal would die at the foot of Carmel. Ahaziah and Josiah met their untimely deaths in this valley. Hordes of Assyrians, Babylonians, and Egyptians waged bloody battles here. Thousands of Jewish captives strung together with fishhooks through their noses were herded into captivity in Assyria through this place. Invading armies of the Greeks and Romans would march this way. Caravans of merchants from the East traveled down "the way of the Sea" on their journey to Egypt. Bands of robbers who abounded here were renowned for their brutality.

Islamic armies came this way, and crusaders from Europe proudly marched here on their way to Jerusalem, where they burned the Jews in their synagogues, while brandishing crosses and singing hymns. Napoleon led his French army against the Turks on this plain. It was here that the British army officer, Orde Wingate, trained Jewish immigrants to fight against Arab armies.

I have walked along the banks of the now polluted Kishon. Rusted and decaying ruins of railway tracks and an oil pipeline that were to connect Haifa with Damascus and Baghdad pay silent testimony to another time, a faded dream, when Jews and Muslims thought they might live together in peace. We once investigated the possibility of purchasing and refurbishing a deserted railroad hotel here to use for a rehabilitation center.

I have stood at Muhrakah and been startled by the sudden deafening roar of Israeli warplanes taking off from a hidden air base. Yes, this is a place of conflict, battle, and war. As one ancient scholar put it, "hardly an equal area of earth can so often have been drenched with the blood of men" (*International Standard Bible Encyclopedia*, Vol. II, p.994).

From Muhrakah you can also see Nazareth where Jesus grew up. Did He ever stand on the cliffs at Nazareth where He would be rejected by His own neighbors and ponder the events that had taken place, and will take place here? The young Jesus could have stared at majestic Tabor where most scholars believe He was transfigured. The translated Elijah would make his last appearance here as the glory of God shone from our Savior. Is it here that He will intervene in the coming Gog and Magog war? (See Chapter 15.)

"CALL ALL ISRAEL TO MOUNT CARMEL"

Throngs of people from the ten northern tribes obeyed Ahab's call and came from the towns and villages of Galilee and Samaria as they walked or rode on donkeys across the Jezreel Valley. They came by the thousands—parents, grandparents, children and widows—making their way to Carmel. Some crossed the narrow Kishon at the foot of the mountain and climbed the slope to the open level area that resembles a natural amphitheatre. Others stayed below on level ground where they were afforded an open view of the proceedings about to take place on the stone promontory above. They had been ordered by their king to attend a national convocation at the place of "the sacrifice."

Each tribe of Israel assembled together under their respective tribal banners. From all sides the eager crowds surrounded the place. Were they to see a miracle? Was the long-hoped-for rain about to fall? Mounted troops of the king's army took their appointed places. The crowd made way again, and through their midst with great pomp and splendor arrayed in colorful, costly robes and tall, pointed hats, the four hundred and fifty prophets of Baal marched to their assigned positions. From the text it appears that the four hundred prophets of Asherah under the patronage of Jezebel were not there. Were they with her? Did she suspect what was about to happen?

Then through the still morning air, the blasts of shofars (rams' horns) were heard. The crowd turned to view King Ahab as he arrived in the royal chariot. Ahab dismounted, and with his palace guards passed on to his central seat of honor, marked by a spear fixed upright in the ground. The entire society was represented ("all Israel")—the tribal elders, the ten tribes, the military, as well as the civil and religious authorities. It was the largest gathering in the half-century history of the northern kingdom.

There was great excitement among the crowd, talking and chattering, as rumors abounded that the prophet Elijah was to reappear. He had not been seen in three and a half years, since he had declared the drought for which many hated him. Others wondered if he would even come, or was he afraid? Had he seen this awesome pageant from a distance and already given up the contest?

As the people waited in anticipation, several of the assembled soldiers turned and began to look up toward the crest of the mountain. A buzz of whispers rippled through the crowd as all eyes turned toward the mountaintop. People scrambled for a better view, and curious children were hoisted onto their father's shoulders. Then a hush descended upon the huge throng. Above them on the shoulder of the mountain stood a man. The name "Elijah" was heard in muted whispers running from tribe to tribe. It was indeed the man of God, fresh from communion with Jehovah.

The assembled soldiers slowly divided their ranks to make an entranceway for the prophet. Through the glittering assembly the lone man slowly walked, his simple garment and rough mantle in stark contrast to the gaudy surroundings. He carried the air of one who had a solemn work to do. He paused as the piercing gaze of his eagle-like eyes of the seer confronted the idol-serving priests in their splendid attire. He moved on and took his place opposite his powerful adversaries. The participants were all there, as Elijah paused to survey the scene.

Suddenly, like a shofar blast, the powerful voice of the prophet rang out over the assembled multitude. "How long will you falter between two opinions? If the LORD is God, follow Him; but if Baal, follow him" (1 Kings 18:21). The words from the man of God reverberated in the distance, and finally died out. A great silence pervaded the scene.

The hush continued as the prophet waited. No voice responded. No one moved. No one dared. Not one person stepped forward and proclaimed, "I will follow Jehovah!"

Perhaps expecting such a response, the prophet proposed a daring and dramatic contest. He addressed the nation a second time: "I alone am left a prophet of the LORD; and Baal's prophets are four hundred and fifty men. Therefore let them give us two bulls; and let them choose one bull for themselves, cut it in pieces, and lay it on the wood, but put no fire under it" (1 Kings 18:22-23). Then turning to the four hundred and fifty prophets of Baal he challenged them: "Then you call on the name of your gods, and I will call on the name of the LORD; and the God who answers by fire, He is God" (v. 24).

Elijah turned back to the people for a response. Suddenly as one voice the people cried in Hebrew, "Your word is good!" Baal's prophets had no choice. They were trapped. The *agon* had begun.

The false prophets went first. A bull was brought into the center of the gathering. They butchered the huge animal, and placed the large bloody pieces of flesh on branches and sticks they had laid on a stone altar to Baal. Then they began to cry out to their god. The name, "Baal! Baal!" ascended from four hundred and fifty voices over Mount Carmel. They called on their god of nature to send fire. On and on they went, shouting, chanting, singing. Occasionally, they would stop. As they rested, the people murmured among themselves.

Again the brightly clad priests cried out, and began to spring and jump and roll upon the ground. They screamed as their dancing became more frenetic as they leaped around the altar and worked themselves into a frenzy. Finally, at noon, the exhausted participants stopped and rested again.

Elijah once more came forward, and began to heap scorn on the false prophets in front of the king and his subjects.

"Shout louder," the prophet suggested. "Maybe he is sleeping and must be awakened" (1 Kings 18:27, NIV). The insulted and enraged priests were provoked to another attempt to arouse their dormant god. Once more they shrieked and leapt and danced and banged on instruments, as a hellish din arose over the people. Finally, they began to cut themselves with knives. Blood stained their priestly garments. Some began screaming prophecies about fire. Others rolled in the dirt in convulsions. The king, the army, and the assembled nation watched the mad spectacle as these dervishes finally began to subside. Some collapsed or crawled to the side while others attended to their wounds. The parts of a slaughtered bull lay on a bloody altar surrounded by blood-stained pagan priests. The only sound was of moaning and panting. There was no response from Baal. "There was no voice; no one answered, no one paid attention" (1 Kings 18:29).

ELIJAH HEALED THE ALTAR OF THE LORD

Now it was Elijah's turn. He called to his people to come nearer to make sure they could see clearly what he was about to do. The prophet then walked over to some unnoticed stones overgrown with weeds that had once been an altar to Jehovah. Jezebel had ordered the altars to the God of Israel to be thrown down. Who had once erected this ruined altar to the true God? Was it Joshua when he conquered the king of Megiddo nearly five centuries earlier? Or had the altar been erected by the tribe of Asher whose land this was by allotment, covenant and inheritance? Was there still a hidden remnant of true believers in the midst of the flood of idolatry in the land?

The prophet then "repaired [in Hebrew "healed"] the altar of the LORD that was broken down" (1 Kings 18:30). What a contrast we have before us to the wild madness of the false prophets! Calmly and deliberately the prophet began to move the ancient stones one by one into place, as the people watched with great interest. With the stones he rebuilt the altar to the God of Israel. As the prophet finished his task, some of the people counted the stones and realized there were twelve. This was the sacred number of the tribes of the sons of Jacob whom God had renamed "Israel." The ten northern tribes had forsaken the tribes of Judah and Benjamin, and had usurped the name "Israel." The prophet was now addressing a shattered people with a prophetic gesture of unity and completeness. He was taking them back to the roots of their own history and identity.

Confused, double-minded, and faltering between two worlds, the people were being confronted with their call to be a holy people chosen by Jehovah as a light to the nations. Lost among their idols, they were witnessing not a contest between two gods, but an agon between the God of Israel and their delusions. The people were fascinated as they watched the prophet dig a trench around the altar. He then put wooden tree branches upon the stones. With a sword he butchered a second bull, and laid the bloody pieces on the wood. Elijah ordered some onlookers to take four water pots and fill them with water from the covered well nearby. Three times they drenched the bloody sacrifice, the wood and the stones with water, as the trench filled up.

FIRE FROM HEAVEN

It was now about three o'clock in the afternoon, the time of the evening sacrifice at the temple in Jerusalem. At that strategic hour, Elijah the prophet calmly approached the restored altar and addressed his God: "LORD God of Abraham, Isaac, and Israel, let it be known this day that You are God in Israel and I am Your servant, and that I have done all these things at Your word. Hear me, O LORD, hear me, that this people may know that You are the LORD God, and that You have turned their hearts back to You again" (1 Kings

18:36-37). The people held their breath and watched. The Creator of the universe heard the simple, bare, and essential prayer of His servant. Suddenly the heavens opened above the mountain. A shaft of supernatural fire hurtled down toward the altar. The bloody sacrifice burst into flames for all to see, as a collective scream came from the assembled nation. All were aghast. The nearest onlookers staggered backward away from the fire. The wood began to burn. Then the stones of the altar caught on fire. Even the water in the trench flamed up. Everything was consumed in the fire of the Lord. Within seconds all was ashes.

The people stared, stunned by what they were witnessing. The fear of the Lord swept through the camp. Jehovah had manifested His burning jealousy for His people. Throughout the crowd people began to fall on their knees and prostrate themselves before the Lord. Soon the soldiers were on their faces in terror before the Holy One of Israel. As one man, the people cried out, "The LORD, He is God! The LORD, He is God!" (1 Kings 18:39). All-consuming fire from Heaven had visited the people of Israel again!

Since the days of Cain and Abel, God has challenged people everywhere to decide between true and false worship by means of sacrifice. Elijah's sacrifice had been accepted. The awful, divine response to God's servant had overwhelmed the king and his false prophets with shame, confusion, and truth in the presence of the king's subjects. The people surely had heard how God had accepted the sacrifice from Moses and Aaron and how "fire came out from before the LORD and consumed the burnt offering and the fat on the altar. When all the people saw it, they shouted and fell on their knees" (Leviticus 9:24). They had heard, and perhaps some of the elderly had even witnessed, how fifty years earlier King Solomon had prayed at the dedication of the Temple. God had answered with fire from Heaven, which "consumed the burnt offering and sacrifices; and the glory of the LORD filled the temple" (2 Chronicles 7:1). Yes, the One who is "glorious in holiness, fearful in praises, doing wonders" (Exodus 15:11) had again manifested himself to His people.

BURNT STONES

The fire of God actually burnt up ("consumed") not only the bull and the wood, but also the twelve stones! There was nothing left. We are called to be "living stones," who "are being built up a spiritual house, a holy priesthood, to offer up sacrifices acceptable to God through Jesus Christ" (1 Peter 2:5). God wants to burn up the dirt and chaff in our lives with the fire of His holiness and love. Jesus said to His disciples, "I came to send fire on the earth, and how I wish it were already kindled!" (Luke 12:49). We are to be His fire-bearers. The tongues of fire which came upon the disciples at Pentecost were a sign that the perfect sacrifice of Jesus had been accepted. The Church was ignited with holy fire. This is what we are desperately crying out for today. "Lord, send the fire of your holy presence to Mount Carmel again!"

"SEIZE THE PROPHETS OF BAAL"

But Elijah wasn't finished. He ordered the soldiers to seize the terrified, defeated, and cowering prophets of Baal and bring them down the rocky slope to the Kishon. There Elijah took a sword and struck the leader. The soldiers followed Elijah and executed the four hundred and fifty false prophets, even as Jezebel had slaughtered the prophets of God. Elijah was performing what the Torah required. False prophets who led the people into idolatry were to be "cut off" (Deuteronomy 17:2-3). By executing the false prophets, Elijah was attempting to deal a deathblow to the false worship in his nation. He wanted to remove the cause of the curse of drought and famine which had come upon the land.

A DIVIDED HEART

Mount Carmel is the Mountain of Decision. The mighty controversy between Jehovah and Baal had been dramatically settled for all to witness. But, as we shall see, even the visible fire of the presence of the Holy One of Israel was not enough to scorch out the roots of idolatry so deeply imbedded in the hearts of the people. The problem was and has always been a divided heart. The people had broken the first commandment to love the Lord their God with all their heart. They were still naming the name of the Lord while faltering, or stumbling between two opinions or ways of life. The prophet Hosea, who witnessed the apostasy of the northern kingdom firsthand, put it simply, "Their heart is divided" (Hosea 10:2). King David called the eternal problem "a double heart" (Psalm 12:2). In Hebrew it means to have two hearts, "a heart and a heart." The people were calling on the name of Jehovah and Baal at the same time.

God abhors mixture and compromise. He commands us to walk with Him with a blameless heart, not a double heart. I once preached a message on a "divided heart." Later an Arab woman told me she had to leave the meeting, because she knew she had two hearts. A backslidden Jewish man told me he was so convicted he gave his whole heart to the Lord that day. We all have the same struggle.

Elijah had pleaded with God, "Turn the hearts of the people back to You again." God's fiery response was a manifestation of his judgment against every form of compromise and contamination that had entered the hearts of His people. The fire of Jehovah that incinerated the sacrifice on Carmel was the fire of the jealousy of God for the hearts of His children. The root of "jealousy" in Hebrew means "burning." God was longing for communion and fellowship with His people. They, indeed, fell on their faces in fear and worship at the terrifying display of His Presence. But, even after such an awesome experience, as we shall see, most continued on their double-minded path.

DOUBLE-MINDED BELIEVERS

It is too easy for us to point the finger at the people of Elijah's time. In the Lord's body today there is mixture everywhere. A house divided against itself simply will not stand. James (*Ya'acov*) the brother of Jesus wrote that a "double-minded person will be unstable in all his ways" (James1:8). He challenges us with the same issue with which the Lord confronted Israel on Mount Carmel. "Adulterers and adulteresses! Do you not know that friendship with the world is enmity with God? Whoever therefore wants to be a friend of the world makes himself an enemy of God" (James 4:4). These words are written to the church of Jesus Christ. He continues, "The Spirit who dwells in us yearns jealousy" (James 4:5).

The people of Israel had not been given the Holy Spirit as we have. We are worse than they are when we grieve the Holy Spirit by still desiring or participating in the evil of the world's system. The Apostle John put the issue this way: "Do not love the world or the things of the world. If anyone loves the world, the love of the Father is not in him" (1 John 2:15).

The execution of the false prophets by Elijah is also instructive for us. Our war, of course, is not "against flesh and blood ... but against the rulers of the darkness of this age" (Ephesians 6:12). We are to renounce and repent for our idolatry and "have no fellowship with the unfruitful works of darkness, rather expose them" (5:11). We are to take "the sword of the Spirit, which is the word of God; praying always with all prayer and supplication in the Spirit" (6:18). It was Elijah's prayer from his undivided heart desperate for God which brought the victory on Carmel.

THE SOURCE OF ELIJAH'S COURAGE

The courage of Elijah is a great challenge to us. To what can we attribute the courage of a single man publicly standing against an entire nation? We don't know that Elijah was naturally courageous or confrontational. I believe the answer can be found in the prophet's simple prayer on that memorable occasion. He implored "the LORD God of Abraham, Isaac, and Israel" to hear and respond to him, because "I have done all these things at Your word" (1 Kings 18:36). Every word and action of Elijah on that day was dictated and directed by the Lord. God told him specifically what to do—the twelve stones, the trench, all of it. Prophets walk in the power of a word not their own, but from God. "Your word is a lamp to my feet and a light to my path," the psalmist could proclaim (Psalm 119:105).

The source of Elijah's courage was his absolute obedience to a word from God. He knew that God watches over His Word to perform it. The prophet had also been refined for over three years since giving his last public prophetic word. In the Lord's economy purity always proceeds power. Elijah heard, obeyed, and prayed a simple prayer, and God manifested His presence.

Many centuries later General William Booth, the founder of the Salvation Army, caught the heart cry of the Elijah legacy with this song:

SEND THE FIRE

O God of burning, cleansing flame
Send the fire
Your blood bought gift today we claim
Send the fire today.
God of Elijah, hear our cry.

Send the fire
And make us fit to live or die
Send the fire today.
To burn up every trace of sin
To bring the light and glory in ...
Send the fire today!

ELIJAH HAS LEFT US THE LASTING LEGACY OF THE
POWER OF PREVAILING PRAYER.

6

Restoring the Altar
of the Lord

The restored altar of the Lord on Mount Carmel is a prophetic type and metaphor which carries deep significance for our instruction, and a serious warning for the Church and Israel in the last days. The confrontation on Carmel was a foreshadowing of things to come. The showdown between Jehovah and Baal points us toward something greater than even the events of that memorable day.

I would like to examine four of the ramifications of the contest on Carmel which I see as most important for us at the beginning of the twenty-first century. I believe that the sacrifice the Lord accepted on His restored altar represents a powerful depiction of four significant truths:

(1) the Cross of Jesus Christ
(2) the New Covenant
(3) the restoration of Israel
(4) the end-time fullness of the Church and Israel manifested as the "one new man in Christ"

THE CROSS OF CHRIST

The sacrifice Elijah offered on Carmel is a clear representation of the Cross of Christ. In this respect the typology of the prophetic event is graphic and unmistakable.

The wood on the altar points to the cross upon which Jesus was crucified. The slaughtered bull was the sin offering, even as Jesus was pierced and crushed for our iniquities. As people stared at the burning, butchered bull, they had been taught to understand that the bloody animal represented a substitutionary sacrifice for their sins. Jesus embodied the substance of that shadow, when He willingly was "led as a lamb to the slaughter" who died in our place, as "the LORD laid on Him the iniquity of us all" (Isaiah 53:6-7).

The blood of that animal was a foreshadowing of Christ's atoning and life-giving blood poured out for the sins of the world. The water that drenched the sacrifice and altar points to the water that gushed from our Savior's side pierced by a Roman spear. It is also a picture of the Word of God which still washes us. The fire of God's holiness and His wrath against sin fell upon His beloved Son on another mountain in Israel called the place the "place of a skull." Even the time of both sacrifices was identical. Calvary was the hour of the world's evening sacrifice. On that bloody afternoon in Jerusalem, as the Passover lambs were being slaughtered, "the sun was darkened and the veil of the temple was torn in two" (Luke 23:44-45). Mankind now had access to the throne room of God "by a new and living way which He consecrated for us, through the veil, that is His flesh" (Hebrews 10:20).

As the assembled nation on Carmel watched the holy fire consume the sacrifice they lay prostrate in worship. True worship was being restored, which also reflected another aspect of the meaning of the Cross. Not only was Jesus crucified that day, but He also took His corporate body (us) with Him: "Knowing this, that our old man was crucified with Him, that the body of sin might be done away with that we should no longer be slaves of sin" (Romans 6:6). By faith we need to "reckon ourselves to be dead indeed to sin, but alive to God in Christ Jesus our Lord" (v. 11).

This is the transforming power and wonder of the Cross. It is the great exchange. We give Him our old, corrupt life, and He gives us His new life. I was once asked to speak to a missionary association on the subject of the Cross. The pastor who invited me said, "We hear you preach the Cross. We need that." Shouldn't all pastors be preaching the Cross, as Paul did?

When Jesus saved me out of alcohol, drugs, show business and everything else that went along with such a "fast-lane" life-style, the Cross became powerfully real to me. My first message to addicts and street people in New York City is really the only message: "God forbid that I should boast except in the cross of our Lord Jesus Christ, by whom the world has been crucified to me, and I to the world" (Galatians 6:14). The centrality of the Cross of Christ must be restored to His church. A Cross-less Christianity is a false Christianity.

THE NEW COVENANT

Secondly, the momentous events that transpired on Mount Carmel are a dramatic foreshadowing of the New Covenant. In the Tanach (Old Testament), there are many wonderful "covenant conversations" between the Father and the Son. For instance, in Isaiah 49:8-9 the Father tells Jesus:

> In an acceptable time I have heard You; and in the day of salvation I have helped You; I will preserve You and give You as a covenant to the people, to restore the earth, to cause them to inherit desolate heritages; that You may say to the prisoners, "Go Forth."

In eternity, Jesus volunteered and asked the Father when He could come to Earth in the form of a man and die an innocent death and shed His blood for us as a covenant for the people. He is the New Covenant. A covenant is a solemn

69

binding contract between two parties ratified by blood. A covenant must be "cut," like circumcision. In Genesis 15, God cut an unconditional covenant with Abraham contracting the land of Canaan to the patriarch and his offspring forever. Animals were dismembered and the bloody pieces were laid on the ground of the covenant.

Abraham was asleep when the Lord manifested Himself as "a smoking oven and a burning torch" (Genesis 15:17), and ratified His covenant with the patriarch. God initiated the agreement and covenanted himself to fulfill it. Our God keeps covenant.

In Isaiah 49:8, the "day of salvation" in Hebrew is the "day of Yeshuah," the same root as the Hebrew name for Jesus. It means "redemption," "deliverance," and "wholeness." Jesus is the promised *brit am*, or "covenant for the people" ("cut one"), who became our eternal substitutionary sacrifice. His precious blood has once and for all fulfilled the meaning of the rivers of animal blood shed under the old covenant.

In another covenant conversation in eternity, Jehovah vows to Yeshua: "I, the LORD, have called You in righteousness, and I will hold Your hand; I will keep You and give You as a covenant to the people, as a light to the Gentiles, to open blind eyes, to bring out prisoners from the prison" (Isaiah 42:6-7). The New Covenant was agreed upon in eternity between the Father and the Son, "Behold, the former things have come to pass, and new things I declare; before they spring forth I tell you of them" (v. 9).

When we enter into this New Covenant by faith through the blood of Jesus, all the promises to the Son become ours. We are co-heirs with Jesus (Romans 8:17). He will save us, restore us, heal us, guard us, open our eyes, love us, and hold our hand as a loving Father. The benefits are endless even as He loved us before the foundation of the world.

When Jewish people challenge us to show them Jesus in the Old Testament, we take them to these Scriptures, and to many more, like Psalm 22, or Psalm 89, and Isaiah 53. It is wonderful to see the veil upon a Jewish heart removed as he or she sees Messiah as the covenant for the people. For Muslims, the revelation that God is a loving Father who would sacrifice His own Son for them is overwhelming. God has sworn by His holiness on His everlasting covenant. (See Psalm 89:35.)

WE ARE "NEW," NOT "RENEWED"

Some voices in Messianic Jewish circles would have us believe this is a "renewed" covenant. This is simply not true. It is also a most important distinction. The New Covenant liberates the believer from dead works, and Christ becomes central and preeminent. When we enter into the New Covenant relationship with Yeshua we are not "renewed," we become "new" (kainos) fresh, pure, innocent, never before used. In the greatest of miracles, through the divine power of the covenant, there has been "given to us exceedingly great and precious promises, that through these you may be partakers of the divine nature" (2 Peter 1:4). The divine power and promises of this New Covenant were seen from afar by the Old Testament saints. Prophets, kings, and even angels have desired to understand what we now see (Luke10:24;1 Peter1:10-11).

As the Lord opens to us deeper understanding of the New Covenant, we can begin to see it prophesied and foreshadowed in numerous places in the Old Testament. We are given the privilege of listening in on the eternal counsels of the Godhead. For instance, in Proverbs 8 there is recorded for us another detailed intimate conversation between the Father and Son:

> The Lord possessed me at the beginning of His way, before His works of old. I have been established from everlasting. When He prepared the heavens, I was there. Then I was beside Him as a master craftsman. And I was daily His delight, rejoicing always before

This is Jesus along side the Father at the very beginning

Him, rejoicing in His inhabited world, and My delight was with the sons of men. (Proverbs 8: 22-31)

This personification of Wisdom is a beautiful picture of Jesus longing for deep intimate fellowship with us. "Of Him [lit. "by His doing"] you are in Christ Jesus, who became for us wisdom from God—and righteousness and sanctification and redemption" (1 Corinthians 1:30). What glorious benefits are ours from the New Covenant!

JESUS SPOKE OF THE CROSS TO ELIJAH AND MOSES

The last time we see Elijah is not when he ascended to Heaven in a fiery chariot. It is on another mountaintop in Galilee, probably Tabor, in clear view from Muhrakah on Carmel. Jesus took Peter, James, and John there to pray. "As He prayed, the appearance of His face was altered, and His robe became white and glistening. And behold, two men talked with Him, who were Moses and Elijah, who appeared in glory and spoke of His decease, which He was about to accomplish in Jerusalem" (Luke 9:29-31).

What were Jesus, Moses, and Elijah talking about on the Mount of Transfiguration? They were discussing the coming death and resurrection of Jesus, literally "the exodus He would make," or "accomplish" in Jerusalem. This celestial conversation was about the Cross and the meaning of the New Covenant. We see the great lawgiver and greatest of prophets listening to the Son of God describe to them His coming crucifixion as the Passover Lamb of God slain before the foundation of the world. Was it then that Elijah began to understand some of the fuller meaning of what had happened when the fire of God had consumed the sacrifice on Mount Carmel eight centuries earlier? Moses (the Law) and Elijah (the Prophets) were realizing that Jesus is the fulfillment of the Torah. O, may we hunger for continuing revelation of the wonder of the New Covenant.

THE INGATHERING OF THE TWELVE TRIBES—ISRAEL RESTORED

Thirdly, the twelve stones of the altar of the Lord on Mount Carmel confront us with an objective picture of the final ingathering of the twelve tribes of Jacob and the restoration of the nation of Israel in our day. "Elijah took twelve stones, according to the number of the tribes of the sons of Jacob, to whom the word of the LORD had come, saying, 'Israel shall be your name'" (1 Kings 18:32). This was an obvious prophetic act when Elijah knowingly rebuilt the altar with twelve stones, even though the northern kingdom was divided from the two southern tribes. But that does not exhaust the meaning of the prophet's actions.

The Hebrew prophets were often not aware of the full eschatological meaning of what God told them to say or do. For instance, when Jeremiah prophesied the New Covenant in Jeremiah 31, he did not understand the specifics of how this would be fulfilled. At the Passover Seder, on the night that He was betrayed by Judas, Jesus explained the fulfillment of Jeremiah's prophecy. He held up the Passover cup of redemption, and said, "For this is My blood of the new covenant, which is shed for many for the remission of sins" (Matthew 26:28).

The assembled disciples in the upper room with Jesus, who partook of the bread and fruit of the vine, did not understand the full meaning of what they were doing. Fifty days later at Shavuot (Pentecost) when they were filled with the Holy Spirit, they began to understand these prophecies. Today we are still gleaning deeper insights into the mystery and power of the New Covenant in Jesus' blood.

Likewise, Elijah did not know of the judgment, exile and subsequent re-gathering of His people. But he did know exactly what God had told him to do, as he said, "I am Your servant and I have done all these things at Your word" (1 Kings 18:36).

In these last days, God has called the children of Israel back to the land which He gave them by covenant. He still has a controversy with them and He will confront them one last time in the land of Israel when the Jewish people will finally recognize and receive their Messiah.

> And I will pour on the house of David and the inhabitants of Jerusalem the Spirit of grace and supplication; then they will look on Me whom they have pierced. Yes, they will mourn for Him as one mourns for an only son, and grieve for Him as one grieves for a firstborn. (Zechariah 12:10)

God's ancient covenant people will look to Jesus and repent before He comes back. Jesus clearly prophesied as He wept over Jewish Jerusalem, "You shall see Me no more till you say, 'Blessed is He who comes in the name of the Lord!'" (Matthew 23:39). In Hebrew these words are *"Baruch haba beshem Adonai."* That is why we sing them prophetically with such fervor. Jesus said He will not return until He is welcomed by His own people in Jerusalem. Peter preached the same message to the Jews in the temple:

> Repent therefore and be converted, that your sins may be blotted out, so that times of refreshing may come from the presence of the Lord, and that he may send Jesus Christ, who was preached to you before. (Acts 3: 19-21)

Yes, the people of Israel have an appointment with Yeshua. They are turning to Him now in greater numbers than at any time since the Book of Acts. At almost every Shabbat we see someone praying for salvation. There are now over forty Messianic Jewish congregations from Dan to Beersheva. It is here on Mount Carmel and throughout the land that He promises:

> I will sprinkle clean water on you, and you shall be clean; I will cleanse you from all your filthiness and from all your idols. I will give you a new heart.... I will pour my Spirit within you and cause you to walk in My statutes.... Then the nations which are left around you shall know that I, the LORD, have rebuilt the ruined places ... I, the LORD, have spoken it, and I will do it. (Ezekiel 36:25-27, 36)

These and many more new covenant promises are being fulfilled in Israel today. God is keeping His appointment with His chosen people in their ancient homeland.

REPLACEMENT THEOLOGY

Today there is an increasing controversy over the place of national Israel and the Jewish people in the plan of God. The heresy of replacement theology (that the Church has replaced Israel) became official Church policy at the Council of Nicea in 325 A.D. The Romanized State Church officially cut off the Jewish roots of our faith, labeling the Jewish people "polluted wretches," and therefore withdrawing from what they described as, "that most odious fellowship." By ratifying this position, the Council officially established an anti-Judaic foundation for the doctrine and practice of the Church. The Council declared that separation from the Jews was the only acceptable Christian behavior. It was only a short step from division to persecution, to pogroms, inquisitions, crusades and the Holocaust, all of which became part of the horrible history of the Church towards the Jews. I grew up in the Roman Catholic church, where as a boy I was exposed to the poisonous lies of anti-Semitism. The ugly tide of anti-Semitism is rising again.

Those who espouse replacement theology have aligned themselves with the heritage of hatred of the Jews practiced in the Roman Catholic and Greek and Russian Orthodox churches. Romans 9:1-5 and Romans 11 should be mandatory study for all of us. I once sent a copy of Romans 11 to an anti-Semitic relative who insisted on calling Israel "Palestine." When I asked her what she thought of the passage, the response was, "Our priest thinks some of what Paul wrote was okay, but some of it wasn't."

When Karen and I were living in Jerusalem in 1989, we spent an evening with an American missionary couple who were working with Muslims. The man had been a brilliant student in Bible school and was a genuine scholar. As we talked, the chill wind of anti-Semitism blew across our fellowship. This brother had memorized Scriptures for years, and seemed to be on a vendetta against the Jews. He even questioned the facts and magnitude of the Holocaust. We couldn't pray together. One of his colleagues had mocked the Jews and Israel in the presence of my Jewish wife. This predisposition can be so ingrained that it becomes part of a person's character, and often the person may not even be aware of it.

This contention over the place of Israel today is polarizing the body of Messiah. As anti-Semitism increases, especially in Britain, continental Europe, and the Muslim world, it will take greater courage for the Church to stand with Israel. But those who align themselves with God's Word and purposes concerning the Jews will be blessed.

MESSIANIC MILLENNIALISM

On the other side of the theological spectrum, some Messianic Jews do not consider themselves part of the Church. Some believe, teach and write that Jewish believers will rule the Earth for a thousand years from a new temple in Jerusalem. They say Jesus will also have His throne there, but that animal sacrifices will be re-instituted. These Torah-observant believers—who keep different parts of the Mosaic law—teach that Gentile millennial believers throughout the world will also be Torah (Law)-observant, quoting such verses as, "Out of Zion shall go forth the law" (Isaiah 2:3). What happened to the Cross and the New Covenant?

I believe this is an overreaction by some Messianic Jews to a Gentile Church that has lost its Jewish roots. Such separatist, exclusivist positions have caused many believers who love Israel to back away from some Messianic Jews. I also believe such a dogmatically held and promoted dispensationalist position is not "the testimony of Jesus which is the spirit of [true] prophecy" (Revelation 19:10). The restored altar on Carmel points to the *completion of the Church with saved Israel.* A Jewish rabbi named Paul wrote, "There is one body and one Spirit ... one hope ... one Lord, one faith, one baptism, one God and Father of all, who is above all, through all, and in you all" (Ephesians 4:4-6). I would add, "What God has joined together, let no man separate." Jesus told His Jewish disciples, "I will build My church, and the gates of hell shall not prevail against it" (Matthew 16:18).

ONE NEW MAN

Lastly, Elijah was a forerunner who prophetically and practically prepared the way for the "one new man" of Jew and Gentile in one body. He went to the foreigner and became family with a widow and a fatherless boy—a picture of the Lord's true end time church. Jesus died to make us one.

I see it happen with Jewish and Arab drug addicts and alcoholics. When they love Jesus, then they begin to love each other. The Cross and New Covenant in His blood is the only thing that can heal the world's longest running family feud between half-brothers, the sons of Abraham—Ishmael and Isaac.

Once Karen and I were treated to a wonderful Erev Shabbat (Friday evening) dinner at House of Victory. It was cooked by an Arab chef who had been on drugs for thirty years. At the dinner table were three Arabs, eight Jews (including Karen) and me. It was just a little taste of being reconciled "in one body through the cross" (Ephesians 2:10).

TWELVE STONES

The number twelve represents multiplication, fullness, and completeness. Other examples are the twelve apostles, the twelve tribes and the twelve gates of Jerusalem. Do the twenty-four elders in Revelation 4 represent the Church and Israel as one? For the believer, the altar also represents our heart, where the Lord should be reigning upon His throne in His temple, which He bought with His blood. The altar that Elijah restored points to the healed and undivided heart of a New Covenant believer. The idols in our heart need to be torn down. Even as Elijah executed the idol-worshipping priests who had usurped the altar of God, we are to cut off by the Spirit "every high thing that exalts itself against the knowledge of God, bringing every thought into captivity to the obedience of Christ" (2 Corinthians 10:5).

The latter-days Church needs to move in "the Spirit and power of Elijah" by restoring the ancient stones of the Cross, the centrality of Jesus and the crucified life. When we embrace the New Covenant by faith, the Lord pours more of His character into us and more of His compassion is released through us to others. We once did a series of meetings in

Finland on "Restoring the Altar of the Lord." Each night our translator would eagerly ask, "Which stones are we going to speak about tonight?" We need them all.

In Jeremiah chapter 31, God's Word clearly proclaims that He will gather His people from the ends of the Earth and He will Father them and Shepherd them in Israel. He says He will cut a "new covenant with the house of Israel and with the house of Judah" (v.31). God vows that He will "forgive their iniquity, and their sin I will remember no more" (v.34). The Creator of the universe then takes a solemn oath that if the laws that regulate the sun, moon, stars and sea depart from His control, then "the seed of Israel shall also cease from being a nation before Me forever" (v. 36). These are serious words indeed from the Lord of Hosts concerning the nation of Israel, the "apple of His eye." The destiny of Israel is to become a New Covenant nation. And He has made us "ministers of the new covenant" (2 Corinthians 3:6).

The restored altar on Mount Carmel represents the undivided heart of Jew and Gentile believers—"living stones" in one body—made possible by the Cross and the New Covenant. As we enter into the fullness of the mystery of the "one new man" of Jew and Gentile, those who long to sing Heaven's new song cry out together: "You have redeemed us to God by Your blood out of every tribe and tongue and people and nation" (Revelation 5:9).

THE LIVING LEGACY OF ELIJAH IS A RESTORED ALTAR OF LIVING STONES OF JEWS AND GENTILES WORSHIPPING JESUS IN ONE BODY IN THE LAST DAYS.

-7-

THE SOUND OF ABUNDANCE OF RAIN

After the execution of the four hundred and fifty prophets of Baal, Elijah still had more of the Lord's work to do that day. God had told him to confront Ahab and then He would end the drought and send rain to Israel. The king and his entourage went back up the mountainside to the place where the ashes of the burnt altar were probably still smoldering. There they ate and drank the customary ceremonial meal after a religious sacrifice.

But Elijah didn't join them. He continued up Mount Carmel to the crest of the mountain. There "he bowed down on the ground, and put his face between his knees" (1 Kings 18:42). Prostrating himself, the prophet was actually in a fetal position, on the ground, beseeching the Lord to send the promised rain. Previously we have seen Elijah stretched out in compassionate intercession for the life of the widow's dead son. We saw how God responded by answering his petition with miraculous new life. Now again, Elijah was stretching himself out to God, but this time for the land and the nation. The prophet then sent his servant up to look toward the Mediterranean for rain clouds.

THREE KINDS OF BELIEVERS

I see in this scene a picture of three kinds of believers. First, there is Ahab who experienced the awesome manifestation of the fire of God's presence and saw the people fall on their faces in worship before Adonai. Then four hundred and fifty prophets of Baal he had been worshipping were slain according to the Torah. Even now as thousands of his subjects were making their way home, they must have been discussing and considering the terrible events of the day and what they meant. Would the king now take a stand against his absent wife and her imported idolatry? Had the demonstration of God's power changed the king? Ahab sat at the very place of the sacrifice, eating and drinking. As his future actions would reveal, nothing had changed for him. It was business as usual. Even the terrifying display of the Holy One of Israel had not penetrated his hardened heart. The Spirit of the fear of the Lord might have still been hovering over his people, but not over him.

Nearby lay the man of God crying out for his land and his people. Ahab "went up to eat and drink" (v.42). Elijah "went up" into the presence of God and was feeding on the Lord's promise. Was he also fasting? One man went up to eat. Another went up to pray. The third man in this scene, Elijah's servant, obeyed his master by "going up" to the top of Carmel seven times. Here we see carnal, compromised Ahab eating with friends after a powerful meeting, yet himself untouched by God. The busy servant was also missing the deepest essence of what God was doing. But the man of prayer, Elijah, was in deep communion with his God. Only this one heard the sound (or "voice" in Hebrew) of the coming abundance of rain, or God's blessing. How sad that so many of us miss the deep things of God because we are not stretching ourselves out to Him in prayer. Three men "went up." Only one heard God.

(George Whitefield, the British evangelist who ushered in the Great Awakening in the American colonies in the 18th century, said that his whole life was "on the stretch for God.")

The rest of the nation was on the way home, perhaps wondering if true worship would be restored. But still one man remained in the "secret place," even in public. His words are not recorded this time, but we know what was coming from his heart. He was praying for the promised rains, for blessing for his nation after the judgment of drought. The prophet was reminding God of His word, "Go present yourself to Ahab and I will send rain on the earth" (1 Kings 18:1). Elijah had certainly obeyed the Lord by confronting Ahab. But even so he would not let go of God until the promise came. He was "praying through."

When we pray the promises of God, we become His "remembrancers." We are reminding Him and crying out for His response. In Chapter 62 of Isaiah, the watchmen on the walls of Jerusalem are told never to hold their peace and to "make mention" or remind God and give Him no rest "till He makes Jerusalem a praise in the earth" (v. 6-7). The word for "make mention" means to remind. It has the same root as the word for "secretary." We are to be "God's secretaries" in prayer. That's what Elijah was doing.

But there was also much more involved. It was as though he had become pregnant with the prayer. He was crumpled over in pain and travail, as if he was birthing a baby. He was agonizing in prayer until the answer came.

"LIQUID PRAYER"

Once a Salvation Army team in France sent a wire to General William Booth in London. They reported that there were no results from their evangelistic street outreaches. Booth wired back two words: "Try tears." The lives of the

great revivalists like John Wesley, George Whitefield, D.L.
Moody, and Charles Finney all attest to the fact that God's
cure for complacency is tears—a broken heart for the lost.
They all knew the secret that Elijah was learning: "Those who
sow in tears shall reap in joy. He who continually goes forth
weeping, bearing seed for sowing shall doubtless come again
with rejoicing, bringing his sheaves with him" (Psalm 126:5-6).
Prophets weep with God for the lost. Travail brings triumph.
Charles Spurgeon called it "liquid prayer."

It was the prevailing prayer of people like John Hyde
that brought revival to India. On the hills of Wales, the little
prayer groups crying out in the night ushered in the mighty
Welsh revival. There are numerous "prayer mountains" and
prayer watches in South Korea that have been instrumental in
changing that nation.

Before we moved to Israel, I had a vision in a prayer meeting
in New York City. I saw a large, white, fleecy cloud covering
over Galilee from the Golan Heights to Mount Carmel. I
asked the Lord what it was. He replied, "It is the prayer of
the saints for Israel. I am waiting for a remnant I can trust and
then I will pour out my Spirit on northern Israel." One of the
new worship songs the Lord has given us on Mount Carmel is
based on these confirming verses from Psalm 68:32-35:

Sing to God you kingdoms of the earth ...
To Him who rides on the heavens ...
He sends out His voice, a mighty voice.
Ascribe strength to God; His excellence is over Israel,
And His strength is in the clouds.
O God, You are more awesome than Your holy places.
The God of Israel is He who gives strength
and power to His people. Blessed be God!

In October of 1998, I told northern congregational leaders
at our annual summit meeting on Carmel that I believed

we were entering a season of drought. Three years later, in winter 2001-2002 the worst recorded drought in Israel's modern history ended. Israel has begun to purchase water from Turkey. The Sea of Galilee, our major reservoir, was at its lowest recorded level ever. The country was desperate for rain.

A DOWNPOUR IN SINGAPORE

In the Fall of 2001, we were in Singapore for a conference beginning on the eve of Succot, the Feast of Tabernacles. The opening event was an outdoor celebration held on a covered stage erected on the large, open grounds of the Anglican Cathedral in the midst of the high-rise buildings of the financial center in downtown Singapore. Traditional Succot booths were built, as well as seven large, metal menorahs (seven-branched candelabra) erected for the festival. There were also food booths and Christian music and book stalls. It was amazing to see Karen and our team leading thousands of Asian Christians as they worshipped Jesus in Hebrew. Just as the Singapore leaders were preparing to take an offering for God's work on Mount Carmel, the most powerful rainstorm I can remember descended upon the open meeting. Within minutes, the water was up to people's ankles. Many of the people simply put up umbrellas or plastic bags over themselves and their children, and kept praising God. I will never forget the sight. One of the large gas-filled, seven-branched candlesticks kept burning brightly throughout the downpour. We told them this was "the sound of abundance of rain" for Israel. Finally, ushers took up a collection in the pouring rain with plastic bags. We later found out this was the largest single offering we've ever received for Carmel Assembly. (They did not know it, but our congregation was in desperate need of funds.)

When we returned to Israel at our next Shabbat meeting we reported what had happened in Singapore. We said that we believed the drought was over, and then prayed for rain. At the end of the meeting the rain came. People had to run through the downpour to get to their cars. By faith, I had brought an umbrella! In another meeting as I was talking about the rain, it came down so hard and loud on the skylight over our altar the people couldn't hear me. We just laughed and prayed and thanked God.

The drought was finished. This early rain points to a coming outpouring of the Holy Spirit. In the spring of 2002, Mount Carmel had received 30% more rain than its annual average. Rain continued to fall even as late as the end of April, and even into May that year, which is unheard of in Israel.

SHOWERS OF BLESSINGS

We believe that we are moving into a season of great blessing as we continue to hold onto Ezekiel chapter 34, even as Elijah was holding onto his word from the Lord. Here are some of the promises that are being fulfilled on Mount Carmel today:

> I will seek out My sheep and deliver them from all the places where they are scattered on a cloudy and dark day. And I will bring them out from the peoples and gather them from the countries, and bring them to their own land ... I will feed them in good pasture, and their fold shall be on the high mountains of Israe ... I will seek what was lost ... bind up the broken and strengthen what was sick ... I will make [cut] a covenant of peace [shalom] with them ... I will make them and the places all around My hill a blessing; and I will cause showers to come down in their season; there shall be showers of blessing. (Ezekiel 34:12-26)

These showers of blessing have begun and are increasing as we move into more of the Lord's abundance. God says He will do it. We believe Him.

"LEBANON SHALL BE A FRUITFUL FIELD"

One of the places where the Lord is beginning to pour out blessing around His "hill" is in a town just north of us near the Lebanese border. In the middle of the night, on May 23, 2000, the Israeli army pulled out of the security zone in southern Lebanon and moved across the border into Galilee. Since the 1980s, the South Lebanese Army (SLA), who are mainly nominal Christians, had welcomed the Israeli army to their towns and villages. Together they fought against different Muslim terrorist groups, most notably Yasser Arafat and the PLO. Arafat was trying to take control of a country bordering with Israel by building an international terror network and a military infrastructure there. (Previously, in 1970, King Hussein's Jordanian army had driven Arafat out of Jordan in bloody battles in what is now called "Black September.") After Israel drove the PLO out of Lebanon and Arafat found asylum in Tunisia, the SLA and the Israel Defense Forces (IDF) fought together in southern Lebanon against the Hizbullah ("army of Allah").

Hizbullah, like the PLO, is a terrorist organization dedicated to the destruction of Israel. They are supported with massive finances, training and weapons by Syria and Iran. Today ten thousand of their missiles are aimed at northern Israel. They are also on the U.S. list of international terrorist organizations. Together, the IDF and the SLA attempted to guard the Christian towns and villages of South Lebanon, while protecting Israel's northern border. A Jewish believer in our congregation grew up in Galilee, where PLO terrorists from Lebanon invaded her town and slaughtered school children. She still has nightmares of sleeping in the town bomb shelter as a young girl during rocket attacks from across the

Lebanese border. Our two foster sons experienced the same thing as children growing up in northern Galilee.

Over the years we have prayed much for Lebanon. One precious young pastor I met from Lebanon had his leg blown off when he stepped on a mine while serving in the SLA. He told me he cried out to Jesus to save his life, and became a believer that day. Later on he led a dozen Hizbullah (Muslim terrorists) to the Lord, before having to leave Lebanon because his life was in danger.

One of the Scriptures we have stood on is from Isaiah 35, which speaks of the "highway of holiness"—one of the foundational teachings of our congregation. In verse 2, it says that Lebanon and Carmel "shall see the glory of the Lord." We knew that if the IDF pulled out of South Lebanon, the SLA would be defenseless against Syrian and Iranian equipped terrorists like Hizbullah. So we prayed that when Israel would leave Lebanon our government would open the door for our South Lebanese allies to come into Israel, rather than face sure slaughter. And that is what happened on the night of May 23, 2000.

We heard the news the next morning. The Israel Defense Forces had surprised Hizbullah by withdrawing suddenly back into Israel. There were no casualties. With the IDF came thousands of SLA members with their families (7,000 total), and by morning they were all safely in Galilee. Overnight, these South Lebanese had left everything and were being temporarily settled on kibbutzim on the Sea of Galilee and other areas in Israel. We began praying, "Lord, show us which group to go to. Open a door." He did just that.

7,000 LEBANESE IN GALILEE

On a "spying out the land" trip to Israel back in 1989, before we moved here, I had met a young Arab believer from Haifa, named Joseph Haddad. The Lord told me then that we would work together. For years now, Joseph has served on the staff at House of Victory. His wife, Ibtisom, is from Lebanon. In the mid-90s, they had visited her family there and led Ibtisom's sister, Rita, to the Lord. Rita's husband was an officer in the SLA. When the Lebanese came into Israel, Joseph located Rita and her husband on a kibbutz near the Mediterranean, less than a mile south of the Lebanese border. Some of our congregation loaded up three vans and several cars with diapers, baby milk, other food, clothing, and toys, plus a box of Arabic Bibles. We drove north from Haifa in a mini-caravan, to visit Rita and the Lebanese refugees.

On arriving at the kibbutz, it was immediately clear that the Lebanese soldiers and their families were in shock. They were understandably suspicious of us. Ibtisom found her sister Rita, whom she then introduced to Rita Tsukahira, the Jewish wife of Pastor Peter Tsukahira. I'll never forget the "one new woman" embrace of the two Ritas! Elijah had gone to Lebanon, but some Lebanese had come to us!

We put the boxes of diapers, food, and toys on picnic tables under some trees. Gradually the Lebanese soldiers and their parents, wives, and children began to gather around curiously. Our people started to distribute the things that were so desperately needed. Some young Israeli soldiers looked on in approval. There were about two hundred Lebanese living in the small cabins of the kibbutz. Three young widows whose husbands had just been killed were dressed in black. Quite a crowd began to gather. They spoke mostly Arabic, with a little English and Hebrew. (Many Lebanese are not Arabs, claiming descent from the Phoenicians who lived there in the time of Elijah and Jesus. After the Muslim invasion of the seventh century A.D. the language was changed to Arabic.)

After a while, I asked Ibtisam to set up her keyboard. We passed out some Arabic songbooks, and began to worship *Yesua* ("Jesus" in Arabic). More people gathered around us.

"TODAY THESE SCRIPTURES ARE BEING FULFILLED"

There was a sweet presence of the Lord on this beautiful May morning in Galilee. After several songs, we then gave out Arabic Bibles to the adults and children's Bibles with pictures for all the curious children. I was asking the Lord what I should share with them. Joseph began to translate for me as I asked them to turn to Isaiah 29. They just stared at me. They had probably never even heard of Isaiah. They certainly didn't know where it was. An Arab believer named "Jihad" from Beit Jala (next to Bethlehem) who had come off drugs with us told them the page number. When everyone had found the page, these precious Lebanese people heard in their mother tongue these words for the first time:

> Is it not yet a very little while
> Till Lebanon shall be turned into a fruitful field
> ["Carmel" in Hebrew and Arabic]
> And the fruitful field ["Carmel"] be esteemed as a forest?
> In that day the deaf shall hear the words of the book, And the eyes of the blind shall see out of obscurity and out of darkness.
> The humble also shall increase their joy in the Lord, And the poor among men shall rejoice
> In the Holy One of Israel. (Isaiah 29:17-19)

I looked at all these people who had just lost everything and told them that God loved them so much He even put them in the Bible. Then I said to them, "Today these Scriptures are being fulfilled." A few began to cry, then others. Soon everyone was crying, including me. Tough soldiers who had known nothing but war since their childhood were weeping in front of their families. I told them about the love of Jesus and then gave an invitation for salvation. About half the group or more came forward, as our team prayed with them.

The Israeli soldiers who had been watching and listening, now were interested—probably wondering how Lebanon got into "their" Bible. Rita Tsukahira and other Jewish believers with our team began sharing with the Israelis. It became a glorious "one new man" Pentecostal meeting! Jesus was indeed returning "in the power of the Spirit to Galilee, and news of Him" was about to go "through all the surrounding region" (Luke 4:14).

We began holding weekly outdoor meetings at the kibbutz. Relationships developed between a group from our congregation and the Lebanese. At each meeting, different people would pray to receive the Lord. Even several Shiite Muslims accepted Jesus. One family of Muslims became believers when their teenage daughter had visions of Jesus. After some months, the Israeli government began to settle the Lebanese into apartments in nearby Israeli towns. Three hundred Lebanese families were given apartments and subsidies in the Nahariya ("rivers of God") area near the kibbutz where we first met. We moved the weekly meetings to the new home of a high-ranking SLA officer. He had been wounded by the PLO and Hizballah. His wife and children have become believers. When we outgrew his living room, we moved the meeting outside into his spacious yard, where we would meet under his olive trees.

THE ELIJAH-LEBANESE CONNECTION ("ELIAS")

As we got to know our new brothers and sisters, another connection with Mount Carmel emerged. Elijah is a specially revered saint among Lebanese Christians, perhaps because he lived with the widow and her son in their country. Many Lebanese Christians are named "Elias," Arabic for "Elijah."

The oldest "Elias" of this group left Lebanon in the middle of the night in his pajamas. When we first met him, those were the only clothes he had with him. He also left his false teeth in his Lebanese home. The Israeli government provided him with a new set of teeth. I told Elias, now that he has Jewish teeth he is really "one new man" in Christ. Sadly, in June 2002, he went back to Lebanon where he was thrown in jail and tortured.

I had the privilege of performing the marriage ceremony of a young Lebanese officer and his bride in our new building. This man is one of a number of SLA officers who have become believers. Our prayer is that the 35,000 Syrian troops who currently control Lebanon will end their occupation and go back to Syria. Then one day, these Lebanese people will return to their own country and impact their people with the gospel. They will be literally following in the footsteps of Elijah and Jesus.

After helping establish this growing work for a year, we turned the new ministry over to Joseph and Ibtisam. The Haddads make many home visits and bring needed humanitarian aid to our new friends. Some Lebanese families in Haifa have also recently become believers and attend our meetings at Carmel Assembly. One of these young men had been tortured in a Syrian prison. I watched him tenderly feed a Jewish baby at a Shabbat meeting recently. The Lord has now given us a large meeting place north of Haifa for the Lebanese. On Christmas Day 2001, we held a special meeting and celebration. Over one hundred Lebanese attended. They now meet in a rented home on the main street of Nahariya.

A LIGHT IN BETHLEHEM

Our Shabbat meetings are held in Hebrew, Russian, Arabic, and English. This presents quite a challenge to Karen and our worship team. The message is usually in Hebrew or English with a second language translated on the platform, while the other translations are done by headphones. In November of 2001, we invited a friend of ours, a pastor from Bethlehem, to speak to our congregation in Arabic. He described to us how Muslim militants from Yasser Arafat's Fatah branch of the PLO demanded the use of the roof of his church to shoot at Jews who visit Rachel's Tomb nearby. He refused. Muslim gunmen routinely force their way into Arab Christian homes and churches in Bethlehem and Beit Jala and fire upon Israeli troops and civilians in the Gilo neighborhood of Jerusalem. When Israel responds in defense, the biased news media make it look like Jews are attacking Christians. In the past several years, hundreds of Christians from Bethlehem have left for Canada, the U.S., Europe, and Australia.

This pastor told us that his brother had also been outspoken about his faith in Jesus, and that Muslims had hacked him to death with axes on the Mount of Olives. This fearless Arab pastor continues to preach the gospel in Arabic on the radio, even though the Palestinian Authority has told him to stop. Ninety-five percent of his church are out of work. Jewish believers, including our congregation and others, regularly send food and support to his church. The PA won't give jobs to born-again believers, and because of the latest outbreak of terrorism and violence condoned and promoted by Chairman Arafat, there is no tourism in Bethlehem.

In December 2001, Israel would not allow Arafat to go to Bethlehem for the annual Christmas midnight mass, unless he arrested the four murderers of former Cabinet Minister Rehavam Ze'evi. The murderers were in Ramallah, about two hundred meters from Arafat's compound. Mr. Arafat's attempt to portray himself as a champion of Christianity is, of course, preposterous. He has used Christians as human shields in Beit Jala and Bethlehem, and Christians have been fleeing the PA at four times the rate of Muslims. The PA imprisons

Muslims who accept Jesus. We hid one young ex-Muslim from the Ramallah area.

Our friend is the only Arab pastor on the West Bank or Gaza who publicly acknowledges God's covenant with the Jewish people for the land of Israel. Other believing leaders either espouse replacement theology, or have adopted an extreme dispensationalist doctrine to support their pro-Palestinian stance. Some missionaries to the Arabs are overtly anti-Semitic.

This Arab pastor came out strongly against replacement theology in his message to our congregation. He also shares his faith with Jewish soldiers at checkpoints, and gives them the New Testament in Hebrew. He later told me that he had warned Prime Minister Yitzhak Rabin about the danger of giving Bethlehem and other large cities to the PLO. In 1995, Rabin was assassinated by an ultra-orthodox Jew.

Perhaps a brief description of the background will help shed some light on the situation. Israel gave Bethlehem, located five miles south of Jerusalem, to the Palestinian Authority in 1995. Yasser Arafat and his spokesmen promptly promoted the lie that Jesus was a Palestinian, not a Jew. The historical fact is that Jesus was a descendant of King David, born in the City of David, in Israel. (See Micah 5:2, Matthew 1:21, 10:23, etc.) There was no place called "Palestine" at the time of Jesus. The Romans destroyed the Jewish Temple and brutally murdered thousands of Jews in 70 A.D. In 135 A.D., the Romans changed the name of Israel to "Palestina" after the Philistines, the ancient enemy of Israel. This was an attempt to eradicate the Jewish people who rejected the Roman religion. (Haman, Herod, Rome, and Hitler have all tried to destroy the Jews.) The Philistines were a seagoing people from Crete who lived along the shore of what is now the Gaza Strip. By contrast, people who now call themselves Palestinians are originally Arabs who came from the Arabian Peninsula, beginning with the Muslim invasion of the seventh century A.D. After World

War I, many Arabs immigrated to Palestine from Syria, Iraq, Saudi Arabia, Jordan, and Lebanon, because Jewish immigrants had begun creating agriculture and industry in pre-state Israel in areas previously uninhabitable.

THE SOUND OF RAIN IN PALESTINIAN TERRITORIES

The land currently called the "West Bank" is situated on what the Bible calls "the mountains of Israel" (Samaria, Benjamin, Ephraim, and Judah). God is going to pour out His Spirit there. We know of some Muslims there who have already accepted Jesus. Their lives are in danger. Here is an accurate report from April 26, 2002, entitled, "Hurting Palestinians Hungry for God":

"My people are hungry and thirsty for God," our friend S. told us this week as he came to share his wonderful deliverance from jail in Nablus as a result of the IDF operation there. (He is a Palestinian who became a believer through the witness of Messianic friends, and was imprisoned by the Palestinian Authority because of his faith nearly two years ago.) His inspiring testimony confirms other reports of unprecedented interest in Christianity amongst Palestinians, who are suffering greatly under the despotic rule of Chairman Arafat and the gangs of gunmen who control local towns and villages through fear and force. Grisly public executions of suspected "collaborators" by masked gunmen in Jenin, Ramallah, Bethlehem and Hebron this week have been a grim reminder to the people of who is boss in Palestinian areas. (Parents in Gaza have also been shocked by the deaths of three children attempting a terror attack, as a result of the culture of violence and glorifying of martyrs in schools.) Political correctness demands an enthusiastic outward response, but inside, there is a spiritual vacuum. Right now there is an open window of opportunity for a mighty move of the Holy Spirit amongst the Palestinian people.

Praise God for S's release and pray for the many lives he was able to touch through his vibrant witness to the Lord in prison. Pray for him, his wife and eight children as they have been reunited, and ask the Lord to guide them into His plan for the next stage of their lives. S. can't return to his home village as his life is in danger.

"For as the rain comes down, and the snow from heaven, and do not return there, but water the earth, and make it bring forth and bud, that it may give seed to the sower and bread to the eater, so shall My word be that goes forth from My mouth; it shall not return to Me void, but it shall accomplish what I please, and it shall prosper in the thing for which I sent it" (Isaiah 55:10-11).

Yes, God is beginning to move among the Palestinians.

WE DEDICATED MOUNT CARMEL TO JESUS

In Israel we are surrounded by deep darkness, but like Elijah we see the little cloud and hear the sound of the abundance of rain. There are two Carmelite monasteries on Mount Carmel. These Catholic priests and nuns believe the little cloud that Elijah saw was an apparition of Mary, the mother of Jesus, whom they believe is the "queen of heaven." Each year Arab Catholics from Galilee hold a parade in Haifa honoring Mary. Israeli police hold back traffic as "Christians" carry a statue of Mary through the streets of Haifa and up Mount Carmel where the statue "rests" for the winter. Jews from Haifa watch this idolatry. We have to explain that we are not Catholics and do not worship Mary. It is difficult for Galilee Arabs to admit that Mary (Miriam) was a young devout Jewish virgin who grew up in Nazareth. I recently saw the Pope (on TV) call on Mary to bring peace to the Holy Land.

On January 1, 2000, members from several Haifa congregations—Jews, Arabs, and Gentiles—met in front of the statue of Mary at the Stella Maris monastery overlooking the port of Haifa. This spot is literally one hundred meters from where the Lord visited me in the rental car years ago. We renounced this idolatry to Mary and rededicated Mount Carmel to Jesus. We then marched down the mountain to hold a prayer meeting in an Arab church.

"A CLOUD AS SMALL AS A MAN'S HAND"

As Elijah continued to travail for the promised rain, his servant obediently went back to the top of Carmel a seventh time. Then, the exhausted man came running back to the still prostrate prophet, and shouted excitedly, "There is a cloud, as small as a man's hand, rising out of the sea!" (1 Kings 18:44). The Hebrew description is of a hand stretched out in supplication. Seven is the number of completion. His prayer had been specific, fervent and persistent—and now it was becoming effective. The prophet had "prayed through." After three and a half years, the rain was finally coming!

As Ahab mounted his chariot for his return home across the Jezreel Valley, "the sky became black with clouds and wind, and there was a heavy rain" (v.45). "Then the hand of the Lord came upon Elijah" (v.46). The Holy Spirit came on the prophet and, with supernatural power, he ran ahead of the king's chariot to the entrance of Jezreel. A servant running ahead of a king was a picture of homage and humility. Was Elijah still trying to let the king know that if he would only turn to God, the prophet would serve him? One thing is for certain, the hand of the Lord was directing Elijah to Jezreel and a confrontation with Jezebel.

We hear the sound of abundance of rain on Mount Carmel today. It is harvest time and the Lord's barns will be full. We hear the rain of coming revival.

THE ELIJAH LEGACY RELEASES THE RAIN.

8

Commissioned in a Cave

Through the rainstorm, wind, thunder, and lightning, we see the prophet running before the chariot of his king. "The hand of the Lord," or the power of God, had come upon Elijah. God empowered His servants for special assignments, as He did when Ezra led the exiles back to Jerusalem: "The hand of our God was upon us, and he delivered us from the hand of the enemy" (Ezra 8:3 1). After the outpouring of the Holy Spirit at Shavuot (Pentecost), "the hand of the Lord" would come corporately upon the early Church with the result that "a great number believed and turned to the Lord" (Acts 11:21). The "hand of the Lord," the divine inspiration, presence, and empowerment of God, was supernaturally driving Elijah forward to his next assignment.

He ran over twenty miles through the downpour to the city of Jezreel. The ancient town commanded the northern entrance to the valley of the same name. Jezreel means, "God sows." The fortified tower there was one of Ahab's military strongholds, and one of his royal palaces was also in this city. Under the influence of Jezebel, institutions for the worship of Baal had been founded there. In fact, Jezreel had become Jezebel's stronghold.

JEZEBEL'S RAGE

After the king and prophet arrived at Jezreel, Ahab went to report to his wife. She knew about the confrontation on Carmel, but not the result. She had kept the four hundred prophets under her patronage with her. They were devotees of the Canaanite goddess Asherah, Baal's mythological sexual partner. Jezebel had seen the downpour of rain. Did she actually think Baal had defeated Jehovah and brought the needed rain?

The brief reference to the king's report to his wife is most illuminating concerning his character. "And Ahab told Jezebel all that Elijah had done, also how he had executed all the prophets with the sword" (1 Kings 19:1). In Ahab's report, he left one thing out—God. The king had witnessed the divine judgment of drought and famine, the supernatural falling of the fire of God, as well as the prophet's prayer and the resulting rainstorm. He must have been convinced that all this was from God, but he still was not converted. There are many today who are convinced, but not converted. I believe Ahab was a slave to the demonic spell of his seductive wife. Ahab had blocked God out of his life. Those who continually resist Him and persecute His people will finally be given "over to a reprobate mind" (Romans 1:28). Ahab actually told his wife that Elijah, not Jehovah, was responsible for the fire from Heaven, the rain, and the execution of the four hundred and fifty devotees. Did she think the fire was some kind of trick, such as false prophets and mediums were known to perform?

The rain was the final proof to the nation that Jehovah was supreme, and that Baal was impotent. Imagine the rage of the high priestess of Baal. The harlot queen began to swear by her own false gods. With a hellish oath, she asked her god to kill her if she did not murder Elijah within twenty-four hours. What horrible enmity against the true God from a soul given over to demons. When the human conscience repeatedly resists conviction, wickedness continues to grow. The more it became clear that Jehovah was with Elijah, the more Jezebel hated the man of God. "The bloodthirsty hate the blameless" (Proverbs 29:10). In her rage, she sent a murderous message to Elijah. But, once more we see the hand of God intervene for His servant and His purposes. In her blind fury, this enemy of God made a mistake. She had given Elijah twenty-four hours.

WHY DID ELIJAH RUN FROM JEZEBEL?

And what of our exhausted prophet, who had just concluded one of the fullest days in the service of the Lord ever recorded? As night fell, the inhabitants of Jezreel would be returning to their city. Was Elijah planning to meet with them to continue the revival which had begun on Carmel? Jezebel's messenger found the prophet and conveyed to him the queen's murderous vow. How did this most courageous of prophets react? A sudden and strange transition took place in Elijah. "And when he saw that, he arose and ran for his life" (1 Kings 19:3). The man who had run twenty miles under the hand of the Lord now ran for his life! The fearless man who had confronted the king and the nation now ran from Jezebel. Why? The word for "saw," can also mean he "was afraid." It is often translated that way. (See NASB & NIV.)

I once stood at Muhrakah with a pastor from England. As we looked off toward Jezreel he shook his head and said, "I can't understand why Elijah ran from Jezebel." I have heard and read many opinions about this, including he was tired, or lonely, or God wanted to talk to him in the desert. The original Hebrew text helps clarify what happened. When Elijah saw the situation he was in, he was afraid. His dilemma was indeed terrifying to the natural man. A murderous queen with an army at her disposal had taken an oath to kill him the next day. For once, he fixed his eyes on Jezebel and not God. Not only that, the phrase "ran for his life," also means he "went as on his soul." Elijah reacted out of his soul, not out of his spirit, upon which the hand of God rested.

We are to "walk by faith, not by sight" (2 Corinthians 5:7). Walking by sight always magnifies our difficulties and paralyzes our spiritual activity. Of the twelve spies Moses sent into Canaan, ten reported according to what they had seen, not by faith and obedience. Their unbelief paralyzed the advance of the people of God. Only Joshua and Caleb saw victory in the Spirit, and the people wanted to stone them. These two were the only ones who received the promise of God. It is ever thus with God. Peter was walking on the water of faith when he looked at the storm and began to sink in unbelief. Peter's courage would later fail him in the presence of a maid, even as Elijah's failed him in the presence of Jezebel. Elijah's self-life which the Lord had been crucifying at Cherith and Zarephath was not quite dead and buried.

It is so easy to be critical of God's prophet. We must walk carefully here. After all, God loved Elijah so much that rather than let him die, He just took him. We, too, have encountered the intimidating spirit of Jezebel on Mount Carmel. I have come to believe that it is a ruler spirit that rampages through the unbelieving world. This spirit also hates God's prophets, and has infiltrated the Lord's body. It most often targets God's "point men," those who are pioneering new ground, causing them to want to quit. (We will look at this subject later in Chapter 13.) Here I offer some of my thoughts on what happened at Jezreel that stormy night, which may help us through some of our storms.

A STORMY NIGHT IN JEZREEL

It is clear that the hand of God had sovereignly brought Elijah to Jezreel. The question is, "Why?" I believe the nation was ripe for reformation and renewal after the dramatic events that had just occurred upon Mount Carmel. Ahab had been shaken and publicly humiliated, and Baal's false prophets were defeated and destroyed. Jezebel was the last major obstacle to a return to the worship of the true God. God sent Elijah into her stronghold. Jezreel was where Elijah's presence was needed most, and the Lord's authority was with him there.

The northern kingdom was at a crossroads of decision between the Lord and continued idolatry. "Jehovah is God! Jehovah is God!" was on the lips of the people. They had seen that He was God, and called upon His name. Many were now returning home in the plentiful rain of God. When Jezebel heard what had happened she immediately determined to abort the possibility of a national revival. If the prophet in his extremity had looked to God and not at his life-threatening situation, he would have received God's plan of action. God had left the door open, as Elijah had twenty-four hours. It is too easy to say he was worn out. The "hand of God" was still upon him. He, of all people, knew the power of the God of Israel upon a willing and yielded vessel. His God had never failed him.

I see here a defining moment in the life of Elijah. That night in Jezreel, right at the Devil's doorstep of Jezebel's palace, God's blessing had begun to fall upon Elijah's beloved land and people. The rain was God's answer to the prophet's travail. But for once Elijah didn't pray, he panicked. Had he spread his situation out before the Lord, God surely would have answered him. "Ask, and it will be given unto you" (Matthew 7:7). Perhaps God would have told him to gather the people together as they returned from Carmel. A move of the Spirit of God could have come upon the city, even as the hand of God came upon the prophet. Jezebel and her remaining prophets could have been deposed.

We will never know what might have been that night. I believe that God's highest purpose was to finish off Jezebel then and there. Some years later, Jehovah would indeed deal with her and with the whole degenerate house of Ahab in this same strategic city. Dogs would eat the flesh of the murderous woman. The severed heads of the sons of Ahab would lie in two heaps in the very gate of Jezreel where Jezebel threatened to kill Elijah. But, that night the opportunity was missed.

So Elijah fled from his post and went south to Beersheva which was part of Judah. Jehoshaphat, the righteous king of Judah, had allowed his daughter to marry into Ahab's wicked family. Maybe Elijah didn't feel safe there either. He left his servant and made his way alone into the desert.

UNDER THE JUNIPER TREE

The sudden and strange change we observe in Elijah is most instructive for us. I have found that after a great victory for the Lord, there is often a savage counterattack from the enemy. We say, "Don't forget to close the back door." For instance, King David at the height of his blessing and power was in the wrong place, and fell because of what he saw with his eyes. I usually feel my most vulnerable after a powerful meeting. I try to guard my feelings and my tongue. There is great comfort in knowing the loving heart of the Lord for His struggling servants. The wonderful words He spoke to Paul were also for those of us who may be going through an Elijah-like season of confusion and discouragement. "My grace is sufficient for you, for My strength is made perfect in weakness" (2 Corinthians 12:9).

The forlorn prophet wandered a long way in the wilderness and finally collapsed under a juniper tree. The great prayer warrior had given up, as "he prayed that he might die, and said, It is enough! Now, Lord, take my life, for I am no better than my fathers!'" (1 Kings 19:4). Alone in the desert the despondent prophet fell into a deep sleep.

THORNS

At a national leaders' retreat in the desert, I sat for a time under a scrawny juniper tree (more like a bush) in the desert in the vicinity where Elijah had fled, and meditated on this passage of Scripture. At one point, I stood up to stretch and was pierced in the forehead with a sharp thorn from the tree. I carefully broke off a branch. The thorns were two inches long. Jesus said that thorns represent the "cares or anxieties of this world." Paul had a thorn in his flesh. As I examined those brutal thorns in the desert, I began to think about the crucifixion and what Jesus went through for us. He took our anxieties and burdens upon the Cross. How the Lord must love Elijah, who had served Him faithfully and fully for years. Yes, I believe Elijah had failed the Lord back at Jezreel. But one thing is for sure, God was not finished with His sleeping prophet. Would any of us have reacted any differently? A man mightily used of God now felt so worthless, a failure to the God he loved so much, that he wanted to die. The Father-heart of God heard the prophet's cry of despair.

> The LORD is near to those who have a broken heart, and saves such as have a contrite spirit. Many are the afflictions of the righteous, but the LORD delivers him out of them all. (Psalm 34:18-19)

As the brokenhearted prophet slept for sorrow in the wilderness, the God of Elijah was about to intervene on the prophet's behalf, and deliver him out of his afflictions in a most singular way.

ANGEL FOOD

The sleeping prophet who wanted to die was in for a great surprise. His time to depart from this Earth had definitely not come. The Lord would have a grand exit in store for His now burned-out minister. In the past, Elijah had been fed by ravens and by a starving heathen widow. Now Jehovah sent a divine messenger to minister to the prophet's needs. All of a sudden there was an angel standing next to him. The heavenly visitor touched the man. The word used here for "touched" means, "to approach someone with respect."

What a moving scene we see as the angelic messenger of the Lord gently and respectfully woke up the exhausted prophet. Elijah opened his eyes to look upon the face of an angel! I wonder if he thought his prayer had been answered, and he was in Heaven. But then the heavenly visitor spoke to him in Hebrew. He simply said, "Get up. Eat." As the prophet was probably still wondering where he was, he noticed what seemed to be a cake sitting on some red-hot stones. Next to the cake was a jug of water. The bewildered but thankful prophet silently took a piece of cake. He washed it down with some water from the jug. As the angel stood there looking on in approval, Elijah rolled over and went back to sleep.

I think the angel let him sleep for a while, perhaps knowing what lay ahead for him. However, the angel's mission wasn't complete, so he touched him and woke him up again. Looking at Elijah with compassion and concern, he said, "Arise and eat, because the journey is too great for you" (1 Kings 19:7). What a beautiful example of our Lord's concern and care for us when we are going through a desert experience. "The angel of the LORD encamps all around those who fear Him, and delivers them. Oh, taste and see that the LORD is good; blessed is the man who trusts in Him!" (Psalm 34:7-8).

In his book, *Angels*, Billy Graham wrote that he believes we each have at least two angels watching over us. It is true that the Lord directs angels to strengthen and guard His servants in their time of dire necessity. The Lord sent Gabriel to tell His prophet Daniel that his prayers were answered and that he was "greatly beloved" (Daniel 9:23). When Jesus was going through His greatest agony at Gethsemane and His sweat was like great drops of blood, His best friends were asleep. At that moment an angel appeared to the Son of God, "strengthening Him" (Luke 22:43).

Our loving father will never give us more than we can handle. What He initiates He oversees and empowers. When the journey is too great for us, that is when He reaches out with His great Father's hand and says, "There, my son, let Me help you. Lean on Me. Let's do this together. I am with you." Yes, Elijah's journey had become too great for him, so the Lord lovingly intervened and sent heavenly help.

Elijah ate and drank a second time, and finished the cake and water. He was tasting and seeing that the Lord is good. This cake had some celestial seasonings! The Lord had begun to restore and reassure His servant. Elijah was once again beginning to "see"—meaning a "deep knowledge acquired only by direct personal contact"—that God is good. Gradually the prophet's spiritual sight would come back, even as his body was being restored.

BREAKING BREAD

This great prophet had some of the most amazing meals in the Bible. Ravens fed him. He ate from an empty bowl many times with a boy who had been dead! And now this angel's meal would strengthen him for forty days! When the journey seems too great for us, we also are to "arise, and eat" from the life-giving Word of God. He may even send us an angel.

Another remarkable Bible meal took place in Bethany shortly before the Lord's crucifixion. Martha was serving dinner to the Son of God, while her sister Mary's costly perfume had anointed Jesus and was filling the house with its sweet fragrance. Jesus and His disciples were eating dinner with Lazarus "who had been dead" (John 12:1). On another occasion, on that first Resurrection Day the Risen Savior of the world revealed himself to two of His followers "in the breaking of the bread" (Luke 24:35). He later restored Peter at a fish breakfast on the shore of the Sea of Galilee.

The angel fed Elijah in the desert and the prophet was beginning to be restored physically from the terrible strain he had endured. He was ready to continue his journey in the Master's service. His way now led to Horev, "the mountain of God."

FROM MOUNT CARMEL TO MOUNT SINAI

Mount Horev is a variant name for Mount Sinai. "Horev" comes from a Hebrew root that means "desolate," and also "sword," or cutting instrument. God had an appointment with His prophet at the very place where He had met with Moses and the children of Israel. It was also the place where God's people had worshipped the golden calf, even as they were still doing in the northern kingdom.

The prophet fasted as he made his way to the place of the giving of the Law and the Sinai Covenant. It was at the foot of Sinai that Moses had built an altar and "twelve pillars according to the tribes of Israel" (Exodus 24:4). Oxen had been offered as sin offerings, as Moses took blood in basins from the sacrificed animals and splashed it all over the altar. He then took the scroll of the words which the Lord had commanded, "the Book of the Covenant," and read them to the people, who answered, "All that the Lord has said we will do, and be obedient" (v.7). Then Moses took more basins of blood and splashed it on the people, saying, "This is the blood of the covenant, which the Lord has made with you according to all these words" (v.8).

After a covenant meal with the elders of Israel, Moses obeyed God and went alone up Horev where the glory of the Lord came down "like a consuming fire on the top of the mountain in the eyes of all the children of Israel" (v.7). For forty days, Moses remained in the cloud of God's glory receiving the Law. When he came down the people had already broken the covenant and were worshipping a golden calf. To this place, the Lord God of Israel was now bringing His prophet Elijah. There is no mention of Sinai in the Bible between the time of Moses and Elijah's arrival there.

THE GLORY

Like Moses, Elijah had also fasted for forty days in preparation for an encounter with God's glory on Mount Sinai. In recent years, "the glory" has become a popular topic in some Charismatic streams in the body of Messiah. Such phenomena as tooth fillings turning to gold are considered to be true manifestations of "the glory." The essence of the concept seems to be that the anointing of the Holy Spirit without the tangible, visible, glory of God is not enough. Another way to put this is, we are being exhorted to have old covenant experiences. Frankly, as we cry out for the fire of God's presence in our meetings I hope He does not send literal fire like He did before. I would hate to have to build another worship center after this one was burned up.

What theological foundation there is for this popular notion is sometimes derived from what happened at the giving of the Sinai Covenant, or the Law. We are told that all the people of Israel should have gone up into the glory, but did not because they were afraid. Such a teaching is in error because Jehovah commanded Moses to come to Him alone, as the mediator of the covenant. Moses here is a type of Jesus. In the same way, we must go through Jesus to the glory. The Lord's command to the people could not have been more clear:

> You shall set bounds for the people all around, saying, "Take heed to yourselves that you do not go up to the mountain or touch its base. Whoever touches

the mountain shall surely be put to death." (Exodus 19:12)

The New Covenant application of what happened at Sinai is abundantly clear:

> For you have not come to the mountain that may be touched and that burned with fire, and to blackness and darkness and tempest, and the sound of a trumpet and the voice of words, so that those who heard it begged that the word should not be spoken to them anymore. (For they could not endure what was commanded: *"And if so much as a beast touches the mountain, it shall be stoned or shot with an arrow."* And so terrifying was the sight that Moses said, "I am exceedingly afraid and trembling.") But you have come to Mount Zion and to the city of the living God, the heavenly Jerusalem, to an innumerable company of angels, to the general assembly and the church of the firstborn who are registered in heaven, to God the Judge of all, to the spirits of just men made perfect, to Jesus the Mediator of the new covenant, and to the blood of the sprinkling that speaks better things than that of Abel. (Hebrews 12:18-24)

We are exhorted to run to Jesus, the Mediator, the reconciler, arbitrator, and guarantor of the New Covenant. He is where the glory is, "for our God is a consuming fire" (v. 29). We are called to be ministers of the New Covenant which is far "more glorious" (2 Corinthians 3:8). It "exceeds much more in glory" and is "the glory that excels," and is "much more glorious" (v. 9-11). To chase visible manifestations is to miss the mark. Yes, visible signs of His presence may occur. But let us run hard after the Lord himself.

"SHOW ME YOUR GLORY"

Moses asked the Lord, "Please, show me Your glory" (Exodus 33:18). Jehovah will always respond to such a hungry heart. "Here is a place by Me, and you shall stand on the rock. So it shall be, while My glory passes by, that I will put you in the cleft of the rock, and will cover you with My hand while I pass by. Then I will take away My hand, and you shall see My back; but My face shall not be seen" (v. 21-23). The rock is Jesus. We are to be "hidden in Christ with God" (Colossians 3:3).

I once saw Jesus standing upon the huge bedrock upon which our worship center is now built. I have seen a rainbow coming from the altar of our sanctuary and golden rain descending upon it. I have experienced the fear of the Lord when an assembled people are too in awe to move or whisper in His holy presence. I have been in the presence of God when people either run to the altar or run out the door. As His holy "temples" we are called to have rivers of His glory flowing out of our innermost being. And what is the manifestation of His glory? Jehovah defined His glory for Moses who begged Him to see it. He told him it is His "goodness," His active virtue and manifested kindness. The Lord continued that His glory is "My name," or character, "My graciousness," and "My compassion" (v.33:19). This is God's own description of His glory.

Oh, how we want His true glory! We long for more of His goodness, character, grace, and compassion to roll as rivers of living water through His people on Mount Carmel. We are crying out for Him to send more of the holy fire of His presence—the convicting, purifying, refining fire of the Holy Spirit. We want Him to permeate our meetings as we pray fervently with Elijah, "Hear me, O LORD, hear me, that this people will know that You are the LORD God, and that You have turned their hearts back to You again!" (1 Kings 18:37).

A SIGN IN THE SKY

The roof of our new worship center is the highest point on Mount Carmel. You can see the Mediterranean, Caesarea, Lebanon, Galilee, Tabor, even Jordan and the Judean hills around Jerusalem on a very clear day. It is a wonderful place to pray for the nation and the Middle East. In the fall of 2000, Karen and I were praying on the roof with about fifty intercessors from various nations. We were in a season of Israel's worst recorded drought. I hadn't seen a cloud in months. Suddenly, some of the intercessors began to point to the sky. It was about noon and the sun was directly overhead. A cloud had covered the sun so you could look at it. An incredible 360° radiance was streaming out through the cloud. The sun and cloud were surrounded by two vivid circular rainbows. People started shouting and praying. Some took pictures of this amazing sign in the sky over Mount Carmel. After a few minutes the rainbows and clouds disappeared. We went down into our "Elijah Prayer Cave" to pray about the sign we had all witnessed.

In the cave, the Lord gave me this word from Revelation 4: "Immediately I was in the Spirit; and behold, a throne set in heaven, and one sat on the throne. And He who sat there was like a jasper and a sardius stone in appearance; and there was a rainbow around the throne" (v.2-3). I said that the Lord was speaking to all of us that Jesus must be the center of everything. He is a Man in glory. In the Book of Revelation, Jesus is in the center of the seven candlesticks, His Church. If He is not central in everything we will miss His presence and glory. These Gentile intercessors had come to pray for the Lord's body in Israel. I asked them to intercede for the Messianic congregations, because some tend to de-centralize Jesus, who fulfilled the Torah given at Sinai. It's all right to kiss a Torah scroll, but we must "kiss the Son" first (Psalm 2:12). I have been to Messianic weddings where Yeshua was not even mentioned, or invited to the feast. At least one Messianic congregation teaches that Jesus is not divine.

> For it is God who commanded light to shine out of darkness, who has shone in our hearts to give the light of the knowledge of the glory of God in the face of Jesus Christ. (2 Corinthians 4:6)

Jesus is where the glory is. Elijah was about to encounter the glory of God in a cave.

THE MAN IN THE CAVE

Elijah had come to the mountain of the covenant, and he made his way up higher to spend the night in "the cave." Because of the definite article "the," some commentators theorize that it was the same cleft in the rock where Moses beheld the glory of God pass by. The Hebrew word for "cave" means "to be bare" or "naked." It comes from a root meaning "an opening of the eyes" or "an awakening." Elijah was about to be laid bare before the Lord and receive a new revelation of His glory. Caves in the Bible are temporary dwellings and emergency refuges. I am sure David wrote some of his greatest psalms in caves. They are also places of burial. Our Lord's body was placed in a burial cave as the Shabbat began in Jerusalem. In that sacred cave the Son of God was raised from the dead, and the devil and death were defeated. Caves are also places of resurrection.

The legacy of Elijah is such a wonderful example for those who desperately want more of God. Elijah had walked the crucified life. He had died daily at Cherith and Zarephath. He had experienced the awesome, manifest presence of God on Carmel. In many aspects he was dead to his old self-life. However, the prophet may have been dead, but he wasn't buried. Elijah had now come to a place of burial.

The next morning the Lord spoke to him. He asked His prophet a simple question, "What are you doing here, Elijah?" (1 Kings 19:9). What did the Lord mean by this question? Did He mean, "Why are you here, and not at Jezreel where I sent you?" The Lord has posed a universal question to all of us. What are we *really* doing here? *What* are we doing? What are we doing *here*—on this planet, in our nations, in our cities, our fellowships—at this moment? Are *we* doing what we are supposed to be doing? Are we doing our own thing, or God's thing? I once preached a message in Switzerland called, "What Are You Doing Here?" After the meeting the pastor came to me and confessed that he didn't know what he was doing there. We prayed together and he decided to go on an extended retreat to discover what he was supposed to be doing. He needed to go to a cave.

Elijah was also about to find out what God wanted him to be doing. The prophet poured his heart out to the Lord. The Hebrew clearly states that a divine "He" was in the cave with Elijah. I believe it was Jesus. They were having a covenant conversation in a cave on God's mountain of covenant. The animals which had once been sacrificed there, with the blood poured out on the people, all prefigured Jesus. Moses, the mediator, was also a type of Jesus. Now Jesus was in the cave with Elijah.

Elijah began to explain his feelings and his behavior to his God. Elijah was conversing in a cave with the Lord of Hosts! He said he had been zealous for Him, and he most certainly had. He told the Lord that His people had forsaken the covenant ratified on that very mountain, and he was right. He agonized to the Lord that the children of Israel had "torn down Your altars, and killed Your prophets with the sword . . . and they seek to take my life" (1 Kings 19:10). Everything he said was true. But he added one thing that was not true. He claimed, "I alone am left." He was not alone, as the Lord was about to show him. I believe that a terrible loneliness sometimes overcomes the true prophets of God. We see it clearly in the lives of Moses, Joshua, Samuel, Jeremiah, John the Baptist and Jesus. Near the end of his life, Paul could write to his beloved son, Timothy, "All forsook me ... but the Lord stood with me and strengthened me" (2 Timothy 4:16-17). I know a prophet who has confessed his aching loneliness to me. Elijah may have felt that he was forsaken but the Lord was standing with him in that cave.

Our gracious Lord responded to Elijah's despair (or self-pity, as some have called it) by giving him a command to, "Go out and stand on the mountain before the Lord" (1 Kings 19:11). As Elijah stood there Jehovah "passed by." A tremendous wind of hurricane proportions began to tear up the mountains before the prophet's eyes and "broke the rocks in pieces before the Lord" (1 Kings 19:12). Then the mountain began to shake in a violent earthquake. Supernatural fire came out before the Lord. Elijah must have been terrified. The text says that Jehovah was not in the wind, or the earthquake, or the fire. The awesome manifestations of His power and judgments went "before the Lord." The storm, the fire, and earsplitting noise subsided.

Elijah went back into the cave. It was quiet. He then heard what sounded like the small whisper of a voice. "When Elijah heard it ... he wrapped his face in his mantle and went out and stood in the entrance of the cave" (1 Kings 19:13). The root of the Hebrew word for "mantle" means "glory." Elijah was standing in the entrance of the cave wrapped in the glory of God. The glory wasn't in the hurricane, earthquake, or fire— all biblical manifestations of the awesome judgments of God. The glory, or splendor, of God was manifested to a man who had returned to deep intimacy with Jesus. Elijah was being stripped in the cave to the barest of essentials. He was a man naked before his God. There was nothing there but him and God. This is where true prophetic impartation takes place. The prophet's simple cloak represented the awesome presence of

God. "But we all, with unveiled face, beholding as in a mirror the glory of the Lord, are being transformed into the same image from glory to glory, just as by the Spirit of the Lord" (2 Corinthians 3:18). God was anointing His prophet with a new distinctive calling at the same location where Moses had received his call as lawgiver.

WRAPPED IN THE GLORY

Elijah was wrapping his face in awe at the majesty of God in that cave and out of a sense of his own unworthiness. At the foot of Sinai was also the place where Moses beheld God's glory in the burning bush and "hid his face" (Exodus 3:6). Even the seraphim cover their faces with their wings when they stand by the throne of the Most High. The Lord was whispering to him graciously in a "still small voice." The word for "still" also means "calm." God was calming His prophet's spirit and filling him with a new anointing for a new calling.

First, He had shown Elijah a prophetic panorama of storm, earthquake, and fire. I see these manifestations as prophetic pictures of God's coming judgment upon the idolatrous nation. These terrible shakings and burnings are sharply contrasted with the calming whisper of the mercy of God in the midst of the coming storm.

BIRTH PAINS

We are in a similar situation in Israel today. The judgments and shakings we are seeing now are only the "beginnings of birth pains" (Matthew 24:8, NIV). Birth pains become increasing faster and more severe. The Lord gave me this word for our final Shabbat meeting of 2001:

Behold, the whirlwind of the Lord Goes forth with fury, a continuing whirlwind; it will fall violently on the head of the wicked. The fierce anger of the

Lord will not return until He has done it, and until He has performed the intents of His heart. In the latter days you will consider it. "At the same time," says the LORD, "I will be the God of all the families of Israel, and they shall be My people." (Jeremiah 30:23, 31:1)

As the righteous storm of the Lord goes forth we are called to build the family of God.

A NATIONAL COMMISSION

The Lord was about to give Elijah a much larger spiritual family. The prophet had much more to learn about compassion and fatherhood. The commission the Lord was giving to Elijah was a mandate to raise up spiritual sons in Israel, a younger generation that would hold back the deserved judgments of God upon the northern kingdom. A prophetic impartation of newness of life was being released in a cave.

Once again the Lord spoke to His prophet as he stood in the entrance to the cave. "What are you doing here?" After all, Elijah had fled his post, and his nation was now without the spiritual covering of the prophet. Elijah repeated his explanation of his behavior. The Lord didn't answer him or rebuke him. Instead He conferred upon the prophet a national commission. He was told to appoint Hazael as king of Syria, and Jehu was to be anointed king of Israel. Then God ordered Elijah to anoint a man named Elisha the son of Shaphat of Abel Meholah "as prophet in your place" (1 Kings 19:16).

As God's servant was pondering these commands, the Lord shared with him another piece of information: "Yet I have reserved seven thousand in Israel, all whose knees have not bowed to Baal, and every mouth that has not kissed him" (v.18). There was a remnant in the land whose hearts were open to the Lord. There was a harvest to be reaped. "Surely the Lord God does nothing unless He reveals His secret to His servants the prophets" (Amos 3:7).

Most commentators believe that there were seven thousand hidden believers in Israel then, but the Hebrew verb tense can also indicate the future. The Lord was telling Elijah: "There is a harvest of seven thousand Jews who aren't given over to Baal. They are ripe for a mighty harvest. I am giving you a helper, the servant and son you need. His name is Elisha ["my God saves"]. He will replace you when your service to Me is completed. I am anointing you to raise up disciples, sons, and schools of prophets. My presence will go with you to enable you for this new work. You are My chosen vessel."

The intensity of the anointing, and the glory of God in that cave must have been almost too precious for the restored prophet to bear. He had failed and fled. But His loving, heavenly Father had forgiven him and still had faith in him.

UNDONE

Though nothing like what Elijah must have experienced in that cave, when holy men of God laid hands upon Karen and me as we were being commissioned and sent to Israel, I was undone. I couldn't stand for over an hour. Things were breaking up inside of me. I could not stop weeping as waves of God's love kept sweeping over me. I felt so unworthy, yet He loved me, and for some reason He wanted to use me. I was wrapped in the glory of His goodness, His graciousness and compassion standing on the stage of a Broadway theater, where years before I had attended the Tony Awards as an actor, now it was God's sanctuary, Times Square Church. But for me at that hour it was a cave, and in that cave were just Jesus and me and His glory.

MORNING IN THE CAVE

Elijah looked around the cave. Jesus was gone. The prophet wrapped his cloak more tightly about his shoulders. As the sun came up in the east, a new man emerged from the cave. "So, he departed from there" (v.19).

The end-time Elijah company will be "cave men," wrapped in the presence of God.

THE ELIJAH LEGACY CONTINUED.

9

THE ELISHA GENERATION

Elijah's dark night of the soul on the mountain of God was over. A new day was dawning for the restored prophet. He made his way down the mountain and past the place where God's glory had been manifested to Moses in a burning bush. He walked along ground where basins of the blood of the covenant had soaked the desert sand. It was here that God's people had so quickly broken covenant with Him and worshipped a golden calf. Elijah was walking through the revered place that summed up the painful past of God's chosen people. He turned north to return to the land of his inheritance. "So he departed from there" (1 Kings 19:19).

His searing loneliness and the pain of having failed his God had both been buried in the cave of Horev, where Jesus had ministered to him. For his new assignment Elijah had a divine commission directly from the mouth of God. He was equipped with the full backing, authority, and power of the Commissioner. An Old Covenant prophet-apostle, a "sent one," was emerging from the desert.

As he walked through the wilderness, was he wondering about Elisha, the young man God had appointed to take his place? The older prophet most certainly did not yet realize that in the cave he had also received an anointing of fatherhood. His days of solitude were about to end as he would begin to raise up spiritual sons. Was there any jealous resentment of

God's call on the younger man who would eventually take his place? I think not. Elijah's actions would prove that he had neither insecurity nor envy—two of the deadliest faults that can infect a leader.

PROPHETS WELCOME CHANGE

Elijah now entered into one of those rapid and dramatic transitions for which the prophet's history is so remarkable. Adaptability and flexibility are always marks of the true prophetic. Prophets anticipate, delight in, and welcome change. The status quo can be boring. This is one reason prophets can sometimes appear to be impulsive. They know God is always moving ahead. They also see the changes coming before others do, and sometimes experience intense frustration as those around them take much longer to see or embrace change. A pastor friend of mine refers it to "prophetic frustration." Also, change can be very threatening and unsettling to the insecure. Elijah had come into a place of deeper security in his relationship with his God. The Holy One of Israel had appeared to him and talked to him in the cave. He was sure of his call and mandate.

As he journeyed north, the Tishbite passed the Dead Sea and began to make his way up the Jordan Valley. He passed Jericho, Bethel, and Gilgal to the west. Was he already praying about reaching the seven thousand who had not bowed to Baal? Was he thinking about planting schools of prophets at these historic and strategic places which were now strongholds of idolatry and false worship? His forefathers had entered Canaan at the "city of palm," Jericho. One of Jeroboam's golden calves was worshipped at Bethel ("the house of God"), where Jehovah had renewed the covenant for the land with Jacob. Was the prophet-apostle beginning to feel a longing to train and equip other men? Was God beginning to give him a pastor's heart? Perhaps Elijah was praying for the Lord's vision as he followed his destiny to meet his chosen successor.

THE MEADOW OF THE DANCE

The curtain had come down on the dramatic desert cave events at Horev and the next act in the drama of Elijah's life opened onto a remarkably different scene. As the prophet continued up the Jordan Valley he came to a place called Abel Meholah, literally, "the meadow of the dance." (It can also mean "mourning into dancing.") It was probably used in ancient times for rural harvest festivals. The area is south of the Sea of Galilee, about ten miles south of Bet Shean. It is almost directly across the Jordan from the Brook Cherith, where ravens fed the prophet four years earlier.

This part of the Jordan Valley is renowned for its fertility and fruitfulness. The recent rains must have turned the hard earth into fertile fields where plowmen could follow their oxen as they prepared furrows for precious seed. From a desert scene of storms and earthquakes, Elijah was now entering the pastoral tranquility of a very large meadow bordered by the river. Long ago, it had served as a temporary refuge for the Midianites when they were routed and pursued by Gideon and his three hundred. Now it was the possession of an Israelite named Shaphat ("judge"). Perhaps eager to take advantage of the favorable change the recent rains had brought to his land, the farmer had sent his laborers into the fields to plow.

TWELVE PLOWMEN

The prophet who was accustomed to spending so much time alone entered into a very busy scene. Elijah stood on the edge of the "meadow of the dance" and surveyed twelve men behind twelve plows, each being pulled by a pair ("yoke") of oxen. "Yoke" also means "acre" in Hebrew, indicating this was a large farm, and that the owner, Shaphat, was a prosperous man.

The picture described by the inspired author is not only a busy scene of much activity, but it also portrays a strong sense of hard work and order. The twelve men were involved in laborious, physical work, as they each understood and performed their assigned task. It was a portrait of teamwork. Twelve tillers of the soil had been well trained to do very hard work requiring strong cooperation. The plows they used were not like the modern, elaborate metal plows now pulled by tractors. The rude implements were basically large, strong tree branches from which projected a smaller, sharpened and pointed branch. The plowmen were not spread out across the field as would be done today with modern, mechanized farming equipment. They were following each other in a straight line. In fact, they were going over and over the same furrow. These primitive plows were so light that at first they only scratched the surface of the soil, so the action had to be repeated numerous times until the furrow was deep enough to receive the seed at planting time.

The scene presented to us also has a decidedly social character to it. The farmers could talk, fellowship, and laugh with one another while laboring together performing the same task as they prepared the field for harvest. Upon the edge of this busy, beautiful rural scene stood the lone prophet. Elijah was about to leave behind his solitary life and enter a new dimension of relationship and fruitfulness.

THE CALL OF ELISHA

As the prophet watched the activity taking place before him, he must have been wondering which one of these workers was the son of Shaphat, Elisha. Perhaps he began to notice the young man who was plowing last in the line of the twelve. He was overseeing the work, making sure the furrow being cut was straight. From his position he could observe the entire team and call to any member who might plow a little out of line. It was also the overseer's discretion as to when the furrow was deep enough to receive the seed which would become the harvest.

Each furrow had to be satisfactory before they could move on to the next one. However, the young foreman at the back was not just standing by and watching the others toil, he was doing the same work. Here was a worker and a leader. Elijah had found his man.

The prophet crossed over the field to Elisha, and the twelve men stopped plowing to observe the approaching stranger. They saw the man was wearing the short, rough cloak of a prophet over his shoulders. Some of them recognized this visitor as the prophet Elijah whom they had seen several months before on that memorable day when holy fire fell on Mount Carmel. There in the middle of the meadow the prophet stood face-to-face with his successor. Not a word was spoken. Then slowly and deliberately Elijah removed his prophet's mantle and threw it over the shoulders of Elisha. As the young man clasped the rough garment to his heart, the observing eleven realized what was happening. Their young master was being called and anointed by God to become a prophet and disciple of the famous Elijah. (The casting of the mantle upon another also represented a sign of adoption, just as a father naturally clothed his children.)

The older man turned away and began to walk on. After a moment Elisha ran after him, and cried out, "Please let me kiss my father and mother, and then I will follow you" (1 Kings 19:20). Elijah responded by testing this candidate for the Lord's ministry, "Go back again, for what have I done to you?" (v. 20).

Right there the young Elisha made his decision to accept the call of God on his life. I believe God was fulfilling the deepest desires and longings of his heart. "Delight yourself also in the LORD, and He shall give you the desires of your heart" (Psalm 37:4). From his subsequent history we can ascertain that this was indeed a man who delighted himself in the Lord. God is always looking for young people who love Him with an undivided heart. "For the eyes of the LORD run to and fro throughout the whole earth, to show Himself strong on behalf of those whose heart is loyal to Him" (2 Chronicles 16:9).

Elisha's parents and neighbors were summoned. When they arrived Elisha walked over to the two oxen he had been driving. He took a sharp knife and slit the throat of the first ox. Then he repeated the action with the second animal. With his wooden plow and yoke he built a fire and began to cook the slaughtered oxen. As his mentor-to-be looked on, Elisha was performing an act of complete relinquishment of his former life. He had counted the cost of discipleship with Elijah, and the young plowman chose to plow the spiritual field of the twelve tribes of Israel, rather than "the meadow of the dance." Jesus said, "No one, having put his hand to the plow, and looking back, is fit for the kingdom of God" (Luke 9:62).

Shaphat and his wife along with family and neighbors joined the feast. Elijah also apparently remained. Elisha served the people. When the meal was finished the son of Shaphat kissed his parents, and then walked over to Elijah and stood by him. The two turned and went on their way together. Elisha "followed Elijah, and became his servant" (1 Kings 19:21). Moses had his Joshua. Paul would have his Timothy. Now Elijah had his Elisha.

The older prophet had not only found a servant, a yielded, obedient, young man who would help him and attend to him, but he had also gained one who would become a spiritual son. Elisha entered into a seven-year apprenticeship to his spiritual father, and the Lord had awesome plans for His new father-son team. Did the young man take one last look at the family and farm he knew so well? He was leaving the known, the comfortable, the predictable—for an adventure with God and a man who lived in caves.

THE PREPARATION OF A PROPHET

The three verses that describe Elisha's calling into ministry are packed with meaning and application for us.

First, he was not striving or seeking to establish himself as a minister of the Lord. The call of God came to him. I once read some good advice somewhere which was, "Don't ever go into the ministry, unless you've done everything you can to stay out of it." When two of my pastors told me I was called to ministry, I didn't know what to do about it, or even what that meant. When people come to me and ask me to help them discern the will of God for their lives, I almost always refer them to 1 Thessalonians 4:3: "For this is the will of God for your life, your sanctification." A clean vessel will clearly hear the call of God. Character before commission is the Lord's way. Purity always precedes power. Elisha was certainly not a striver.

I once heard Derek Prince say that in all his decades of ministry (he was in his eighties), he had come to realize that selfish ambition was the most grievous sin among leaders in the Body of Christ. "For where envy and self-seeking exist, confusion and every evil thing are there" (James 3:16). Ambitious, self-willed people are always seeking opportunities for prominence and promotion. I knew a believer like that whose life has left a trail of relational and financial devastation. Before Elijah's mantle was thrown upon him, Elisha was simply excelling in what he was doing. One day as he labored on his father's farm which would be his by inheritance, God came to him and said, "Come, follow Me."

Secondly, Elisha was a hard worker. Plowing up the hard ground of the Middle East with primitive implements is laborious and exhausting work. The Jordan Valley is brutally hot. In the spring of 1991, the House of Victory rehabilitation center was birthed at the end of the Gulf War. We had teams of people pulling out large weeds due to years of overgrowth. The ground was like iron. It was so hot, we began work at five o'clock in the morning, and went inside before noon.

BE AN EXAMPLE

Not only was Elisha a hard worker he was also an excellent leader. All eleven of the men plowing before him were under his direction and supervision. Leaders need to lead by example. Elisha did not ask his laborers to do anything he wouldn't do. Elisha was an inspiring example to his co-workers.

During the early birth pains of House of Victory, we encountered a problem over washing the dishes after meals. I taught our young staff that we all needed to take our turn at washing the dishes, because we were to be examples to those living with us who were coming off drugs. I was informed in no uncertain terms that, "Arab men don't do dishes." I responded, "Here they do." I was told I didn't understand the culture, so I made it clear that at House of Victory we needed to live according to the Word of God, the "culture of the Kingdom." There was some "intense fellowship" over the issue. Finally, the reluctant Arab brother came to me and said, "OK, I'll do it on one condition—please don't tell my wife." There were also so many arguments over food we finally put a sign in Hebrew and Arabic on the wall of the kitchen-dining room which read: "The Kingdom of God is not eating and drinking, but righteousness and peace and joy in the Holy Spirit" (Romans 14:17). It's still there. Now we have it in Russian, too.

One time three social workers visited House of Victory, two were Jewish women and one was a nominal Christian Arab woman. They met with about a dozen students and staff, who all testified to them about how Jesus, the Word of God, and the Holy Spirit had changed them. The Arab social worker asked one of our Arab students to give her an example of how he had changed. He explained that he had just been allowed to spend a weekend with his wife and children in the Old City of Jerusalem. While he was home, much to the shock of his wife, he washed the dishes for the first time in his life. The Arab social worker responded, "Maybe I ought to send my husband here!"

THE SHADOW OF THINGS TO COME

We have a good friend who is a Christian record producer and musician who works with Karen on her recordings. He is also an anointed teacher, and he and his wife direct a leadership school in England. Originally from France, his name is Gabriel Alonso-Martinez. Gaby and Andrea have ministered with us in Israel, Europe and the Far East. I have heard him give an excellent teaching which he calls "The Shadow of Things to Come." His main point is that the things you are naturally good at are only a shadow of what God wants you to do for Him in the light. For instance, Peter was good at fishing and after he laid his livelihood down, Jesus made him a fisher of men. We need to come out of the shadow and into the light of God's call.

Applying this principle to Elisha, we see a hardworking farmer-foreman. He had disciplined his laborers to plow straight, deep furrows for seed that would bring a bountiful harvest. Elisha was fruitful in his endeavors, and now he was being called from the shadow of things to come, into the light, the substance of his destiny. He was going to be discipling men in the deep things of God, teaching them to walk a straight and narrow path. Even though Elisha was "the boss's son," as a leader he set an excellent example to others.

SERVANT LEADERS

Paul charged Timothy, "Let no one despise your youth, but be an example to the believers in word, in conduct, in love, in spirit, in faith, in purity" (1 Timothy 4:12). As we follow Elisha's life we will see that the above quote is an accurate description of his legacy. Our greatest example, of course, is Jesus. On the night that He instituted the New Covenant, He gave the world an unforgettable example of servant leadership, as He, the Son of God got down on His knees and washed the filthy feet of His disciples-in-training.

> If I then, your Lord and Teacher, have washed your feet, you also ought to wash one another's feet. For I have given you an example, that you should do as I have done to you. Most assuredly, I say to you, a servant is not greater than his master; nor is he who is sent greater than he who sent him. If you know these things, blessed are you if you do them. (John 13:14-17)

Next, we can see that Elisha also had a generous spirit. At his farewell feast, it was he who gave the food to the assembled people. He was about to become a dispenser of spiritual food to a great throng of believers in his nation. He would see miracles of multiplication, even as his mentor had seen. Twelve is the biblical number of foundation and multiplication. This whole scene with the twelve laborers plowing with twelve pairs of oxen was a prophetic picture of the coming revival in northern Israel. It could be said of the young Elisha what would be said about the young Timothy, "He was well spoken of by the brethren" (Acts 16:2).

FORERUNNERS AND FINISHERS

Finally, Elisha was a finisher. He was the twelfth, the one who came last and put the finishing touches on the furrows. The greatest athletes are the ones you turn to in the last quarter when the outcome of the contest is on the line. They are finishers. As a child growing up in Washington D.C., I agonized each year with our football team, the Washington Redskins. Our nemesis was the Dallas Cowboys and their great quarterback Roger Staubach. It seemed every year the Redskins would be winning with only several minutes left in the game. But time after time, Dallas would get the ball, and the city of Washington would utter a collective groan. We knew. Here came Staubach, running, passing, improvising, doing whatever it took, and he would lead his team to victory in the final seconds of the game. Roger Staubach also happens to be a leader with the Coalition of Christian Athletes. The Kingdom of God needs finishers.

Paul could say at the end of his life, "I have fought the good fight, I have finished the race" (2 Timothy 4:7). Elisha had the potential of a finisher, but he would need to develop great endurance as he began to follow a man of no compromise, known as the "troubler of Israel." Even as Elisha said goodbye to his family and friends there were war clouds hovering over Israel's northern border, as Syria was preparing an invasion.

When the call of God came, Elisha was prepared and ready to leave everything. He was not a striver, but had proven himself to be a faithful worker, and an excellent example to others. He had a clean heart and a clean reputation. His conscience was clear before God and men. Elisha had a generous servant's heart, and he would also prove to be a finisher.

Elijah had found his man. Together they would be used by God to change the spiritual life of northern Israel in their generation. They were embarking upon a ministry that would shake the gates of hell, release a multitude from bondage, and bring a great revival among their people. They are examples for today.

Behold, I will send you Elijah the prophet before the coming of the great and dreadful day of the LORD. And he will turn the hearts of the fathers to the children, and the hearts of the children to their fathers, lest I come and strike the earth with a curse. (Malachi 4:5-6)

The land had indeed been cursed through the apostasy and idolatry of the government and the people. But through the obedience of two men, a "father and a son," God was about to impact a new generation.

THE HUNDREDFOLD

Elijah and Elisha walked away that day from the pleasant social scene of "the meadow of the dance." The younger man did not know it yet, but over the years as he walked with the Lord he would come to realize the truth of the words of Jesus to Peter and His disciples: "Assuredly, I say to you, there is no one who has left house or brothers or sisters or father or mother or wife or children or lands, for My sake and the gospel's, who shall not receive a hundredfold now in this time- houses and brothers and sisters and mothers and children and lands, with persecutions- and in the age to come, eternal life. But many who are first will be last, and the last first" (Mark 10:29-31).

We can testify to the truth of the Lord's promise. Karen and I love the family of Jews, Arabs, Lebanese and Gentiles He has given us here on Mount Carmel. We also love our extended family of "brothers and sisters and mothers and children" in the nations we've been blessed to visit.

ISRAEL'S "KAIROS" MOMENT

It is clear to me that just as Elijah and Elisha were embarking upon a new season of their lives, the body of Messiah in Israel today has also arrived at a strategic *kairos* moment. *Kairos* in Greek means an "opportune time," or God's set time or appointed time for action. For Elijah and Elisha, a major transition was happening. It was a shifting or turning from the pioneering, individual efforts of Elijah, to fathering and mentoring. After his apprenticeship, Elisha, representing the next generation, would be released as a leader. In the seven (the number of completion, perfection) remaining years of Elijah's life on Earth, he would oversee a transitional season of successful generational overlap. Elisha would be required to develop the foundational work of Elijah into a second phase of duplication and multiplication. I know a number of leaders in Israel and the nations whose passion is to equip the next generation now.

Moses trained Joshua and laid hands on him, passing the anointing of the foundational father to the son. Joshua was to enter the promised land and the promises of God, and even outdo his "father." Joshua took on the giants in the land and was a great warrior for the Lord. He also raised up elders to assist him in God's work. But after their death the nation lapsed into apostasy and idolatry. (See Joshua 24:31.)

GENERATIONAL OVERLAP

Some years ago, Leonard Ravenhill sent David Wilkerson a tape by a young pastor of a small church in western Canada. Struck by the anointing he heard in his message, Pastor David invited Carter Conlon to preach at Times Square Church. The Lord spoke to Pastor David that this young preacher was to pastor with him. Carter brought a word to Pastor David that a shaking was about to occur. Pastor David didn't see it coming, and wondered if he had made a mistake with this young Canadian. Then Times Square Church went through a vicious shaking. Pastor David told me it was the most difficult time of his life.

When the dust had settled, David Wilkerson had found his Elisha. Today, Carter Conlon is the Senior Pastor of Times Square Church, with Pastor David serving as Founding Pastor. This is an example of successful generational overlap. (Pastor Carter had two words for the Missions Department for Year 2002: "Aggressive Missions." They are believing for five hundred more full-time missionaries—including some to Afghanistan—as the multiplication continues.)

Elisha's commission would also entail finding and training a new generation to carry on God's work. The third generation has historically been the place of failure in the advance of the torch of the testimony of God. Elijah and Elisha were now being confronted with such a task. The *kairos* moment between generations is always pivotal in the Kingdom of God, the family, the local church, or any of the Lord's ministries. Jesus succeeded. He poured himself into twelve. Eleven changed the world as they in turn poured themselves into the next generation. Could this be one reason why God calls himself "the God of Abraham, Isaac and Jacob"? It takes three overlapping generations to progress from the new, rugged, pioneering beginning, to a consolidation and consummation of the Lord's purposes.

Elijah called his God "the God of Abraham, Isaac, and Israel." "Israel" represents converted Jacob, the father of the twelve tribes, pointing to multiplication and permanence.

The history of the people of God as recorded in the Bible clearly shows that this fullness is rarely attained. Over and over again we see generational breakdown and rupture, rather than successful transition and overlap. Joshua's legacy was aborted. Eli's children were backslidden. Even Samuel's children were backsliders. What happened to his "schools of prophets?" King David's human legacy was disastrous.

THERE IS A GENERATION MISSING

In the patriarchal society of the Middle East the Church has inherited a major generational problem. I know many Arab pastors from Israel, the West Bank, Lebanon, Syria, Jordan, and Egypt. One of their biggest problems is that they don't make disciples and prepare the next generation. Old patriarchs hold on to their pulpits, and the younger generation rebels against them. It is one of the most painful problems in the Arab churches in Galilee.

A small group of *sabras* (native Israeli Jews) came to the Lord about twenty years ago. One of them, a good friend of ours who had served the Lord for some years in the U.S., returned to Israel in the late 90s. After one of our meetings on Mount Carmel, he told me that he had visited most of the Messianic congregations since he had returned to the Land. Then he said this, "David, there is a generation missing. Dani Sayag is the only *sabra* Israeli leader of his age that I see coming up." Dani is our young pastor whom we have carefully trained and mentored. Dani is now pouring himself into the next generation.

An article in *The Messianic Times*, Fall 2002, was entitled: "The Destiny of Messianic Judaism—In Its Last Days ... or Of The Last Days?" The author contends that the longevity of the movement is in jeopardy because of a deep concern about the small numbers of the "next generation, the children of the baby boomers." Some leaders have concluded that "the movement is in deep trouble." Like Elijah and Elisha, it seems we are at another kairos time in Israel.

THE FATHER AND THE SON

Of course the greatest example of generational overlap is the relationship between God the Father and God the Son. Everything Jesus did on Earth was the result of continual communion with the Father. "My Father has been working until now, and I have been working" (John 5:17). "The works which the Father has given Me to finish—the very works that I do—bear witness of Me, that the Father sent Me" (v. 36).

The wonderful times of fellowship that Elijah and Elisha must have experienced in their seven-year father and son ministry are only a pale reflection of the divine unity of the Father and the Son. "I and My Father are one" (John 10:30). Jesus was totally dependent upon the Father. "Most assuredly, I say to you, the Son can do nothing of Himself, but what He sees the Father do; for whatever He does, the Son also does in like manner" (John 5:19). And how did the Father respond to the Son? "'This is My beloved Son, in whom I am well pleased. Hear Him!' And when the disciples heard it they fell on their faces and were greatly afraid" (Matthew 17:5-6).

Many years later, Peter remembered that defining moment on the Mount of Transfiguration, and testified of the revelation of the oneness of the Father and the Son: "For He [Jesus] received from God the Father honor and glory when such a voice came to Him from the Excellent Glory: 'This is My beloved son, in whom I am well pleased.' And we heard this voice which came from heaven when we were with Him on the holy mountain" (2 Peter 1:17-18).

We, as potential spiritual fathers like Elijah, must also take the dependent stance of sonship like Jesus, doing only what we hear and see from "Abba." We need to raise up spiritual sons and daughters, but we also must wean them away from ourselves, so they are totally dependent on the Father as Jesus was. Elisha would learn this when Elijah was dramatically called to be with the Lord. The Lord began to teach me this truth when demonic attacks assaulted us on Mount Carmel, and it wasn't sufficient to call my spiritual mentor on the phone and ask him what to do. The Father's "phone number" is Jeremiah 33:3: "Call to Me, and I will answer you, and show you great and mighty things, which you do not know." His number is never busy and his computers are never down. He's waiting expectantly for communion with His kids.

A MOST IMPORTANT ASPECT OF THE LASTING LEGACY OF ELIJAH WAS THE RAISING UP OF THE ELISHA GENERATION.

10

RESTORATION OF THE PROPHETIC IN ISRAEL

The intergenerational ministry of Elijah and Elisha quickly began to bear fruit. Young men who were hungry for God began to gravitate to them. The two prophets initiated a circuit of "schools of prophets" in Samaria, Galilee, and on Mount Carmel, as a true prophetic voice was once again being restored in Israel. People who wanted more of Jehovah and not Baal began to join the schools. Families were affected, as wives and children began to hear the word of the Lord from their fathers and husbands. Within a year, a national impact by this new generation could be discerned as anonymous prophets began to speak the word of the Lord.

SUDDENLY A PROPHET

As Elijah and Elisha were quietly going about God's work, Israel was invaded by Syria. The enemy forces came across the northern border and the Golan Heights. Ben-Hadad with thirty-two other kings swept through Galilee with a huge army of 130,000. They moved south and besieged Ahab and his forces at the capital in Samaria. King Ahab was engaged in a bloody war for survival, and the situation seemed utterly hopeless. But then Jehovah intervened. "Suddenly a prophet approached Ahab the king of Israel" (1 Kings 20:13). At the critical moment when Israel was about to fall to the enemy, a man with a word not his own, but from the Lord of Hosts, confronted the king. "Thus says the LORD: 'Have you seen all this great multitude? Behold, I will deliver it into your hand today, and you shall know I am the LORD'" (v. 13).

This dramatic scene has presented problems to some commentators. Having seen the accumulated and grievous sins of Ahab, we might well expect God to have punished the apostate king by removing him and his government through this foreign invasion. But God was not through with Ahab. Our Lord is simply more merciful than we are: "'For My thoughts are not your thoughts, nor are your ways My ways,' says the LORD. 'For as the heavens are higher than the earth, so are My ways higher than your ways, and My thoughts than your thoughts'" (Isaiah 55:8-9).

Not only was God giving Ahab another chance, but He was also watching over His prophetic word to Elijah. There were seven thousand souls to be brought in by Elijah and his young, hardworking assistant, Elisha. Even if Jezebel had heard of the resurgence of the prophets of Jehovah under her hated enemy Elijah, the war with Syria precluded her from trying to stop them. The revival was birthed during the war.

A YOUTH MOVEMENT

Backslidden Ahab, probably still a nominal believer in Jehovah, was incredulous that this presumptuous, unknown prophet would predict victory for Israel against such overwhelming odds. He responded to the prophet by asking, "By whom?" (1 Kings 20:14). In other words, "Who is going to lead us in this preposterous victory you are proclaiming?" The prophet's answer was even more strange. "Thus says the Lord: 'By the young leaders of the provinces.'"

The "young leaders" were teenage servants of provincial rulers, or mayors. The prophet was declaring a youth movement—a national victory led by young, inexperienced servants of local leaders. The dubious Ahab further questioned him as to who would lead all these untried young men, asking, "Who will set the battle in order?" The prophet looked at his king and said, "You" (v. 14).

Through His messenger the Lord was giving Ahab the strategy for victory in an impossible situation. The Lord's plan was definitely unique. The rulers or princes of the provinces (mayors of local villages in our terms) had probably fled to the capital at Samaria as the enemy advanced across Galilee. The "young men" were their young servants unaccustomed to war. The word the prophet used here is the word for "teenagers" today. Ahab was to oversee a group of untried teenagers, who would lead his seven thousand soldiers against 130,000 seasoned Syrian troops! Perhaps Ahab was just desperate enough to attempt such a seemingly foolish scheme. What alternative did he have? "The king's heart is in the hand of the LORD, like the rivers of water; He turns it wherever He wishes" (Proverbs 21:1).

Ahab obeyed the word of the Lord through the unknown prophet. He summoned the teenage servants of the local leaders and put them in charge of his shocked army. Two hundred and thirty-two young men were ready to lead seven thousand. Ben-Hadad and his thirty-two kings were "drinking themselves drunk" all morning. Then at noon, the least expected time for an attack, the youthful leaders led a surprise counterattack against the massive overconfident forces of the army.

The word of the Lord was not only true, but His timing was perfect. These boys courageously "went out of the city with the army which followed them. And each one killed his man; so the Syrians fled, and Israel pursued them" (1 Kings 20:19-20). In a miraculous turn of events a new generation saved the nation as the invaders were driven out of the land. The prophetic word of the Lord was fulfilled and Israel was afforded a much needed interval of peace.

What about Ahab who once again experienced an awesome demonstration of the ways and might of Jehovah? This time the king had been the beneficiary of the Lord's grace and mercy as he and Israel were rescued miraculously by the hand of the Lord. Still the hardened heart of Ahab did not turn to the God of his fathers.

YOUNG SERVANT LEADERS

A fascinating parallel may be discerned here. Young servants of local leaders led a seven thousand man army to a miraculous victory against impossible odds. At the same time, Elijah and Elisha were discipling young servant-leaders, and their goal was a spiritual army of seven thousand. The physical battle for the nation was mirrored by the spiritual war for the people. The word of the Lord by one prophet turned the tide in the war with Syria. This turn of events was reminiscent of the era when the Lord had called the young boy Samuel to be His vessel to inaugurate an earlier prophetic movement in Israel. "And the word of the LORD was rare in those days; there was no widespread revelation" (1 Samuel 3:1).

Elijah also had a sure word of prophecy from God. The resurgence of the prophetic movement in Israel was based on the Word of God. Jehovah had told Elijah to anoint Elisha as his replacement, and that He had reserved seven thousand in Israel for the Kingdom of God. The revival in northern Israel would be led by an older prophet training a younger prophet. The two of them would raise communal groups of the "sons of prophets" at strategic places in Samaria, Galilee, and Carmel, "on the mountains of Israel."

SATAN IS AFTER OUR YOUTH

After the Gulf War in 1991, House of Victory was birthed as the first Bible-based drug and alcohol residential rehabilitation center in Israel. As we ministered to Jewish and

Arab men I began to realize that Satan was trying to destroy a generation of young men. The effects of addiction on a drug addict's family cause devastation, often ending in divorce. Many of the addicts we have ministered to have great potential to be successful, contributing members of our society. Some are obviously called to be leaders. Drugs and alcohol, along with the sins and crimes that usually accompany the lifestyle of addiction are of epidemic proportions in Israel, affecting all sectors of Israeli society. The enemy is trying to wipe out a generation. Now "ecstasy" is the popular drug, and the major international dealers of it are Israelis. Some of the leaders of this cartel were busted in New York in 2001. Drugs, sex, rock 'n roll, rap, heavy metal and trance music, MTV, all-night clubs, "ecstasy" parties in the forest on Carmel—all characterize the war we are in for the souls of a generation of Israelis, both Jews and Arabs. Twenty-five percent of Israeli soldiers have admitted to using drugs while in the army!

Israeli teenagers (male and female) all serve in the army when they graduate high school. There are over seventy believers in the IDF (Israeli Defense Forces). The days of Elijah are still with us, as we battle physical enemies who want to destroy us from without, and spiritual hosts of wickedness who lust to destroy us from within.

NABOTH'S VINEYARD

The obstinacy and degeneracy of Ahab was about to reach its lowest level. The king who was never satisfied coveted a vineyard adjacent to the royal compound in Jezreel. To "covet" means to be dissatisfied with the position God has given one, and to lust after something He has given to another. The owner of the vineyard, Naboth, refused to sell his inheritance to Ahab, as it would have been a grievous sin against the Torah. (See Numbers 36:7.) Naboth had courageously responded to his king, "The LORD forbid that I should give the inheritance of my fathers to you!" (1 Kings 21:3). Naboth had to choose between pleasing the king (and making a handsome profit), or displeasing the King of kings. This God-fearing man obeyed the Law of the Lord. Here was one of God's select seven thousand.

The dejected king went to his palace and threw himself upon his bed where he pouted like a child who is denied his own way. Then Jezebel reappeared at Jezreel where she had taken an oath to kill Elijah several years earlier. The weakness and pettiness of Ahab must have infuriated his pagan, power-hungry wife. She immediately attacked his manhood, as if to say, "You call yourself a king?" Then she told the sulking husband to get out of bed and eat, "and let your heart be cheerful; I will give you the vineyard of Naboth, the Jezreelite" (1 Kings 21:7). "I" is the operative word here. "I, the queen, O weak man, will get the vineyard for you. So cheer up." (Shakespeare must have been reading this scene in his Bible when he created his malignant Lady Macbeth. When Macbeth balks at killing the king, Lady Macbeth cries: "Infirm of purpose! Give me the dagger." She then kills the sleeping king.)

Jezebel now planned a diabolical plot to murder Naboth and steal his vineyard. First, she forged letters with Ahab's name and seal and sent them to the elders and nobles of Jezreel who were neighbors of Naboth. The letter told them to proclaim a religious fast, and then find two liars ("scoundrels"), who would bear false witness publicly against innocent Naboth. The pages of history are stained with the blood of the vilest crimes perpetuated under a cloak of religion—from Mohammedan invasions, to the Crusades, to the Inquisition. September 11, 2001, is only one of the latest.

The elders of the city were to hold a public meeting and instruct the false witnesses to say, "'You have blasphemed God and the king.' Then take him out and stone him, that he may die" (1 Kings 21:10).

The corrupt elders bribed two "sons of worthlessness" and proclaimed a fast and a public meeting. The two liars accused Naboth of blasphemy, or cursing God, and King Ahab. Then they took the innocent man outside the city and stoned him with stones, so that he died (v. 13). They also later murdered his sons, the heirs of the vineyard. (See 2 Kings 9:26.)

The shocking murder of Naboth and the theft of his land was in many ways the culmination of the unholy alliance between Jezebel and Ahab. The holy commandments of God lay shattered in Jezreel, unashamedly broken by a weak, cowardly man dominated by an ambitious, murderous woman. It all began by forsaking the commandments, "You shall have no other gods before Me" and "You shall not take the name of the Lord your God in vain" (Exodus 20:3,7). Finally their rebellious actions against God were manifested by the king and queen willfully ignoring the commands, "You shall not murder. You shall not steal. You shall not bear false witness against your neighbor. You shall not covet your neighbor's ... field ... or anything that is your neighbor's" (v. 13-17).

The deed was done. Of course, Jezebel was not there, as she had cleverly covered up her tracks. While his neighbor and his neighbor's children were being stoned to death, Ahab was still pouting. When Jezebel reported what had happened, she and Ahab exulted that they had obtained ownership of the vineyard free. Or so they thought.

In the place called Jezreel ("God sows") Jezebel and Ahab were sowing their wickedness under a cloak of deception and hypocrisy. Their hands dripped with innocent blood—a sin most hateful to God. (See Deuteronomy 27:24 and 2 Kings 24:4.) This bloodthirsty woman had dragged her husband and the willing elders of the city into the sewer of her satanic crimes. The nobles of Jezreel were evil enough to carry out her schemes. Even though they had seen Jehovah save their city and people from certain slaughter and enslavement twice in the past two years, they willingly broke the commandments of

God and their holy covenant with Him. When the leaders of a society become cowardly and godless that nation has reached a flashpoint of God's judgment. That judgment was about to be announced by the one Ahab most feared and whom Jezebel most hated.

THE MURDERER CONFRONTED

While this horrible plot was unfolding in Jezreel, Elijah was going about his God-given mandate to train Elisha as prophet in his place and to raise up a new generation of godly disciples. Elijah and Elisha were continuing their Kingdom work of preaching to the people, and instructing their younger brethren, "the sons of prophets." Elijah would probably have been very happy never to see Ahab again, but the Lord had one last meeting planned for prophet and king. While the older prophet was thus involved with the Lord's work, God spoke to him about the national scene. Jehovah revealed to His servant the despicable deeds committed by Ahab and his wife. Jezebel thought that no one but Ahab knew of her instigation and participation in these crimes. But Elijah knew, because God told him. "Surely the LORD God does nothing, unless He reveals His secrets to His servants the prophets" (Amos 3:7).

God directed Elijah to return to Jezreel where he had left his post and fled from Jezebel several years before. He was to find Ahab and pronounce the doom of the king and his wife. The Hebrew text indicates that he was in the north, perhaps on Mount Carmel where there was a school of prophets, when the word came to him. I have often wondered if God wanted his restored prophet to literally retrace his steps where he had run in front of Ahab's chariot from Carmel to Jezreel. The prophet obeyed the Lord and went back to Jezreel, the place of his failure, to once again confront the king. This time he didn't run from Jezebel. Our God is a God of second chances.

When Elijah returned to Jezreel he was evidently alone. The Lord told him where to find Ahab who would be looking over the new vineyard he had stolen from his murdered neighbor. In connection with other events in Ahab's recent life God had been sending "junior prophets." But for this word the Lord chose the "father of the prophets." God tends to reserve the most difficult of His prophetic tasks for the more mature of His servants. It took Moses forty years of painful preparation to finally confront Pharaoh. This is a principle leaders need to embrace. Often God will direct the senior pastor to confront the major sin in a congregation. Here Elijah was to charge the king with his hellish crimes and pronounce a sentence of death upon him and his wife.

PROPHETS CONFRONT SIN

I once told a pastor in another city in Israel that a woman in his congregation was about to marry an Orthodox Jew who was not a believer. I suggested he meet with them. He preferred that I meet with them. I told him I wasn't her pastor, that she was just a friend, but he still declined. Karen and I went ahead and met with our friend and her fiancé because we cared about her and wanted to help her. Her pastor clearly did not like confrontation. Most of us don't. But confronting sin in love is part of the mandate from God upon His leaders. It is one of His requirements, lest we disqualify ourselves. The pastor is no longer in Israel. Leaders need to care enough to confront.

Elijah had matured since his night in the cave at Horev. He was learning what all prophets must learn, as the Lord explained to the prophet Ezekiel: "Behold, I have made your face strong against their faces, and your forehead strong against their foreheads. Like adamant stone, harder than flint, I have made your forehead; do not be afraid of them, nor be dismayed at their looks, though they are a rebellious house" (Ezekiel 3:9-10). Micah embraced his prophetic call this way:

"But I am full of power by the Holy Spirit of the LORD, and of justice and might, to declare to Jacob his transgression and to Israel his sin" (Micah 3:8). Elijah was to do the same.

Ahab may have felt that no one would dare rebuke the king for his devilish deeds. The entire city knew of his terrible sin. His seal had been on the false charges against innocent Naboth.

Did any of the Christian pastors who "ministered" to Mr. Clinton after the public exposure of his sexual immorality in the White House confront the president with his guilt as an international role model? Did any of Mr. Clinton's "Christian" friends confront his murderous sin of twice using his presidential veto power to insure that "partial birth abortion" would be legal and sanctioned by the U.S. government? How many innocent babies have had their skulls crushed by doctors as they have emerged from their mother's womb? Did an "Elijah" confront Mr. Clinton with his murderous actions?

Did Ahab not know in his guilty heart that his sin would find him out? The One who is too pure to look upon sin was about to act. Amos, the last prophet the Lord sent to northern Israel before its destruction and exile, saw the Lord in a vision. God told him:

> Though they dig into hell, from there My hand shall take them; though they climb up to heaven, from there I will bring them down; and though they hide themselves on the top of Carmel, from there I will search and take them. (Amos 9:2-3)

Some years ago a Jewish teenager who lived in Haifa read that Scripture. She was being trained to "channel" spirits of the dead by a guru here on Mount Carmel. She showed the passage in the Bible to her guru, who promptly told her to quit reading "that book." Shortly afterward she was dramatically saved and delivered in one of our meetings. She was not able to hide from God on "the top of Carmel." And Ahab should have known he couldn't hide from God either. As the Apostle Paul wrote to the churches in Galatia: "Do not be deceived, God is not mocked; for whatever a man sows, that he will also reap" (Galatians 6:8).

DOGS SHALL LICK THE BLOOD OF AHAB

Ahab had gone to the vineyard of Naboth to take possession of it ("occupy" or "seize by driving out"). Then the last man on Earth he wished to see appeared again. It was the final showdown between the prophet and the king. The guilt-ridden Ahab blurted out, "Have you found me, O my enemy?" (1 Kings 21:20). The king was right about that. Elijah was the enemy of Ahab and Jezebel's pagan religion, which had contaminated the nation. The prophetic word of judgment erupted from the prophet's lips like the thunder on Horev:

> Thus says the LORD: "Have you murdered and also taken possession? In the place where dogs licked the blood of Naboth, dogs shall lick your blood, even yours. I have found you, because you have sold yourself to do evil in the sight of the LORD: Behold, I will bring calamity on you. I will take away your prosperity, and will cut off from Ahab every male in Israel, both bond and free ... because of the provocation with which you provoked Me to anger, and made Israel sin." (1 Kings 21:19-22)

Elijah wasn't finished. "And concerning Jezebel the Lord also spoke, saying, 'the dogs shall eat Jezebel by the wall of Jezreel'" (v. 23). Ahab was an idolator, a thief, and a murderer. But in God's eyes the king's sin was even more grievous. He had provoked the Lord to anger because the leader had "made Israel sin."

O, the reckoning of God upon leaders who refuse to preach against sin and model a holy life for God's flocks. The Lord's righteous wrath upon false shepherds and false prophets is always more severe than upon their misled flocks. "For the wrath of God is revealed from heaven against all ungodliness and unrighteousness of men, who suppress the truth in unrighteousness" (Romans 1:18). After many gracious warnings to His leaders who refuse to hear His voice and repent, the Lord will usually expose their sin publicly. It happened on a national scale in America in the 1980s. It has happened in the body of Messiah in Israel. Hirelings and false prophets or shepherds drag the name and reputation of the Lord and His body through the mud. Jesus had scorching words of warning for those who lead others astray: "But whoever causes one of these little ones who believe in Me to sin, it would be better for him if a millstone were hung around his neck, and were drowned in the depth of the sea" (Matthew 18:6).

The inspired Old Testament writer summed up the corrupt character of Ahab: "But there was no one like Ahab who sold himself to do wickedness in the sight of the LORD, because Jezebel his wife stirred him up" (1 Kings 2 1:25).

"YOUR SINS WILL FIND YOU OUT"

When Elijah finished prophesying the bloody death of Ahab and his wife and children, the king was speechless. There was no word of response or denial, and no attempt at defense or excuse. The sinner had been found out. And he was standing in the vineyard for which he had sold his soul. As the trapped Ahab stared at his old nemesis, he reached up with his two hands and tore his clothes in a sign of repentance. He was now facing the truth that "your sin will find you out" (Numbers 32:23). Was his repentance real, or was he just devastated because he was caught standing among the stolen spoils of another man's inheritance?

Did Ahab accept the enormity of his evil conduct as a king? He actually entered into a season of fasting and wearing sackcloth. I do believe he was shaken with fear at the wrath of God. Every word Elijah had ever spoken had come true. The king didn't arrest Elijah. The prophet delivered his message and left. His mission was accomplished. Ahab actually humbled himself. That is where grace is found. His subjects observed him wearing sackcloth as he "went softly" in mourning for a time. Even the worst sinners are capable of repentance.

Manasseh, the son of godly King Hezekiah, was the worst of Judah's kings. For half a century he reigned in Jerusalem where he built altars to Baal, and erected altars to Assyrian gods in the temple. He practiced witchcraft, sorcery, and child sacrifice, shedding so "much innocent blood, till he had filled Jerusalem from one end to another" (2 Kings 21:16). Manasseh was dragged to Babylon in chains with a fishhook through his nose. There he repented and humbled himself greatly before the God of his fathers. He prayed to Him and the Lord received his entreaty, heard his supplications, and brought him back to Jerusalem. "Then Manasseh knew that the Lord was God" (2 Chronicles 33:12-13). Manasseh is included in the bloodline of Jesus (Matthew 1:10). This is most "amazing grace." The Lord listens and responds to the worst of sinners.

In the summer of 2000, Karen and I were having lunch in New York City with Nicky Cruz and David Wilkerson and their wives. The night before, these two men of God had attended a theatre production based on *The Cross and the Switchblade.* They were kidding each other about the actors who were portraying them in the play. David Wilkerson asked Nicky what had kept him all these years. Nicky promptly responded, "The love of Jesus." He then turned to his wife and added, "And the love of Gloria."

As a little boy in Puerto Rico, Nicky was often beaten by his mother and locked in a closet where he slept in a pool of his own blood. She was a witch. On the streets of New

York, Nicky would stab people, even children, and laugh at the blood. After he was dramatically delivered and saved, he went back to Puerto Rico to see his mother. He forgave her. His mother and his whole family came to know the Lord. I know a former mafia "hit man" who murdered six drug dealers. When he was saved, a pastor took him to a police station where he confessed and turned himself in. At his trial the judge surprised everyone by giving him a suspended sentence. The brother is now married and is a security guard in the house of the Lord. I have seen scores of drug addicts and alcoholics repent and renounce their sins and crimes and be restored with their loved ones. Some of the best pastors I know are former drug addicts.

The Lord spoke to Elijah again about Ahab: "See how Ahab has humbled himself before Me? Because he has humbled himself before Me, I will not bring calamity in his days. In the days of his son I will bring the calamity on his house" (1 Kings 21:29).

God in His mercy stayed His hand upon the king, but the divine sentence was not remitted. Ahab's repentance was superficial and transient. He rent his garments, but not his heart. He had a healthy fear of "God's righteous judgment" but not a heartfelt hatred of his sins. We know this by his actions. He never put Jezebel away or restored the worship of Jehovah. The Lord gave him three more years, "space for repentance," as some of the Puritan writers would call it.

MARTYRS

The other character in this drama of evil and divine retribution was godly Naboth ("fruits"). As much as Jezebel and Ahab stand out as symbols of the satanic world system, innocent Naboth represents a type of our Lord Jesus, and those who will die for His testimony. In the parable of the vineyard, God is clearly the owner (Matthew 21:33-40). The tenants of the vineyard stone and kill the servants of the Lord. Then the Lord sends His son, and the vinedressers conspire together, "Come, let us kill him and seize his inheritance" (v. 38). Naboth and Jesus both died by violent hands for the false charge of "blaspheming God." Each was also slain outside the city. The murderers of both were destroyed by divine justice.

Naboth is also a type of the countless martyrs who have died and are dying today for the testimony of Jesus. "And they overcame him [Satan] by the blood of the Lamb and by the word of their testimony, and they did not love their lives to the death" (Revelation 12:11). Jesus prophesied that a time of persecution and martyrdom will come to His body in Israel. His disciples were persecuted in Paul's day and will be again. As Jesus put it: "Before all these things, they will lay hands on you and persecute you, delivering you up to the synagogues and prisons.... You will be betrayed even by parents and brothers and relatives and friends; and they will put some of you to death and you will be hated for My name's sake" (Luke 21:12,16-17). In that day, will we be able to stand as a testimony to Jesus' gospel, innocent and courageous like Naboth?

IS THERE STILL NOT A PROPHET OF THE LORD HERE?

Three years later, King Ahab decided to attack the Syrians at Ramot Gilead (near what is today called the "Golan Heights"). This is part of the land promised by God to the tribe of Gad (Deuteronomy 4:43, Josh. 20:8). It is also where Elijah came from. Ahab had made an alliance with King Jehoshaphat of Judah, by giving his daughter Athaliah in marriage to Jehoshaphat's son, Jehoram. Before Jehoshaphat would fight with Ahab at Ramot Gilead, he insisted that they first "inquire for the word of the Lord today" (1 Kings 22:5).

Here is the prime intercessory, prophetic principle, "What is the Lord saying today?"

Ahab gathered four hundred prophets together. These were replacements for the four hundred and fifty prophets of Baal who had been slain at the foot of Carmel about six years earlier. As usual, the state-supported prophets told the king what he wanted to hear, "Go up, for the Lord [Adonai] will deliver it into the hand of the king" (1 Kings 22:6).

A most important question needs to be answered here: "Who were these prophets?" They did not prophesy in the name of Baal, but in the name of Adonai, and Jehovah—the God of Israel. Jehoshaphat who feared God, as we know from the rest of his life, discerned that these prophets were "off." He asked, "Is there not still a prophet of the Lord [Jehovah] here, that we may inquire of Him?" (v.7). Ahab replied that there was one named Micaiah ("Who is like Jehovah?"), "but I hate him, because he does not prophesy good concerning me, but evil" (v.8). Jehoshaphat was horrified by Ahab's words and responded: "Let not the king say such things!" (v.8). A messenger was sent to bring Micaiah.

THE THRESHING FLOOR

What a revealing scene we have before us. The two kings of the still divided nation sat on their thrones, clothed in their royal robes, at a threshing floor at the city gate of Samaria, the capital of northern Israel. Every work of God is built upon a threshing floor. The temple in Jerusalem stood on a threshing floor bought by King David who paid "the full price." Jesus is the divine Thresher: "His winnowing fan is in His hand, and He will thoroughly clean out His threshing floor, and gather His wheat into the barn, but He will burn up the chaff with unquenchable fire" (Matthew 3:12). The Holy Spirit was about to thresh out the chaff (worthless debris) of the false prophets.

In front of the two kings and the assembled people of the city the four hundred "prophets of Jehovah" all began prophesying. One of them, perhaps the leader, named Zedekiah ("Jehovah is righteous") was a Hebrew of the tribe of Benjamin. (See 1 Chronicles 7:10.) He had made a set of horns of iron for himself, and put them on his head. He moved around the threshing floor like a bull, performing a "prophetic act." The crowd probably went wild. Then Zedekiah cried out: "Thus says the LORD [Jehovah]: 'With these you shall gore the Syrians until they are destroyed'" (1 Kings 22:11). All the four hundred other prophets agreed.

It seems clear that after the destruction of the four hundred and fifty prophets of Baal on Carmel, Ahab must have installed four hundred more who all prophesied in the name of Jehovah. Most of them were probably Hebrews like Zedekiah. They were all prophesying encouraging, positive and comforting words, which promised great success and reward for Ahab. These were prophecies of confirmation of the desires of Ahab's heart. He was ambitious for gain, as we have seen at Naboth's vineyard. Wasn't there safety in a multitude of prophecies? Isn't that what we often hear today? "What are the prophets saying?" False words were flying fast in Samaria at that meeting of God's people.

As this wild scene was taking place, the messenger brought in Micaiah, telling him: "Now listen, the words of the prophets with one accord encourage [are "good" to] the king. Please let your word be like the word of one of them, and speak encouragement" (1 Kings 22:13). Micaiah responded, "As the LORD [Jehovah] lives, whatever the LORD says to me, that will I speak" (v.14). Thank God for the true, clear, and courageous, and often lonely, prophetic voice in the midst of all the noise and excitement of false prophecy. This is what we desperately need in Israel today—a true prophetic voice.

ALL ISRAEL SCATTERED ON THE MOUNTAINS

In this encounter so reminiscent of Elijah's on Mount Carmel, Micaiah stood alone and spoke the true word of the Lord. He had received a heartbreaking vision of God's pain for His wayward people: "I saw all Israel scattered on the mountains, as sheep that have no shepherd. And the LORD said, 'These have no master. Let each return to his house in peace'" (v.17). Ahab turned to Jehoshaphat and remarked, "Did I not tell you he would not prophesy good concerning me, but evil?" (v. 18).

What Micaiah prophesied was from the heart of God. Jesus himself quoted the word of Micaiah: "But when He [Jesus] saw the multitudes, He was moved with compassion for them, because they were like sheep having no shepherd. Then He said to His disciples, 'The harvest truly is plentiful, but the laborers are few. Therefore pray for the Lord of the harvest to send out laborers into His harvest'" (Matthew 9:36-38).

While these prophets were prophesying falsely, the true prophetic movement led by Elijah and Elisha was doing exactly what Jesus commanded us to do. They were praying for the harvest and sending out laborers into the Lord's harvest field, and bringing in the lost sheep of the house of Israel into the new prophetic communities.

The prophet Micaiah told Ahab what he and the people needed to hear, not what the king wanted to hear. Micaiah had a shepherd's broken heart for the lost. He hoped Ahab would send the people home and not lead them into a disastrous war. But Ahab for the last time rejected the word of the Lord. Micaiah, the seer, realizing that Ahab had not accepted God's word to him, responded by sharing a vision God gave him. Micaiah said he saw Jehovah on His throne in heaven. In the vision God sent deceiving spirits to all of Ahab's prophets. Micaiah continued, "Therefore look! The Lord has put a lying spirit in the mouth of all these prophets of yours, and the Lord has declared disaster to you" (1 Kings 22: 19-23). Micaiah prophesied in front of two kings and a public assembly that Ahab's four hundred prophets were lying. Zedekiah, the man with the iron horns on his head, responded by viciously slapping Micaiah across the face. Ahab ordered Micaiah to be thrown in prison until the king returned from his Syrian expedition "in peace." Micaiah had one last parting shot for Ahab and the assembled people: "'If you return in peace, the Lord has not spoken to me.' And he said, 'Take heed, all you people!'" (v. 28).

The ministry of Elijah had produced men of God who were willing to go to prison or death for the truth. Elijah was concerned for the character of God's people. Ahab was a false shepherd whose false prophets had polluted the land.

God-fearing King Jehoshaphat heard the word of the Lord which he had requested. Why didn't he obey it, and disentangle himself from his unholy alliance with Ahab? I believe the answer can be found in 2 Chronicles 18:1: "Jehoshaphat had riches and honor in abundance; and by marriage he allied himself with Ahab." Jehoshaphat was overly concerned with his prosperity and fame, so he had entered into a covenant with ungodly Ahab for gain. In the ensuing calamitous battle Jehoshaphat cried out to God and was miraculously delivered. He repented and returned to Jerusalem where he began a revival and "brought many of his people back to the Lord God of their fathers" (19:4).

AHAB'S COWARDICE

Ahab proved to be a conniving hypocrite to the end. The coward disguised himself, but told Jehoshaphat to wear his royal robes. In the battle, the Syrians thought Jehoshaphat was Ahab and thirty-two chariots surrounded him to attack; but Jehoshaphat "cried out, and the Lord helped him, and God diverted them" (18:31). God saved Jehoshaphat because of his prayer. Meanwhile, disguised Ahab thought he was safe. But a Syrian archer "drew a bow at random, and struck the king of Israel between the joints of his armor" (1 Kings 22:34).

Ahab's battle became more fierce as the Israelites and Syrians slaughtered each other. Some of Ahab's soldiers propped up the wounded king in his chariot. As the sun was going down on the bloody carnage brought about by Ahab's ambition and rebellion against God, the king of Israel died in a pool of his own blood in his chariot. He was brought to Samaria where he was buried. Micaiah's word from God had come true. The four hundred false prophets had brought disaster upon their own nation. And last, Elijah's word to Ahab in Naboth's vineyard had come to pass:

> Then someone washed the chariot at the pool in Samaria, and the dogs licked up his [Ahab's] blood while the harlots bathed, according to the word of the Lord which He had spoken. (1 Kings 22:38)

PROPHETS TRUE OR FALSE?

During the twenty-two year reign of King Ahab two prophetic movements were birthed, nourished, and flourished. One was false and one was true. The false defiled and brought destruction. The true delivered and brought divine blessing. There is a clear parallel between the days of Ahab and Elijah, and present day Israel. Our nation is filled with idolatry. Rabbinic and mystical Judaism, nominal Christianity and Islam are all demonic strongholds in the "holy" land. New age cults, materialism, and secular humanism are the Baals of today. Sexual immorality abounds in a "spirit of harlotry" as in the days of Jezebel.

The gift of prophecy and the office of prophet which were released by our ascended Lord for edifying or equipping His

Church are necessary for the health of His body (Ephesians 4:11-12). "Equipping" is the English translation for a Greek medical term that means setting a bone in place during surgery. I have broken both my ankles. The snap of one was heard by people sitting in a football stadium. When two large trainers once jammed my separated shoulder back into place, it was no fun either. A broken ankle requires six weeks in a plaster cast, while one hobbles around on crutches. New Testament prophecy is supposed to build up Christ's body by spiritual surgery to make us fit, prepared, and trained to be fully qualified for the Lord's service.

IDOLS IN THE HEART

Ahab had an idol in his heart. An idol is anything we put before God in our lives. The king only heard what fed his idolatry. The Lord clearly explained the problem to the prophet Ezekiel: "Son of man, these men [leaders] have set up idols in their hearts, and put before them that which causes them to stumble into iniquity. Should I let Myself be inquired of at all by them? … I the LORD will answer him who comes, according to the multitude of his idols" (Ezekiel 14:3-4). There is the problem in a nutshell. If someone has set up an idol in his heart and goes to a false prophet, be assured, the person will receive a "confirming word." They will hear what they want to hear. They will even hear what was not even spoken. Why? Because "idols speak delusion" (Zechariah 10:2).

Also if the prophet has set up an idol in his or her heart (fame, power, recognition, honor, money, etc.), that person will prophesy falsely to themselves, as well as to others, according to his idol. For instance, I have known people who were not called or sent to Israel, but came believing they had a "word" from God. Some have brought mostly misery upon themselves and others. Israel is their idol. God answered Ahab according to the idolatry and deception in his heart and it destroyed him. And because he was a leader, many of his followers died with him.

PERSONAL WORDS

I believe there is a widespread misconception concerning the purpose of New Testament prophecy. First, there are the "cessationists" who tell us that the gifts of the Holy Spirit and the office of the apostle and prophet ceased at some point in time. These groups can't agree upon when God's gifts to His Church stopped. Jesus paid the price of crucifixion, and the resurrected and ascended Lord gave these gifts to His Church (Ephesians 4:7-16). If His Church is still here, then so are His gifts to us.

Secondly, many teach that Old Testament prophecy was harsh and judgmental, and that New Testament prophecy is all positive and grace. They are simply wrong. Everyone who was ever saved has been saved by grace, from Abel to us. The message of repentance is God's grace. "The goodness of God leads you to repentance" (Romans 2:4). Any other message is cheap grace. Jesus said that New Testament prophecy began with John the Baptist (Matthew 11:13), because there had been no prophetic voice in Israel for four hundred years. Was John the Baptist giving personal, confirming, comforting words, like most "personal words" today?

If you were walking in sin, you would not have been comfortable anywhere near that prophet. John brought a corrective word to soldiers and tax collectors, not to mention the religious leaders of his day. He was thrown in jail for confronting Herod in his sin. John preached that we should "bear fruit worthy of repentance" (Luke 3:8).

The first word of Jesus when He began to preach was, "Repent" (Matthew 4:17). He called us to turn away from our old life of sin and walk in a new way with Him. That is God's grace. Jesus consistently gave personal prophetic words to

His disciples, and to others who would either reject or receive His warnings and corrections. The rich young ruler rejected Jesus' word to him. The Samaritan woman at the well received his corrective word. Jesus prophesied on several occasions to his apostle-in-the-making, Peter. He told Peter to his face in front of the other disciples that Peter would deny Him. He even prophesied how Peter would die (John 21:19). Peter still continued to follow his Master.

JESUS, THE PROPHET

How would we characterize the prophecies of Jesus to the seven churches in Revelation? To five of the seven He prophesied solemn warnings. Some had left their first love, while others taught false doctrines. One church tolerated a false prophetess named Jezebel. Some had even "known the depths of Satan" (Revelation 2:24). One church Jesus simply called "dead" (Revelation 3:1). Another was lukewarm. He said to all of them, His body, to repent or He would remove His presence, fight against them with the sword of His mouth, come upon them as a thief, or vomit them out of His mouth. He said His Church was "wretched, miserable, poor, blind, and naked.... As many as I love I rebuke and chasten. Therefore be zealous and repent" (Revelation 3:17-19). What can we reply to Him who has "eyes like a flame of fire?" (1:14). The testimony of Jesus is the spirit of true prophecy in the New Covenant church (Revelation 19:10).

The disciple John's mother wanted Jesus to prophesy that her sons would be His right and left hand men in eternity. Jesus gave a different kind of personal word to her boys. "You will indeed drink My cup" (Matthew 20:23). By this He meant divinely appointed suffering would be theirs. When is the last time you heard of a personal word like that? Peter prophesied the death of Sapphira (Acts 5:9-11). The prophet Agabus and others testified to Paul that "chains and tribulations await me" (Acts 20:23). The two prophets Paul and Barnabas came back to Lystra where Paul had been stoned and left for dead. The prophetic word to the disciples there, exhorting them to continue in the faith, was, "We must through many tribulations enter the kingdom of God" (Acts 14:22).

NEW COVENANT PROPHECY

We are commanded to "pursue love, and desire earnestly spiritual gifts, but especially that you may prophesy" (1 Corinthians 14:1). In my experience, there seems to be a confusion over the meaning of prophecy that stems from the interpretation of 1 Corinthians 14:3. The *New King James* translation reads: "But he who prophesies speaks edification and exhortation and comfort to men." We have seen that "edification" can mean to build up by setting a bone in place. Doctors say the repaired bone is stronger. So the person is strengthened. "Exhortation" is defined as "constructive spiritual progress" in the *Amplified Bible*.

John the Baptist prophesied about the Lord's threshing floor and ended with "the chaff He [Jesus] will burn up with unquenchable fire" (Luke 3:17). Luke added: "And with many other exhortations he preached to the people" (v.18). It is the same word that we often water down to mean speaking wonderful positive things about people. Did Jesus flatter people? Paul the prophet was continually warning his flocks. (See Acts 20:28-31, Col. 1:28.) True prophecy will often take the form of a warning for the person's good. Prophets tell people what they need to hear, not necessarily what they want to hear. God's prophets want to please Him, not men.

The prophet Barnabas was called the "son of encouragement." Some people are said to have a "Barnabas ministry" or ministry of encouragement, often meaning just saying nice things about people. But to truly encourage means to put or impart courage into someone. Courage is the ability to conquer fear and despair. Courage requires faith. It could be courage to face a besetting sin and call on the Lord in humility for deliverance. We may need to mend a broken relationship. That too takes courage. That is real encouragement. However, it doesn't mean that as spiritual fathers we don't affirm young believers when they do well, and challenge and inspire them to go deeper with the Lord. Even men of God like Elijah need affirmation. Angels were sent to minister to Elijah and Jesus.

TAKE HEED THAT NO ONE DECEIVES YOU

In Matthew 24, Jesus prophesies about the "end of the age" to His disciples. Three times in the first eight verses He warns us of "deception." To deceive or be deceived means to believe an untruth. Nominal Christianity and all other false religions are deceptions. Millions have been swept into a godless eternity because of deception. But Jesus says the last days will be characterized by delusion in His church: "Then many false prophets will rise up and deceive many … and the [agape] love of many will grow cold" (v.11-12). The Apostle-prophet-pastor Paul prophesied to the elders of that great church at Ephesus that what Jesus had said was about to happen. The Ephesian congregation was evidently already beginning to lose its "first-class agape love" for Jesus and for each other. They were opening the door for deception.

WOLVES

Paul prophesied a solemn warning to those leaders and every other shepherd of the Lord's flock, "among which the Holy Spirit has made you overseers, to shepherd the church of God which He purchased with His own blood. For I know this, that after my departure savage wolves will come in among you, not sparing the flock. Also from among yourselves men will rise up speaking perverse ["misleading"] things, to draw away the disciples after themselves" (Acts 20:28-30). This truly prophetic pastor warned the leaders he had trained. Then they all got down on their knees, and Paul "prayed with them all" (v.36). I would like to have heard those prayers. And how did those leaders respond to Paul's final, prophetic, pastoral warning?

> Then they all wept freely, and fell on Paul's neck and kissed him, sorrowing most of all for the words which he spoke, that they would see his face no more. And they accompanied him to the ship. (Acts 20: 37-38).

Paul said that one of the characteristics of these false prophets in the Church of God was that they would draw disciples of Jesus to themselves. Jesus purchased His Church with His blood. To draw His disciples to ourselves is to displace and decentralize Jesus.

Elijah and Elisha were certainly famous in their day, or infamous to the double minded and idolaters. Their life-style and courageous and uncompromising stand for righteousness didn't draw disciples to themselves. Elisha left everything to follow God as Elijah's servant. He was known as the man "who poured water on the hands of Elijah" (2 Kings 3:11). He had clean hands and a pure heart.

I have often heard mature men or women of God go on and on about some word given by a famous prophet who called someone out of a crowd. The words are invariably very positive. I heard one famous minister who visited Israel dole out "world-wide ministries," like it was a TV game show. A "Thus saith the Lord," not from God is a severe violation of the third commandment not to take God's name in vain. A leader we knew was "called out" in a meeting in the States and was publicly prophesied over that he would impact "thirty-six nations." He did not. As he was dying, the last thing I heard him say in the presence of several other pastors was, "If the body in Israel doesn't grow up, God is going to pass this generation by." I believe that this was a genuine prophetic word. God's word through His dying servant shook me to the core.

THE WORD OF THE LORD

"The words of the LORD are pure words, like silver tried in a furnace of earth, purified seven times" (Psalm12:6). The true prophetic word will always turn the heart of the recipient to God. It will never turn the person's heart to the prophet. A word from the Lord will only glorify God, not man. It will be purified and tried. Godly elders will have a witness. In fact, there is no "Thus saith the Lord" in the New Testament. Why? Because all born-of-the-Spirit believers have the Spirit of Truth, the Holy Spirit residing in us. If we are walking in the Spirit, we should discern the validity of words spoken to us by others. But if we have set up an idol in our heart where the Holy Spirit is supposed to be enthroned we may hear another voice.

The Apostle Paul in his last recorded prophetic words to his "Elisha," Timothy, cried out from a Roman prison:

> Convince, rebuke, exhort, with all longsuffering and teaching. For a time will come when they will not endure sound doctrine, but according to their own desires, because they have itching ears, they will heap up for themselves teachers, and they will turn their ears away from the truth, and be turned aside to fables. (2 Timothy 4:2-4).

A "fable" is a fiction, an untruth. We have been warned over and over again in the New Testament and by Jesus himself, that believers will have "ears itching [for something pleasing and gratifying], they will gather themselves one teacher after another to a considerable number, chosen to satisfy their own liking and to foster errors they hold, and will turn aside from hearing the truth and wander off into myths and man-made fictions" (2 Timothy 4:3-4, AMP). The *New Living* translation puts it this way: "For a time is coming when people will no longer listen to right teaching. They will follow their own desires and will look for teachers who will tell them whatever they want to hear" (2 Timothy 4:3). We have been warned and we have no excuse.

PROPHETS AND SCRIBES

Before I met Jesus and was filled with the Holy Spirit, I had lived the life of an academic scribe, usually studying what others thought. My years of academic discipline would certainly help me as I became a student of the Bible, but this new study was illuminated by the Spirit of God. In early Bible times, scribes were scholars of Jewish law. Their occupation was to study and to copy, as they often wrote down what prophets said. They recorded other people's revelations. Jeremiah heard from God, and Baruch recorded. That's what scribes did, and that was much of what I had done for years.

After serving the Lord on Mount Carmel for nearly twenty years, we have often witnessed the power of the prophetic Word of God. During these years I have come to some conclusions about walking in the prophetic anointing as opposed to living as a scribe.

Elijah and the other Hebrew prophets were some of the most disturbing people who ever lived. That's why they were often rejected, stoned, or crucified. The prophets were watchmen, seers, and messengers of God who gave them divine understanding of human situations. Prophets faced a holy God, then faced men. Elijah was acting in the power of a word that was not his own. It was God's.

Holy Spirit inspired insight is to see and respond to the present, the immediate situation, the now. Believers who would walk in the Spirit, consistently hear and obey what God is saying and prompting them to do now. Eventually it becomes second nature.

Seeing the present through the past can be deadly. It locks us into seeing life only through patterns to which we have been accustomed. Prophetic insight or revelation demands seeking and longing to know the voice of God. Sometimes something is suddenly disclosed, or gently revealed. But it is new—*kainos*—fresh, pure, unused, undiluted. For instance, when the fire fell on Mount Carmel thousands of Israelites were there, but only Elijah heard the "sound of abundance of rain." In the case of Elisha, he saw the chariots of fire, while his servant did not. I believe that most of us simply choose not to pay the price to walk in the dimension of spirituality available to us.

Jesus made this amazing statement to seventy ordinary followers who were not even baptized in the Holy Spirit: "I tell you that many prophets and kings have desired to see what you see, and have not seen it, and to hear what you hear, and have not heard it" (Luke 10:24). Jesus died to save us, but He also sent us the Spirit of truth to "guide us into all truth ... and He will tell you things to come" (John 16:13). We are commanded to "desire earnestly" to live like this.

In my years as a pastor in Israel, and ministering in different parts of the world, I have come to believe that much of the body of Messiah is deficient spiritually because many believers walk only as "scribes." Here are some observations concerning the difference between prophets and scribes, or those continually led by the Spirit and those who are not.

PROPHET	SCRIBE
• Testifies to what he has seen/heard	• Tells what he has read somewhere
• Stands in the inner court of God	• Stays in the outer court
• Lives at the Source	• Looks at secondary sources
• Hears, sees, obeys, initiates	• Copies, imitates others
• Searches and seeks	• Is satisfied
• Feels God's pain, weeps	• Is busy
• Sees from God's point of view	• Sees externals
• Understands causes, roots	• Sees effects, symptoms
• Fears God	• Fears man
• Heralds change	• Fears change
• Is secure in relationship with God	• Is insecure; identity in works, people
• Is a man of the Spirit	• Is a soul man

People walking in the prophetic know what they see and hear. Scribes see or hear what they think they already know. Scribes will usually miss the prophetic urging because of soulish mindsets and habits of thinking. These include preconceptions, pre-judging, and categorizing events and people to fit former or formal understanding. The nature of prophecy is to disturb, to stir up, and to bring about change. Not many of us like change, so prophecy will draw resistance. Elijah's ministry disturbed, stirred up and brought change in his day.

Elijah was not only a prophet of God, but he poured his heart into the Elisha generation which followed him. This great father-figure fostered a true prophetic remnant at a time of national apostasy.

THE CHURCH DESPERATELY NEEDS SUCH AN
ELIJAH LEGACY NOW.

THE RELEASE OF THE DOUBLE PORTION

A FATHER'S FAREWELL

As Elijah's time on Earth was drawing to a close he made a farewell tour of the prophetic schools he had founded. Scripture does not record his final words to the "sons of the prophets" on Mount Carmel or the other schools, but these last meetings must have been very moving. The father was saying a final "until we meet in Heaven" to his spiritual children.

Elisha followed Elijah from Gilgal to Bethel to Jericho. For the third time Elijah told Elisha to stay and not follow him as he continued to the nearby Jordan. Elisha repeated his vow not to leave his mentor. "So the two of them went on" (2 Kings 2:6). This simple statement is filled with beauty and meaning. The son would not leave the father. They were going on together toward the Jordan, the place of humility, cleansing and newness of life. They had originally met further up the Jordan at the "meadow of the dance." Now their remaining time together was short and therefore most precious. The description of this father-son scene has a sense of privacy.

For a moment the inspired writer puts us in the same place as the onlookers: "And fifty men of the sons of the prophets went and stood facing them at a distance, while the two of them stood by the Jordan" (v.7). I have preached many times about this scene, saying that only Elisha chose to go all the way with God. The fifty other Bible students (believers) were lukewarm and hung back at a distance from total surrender and intimacy with Jesus. Only Elisha chose to walk in the light. I have seen the Lord meet with believers and non-believers in Israel and in different nations as they responded to this message, as they have been convicted over their sin and compromise. And I believe all of this is right and true. But I am beginning to see more here. There is such an intimacy between Elijah and Elisha, father and son, who would dare intrude? The other students all knew that Elisha was the "heir apparent." It is similar to Jesus taking Peter, James and John with Him to the Mount of Transfiguration. Did the others insist upon joining them? When Jesus was in rapt communion with the Father did they dare interrupt Him? On the way to Gethsemane when Jesus stopped and "lifted His eyes to heaven," and poured out His sublime "high priestly prayer," who would dare intrude? (See John 17:1-26.)

AN INTERGENERATIONAL TRANSITIONAL MOMENT

Elijah and Elisha stood at the Jordan on the verge of a major intergenerational, transitional moment. The fifty others looked on from a distance perhaps out of respect, maybe even a sense of awe. They were all prophets. Perhaps several were yearning to become Elisha's servant. Were any envious of Elisha because he was younger than some, and because of the obvious anointing upon him? Jesus would have responded to them: "Is it not lawful for me to do what I wish with my own things?" (Matthew 20:15). As Paul told the Corinthian believers: "God has set the members, each one of them, in the body just as He pleased. God has appointed these in the church: first apostles, second prophets, third teachers" (1 Corinthians 12:18, 28a).

Elijah took his rough cloak and struck the Jordan with it. The river opened up and divided. He and his spiritual son "crossed over on dry ground" (2 Kings 2:8). The river closed again and the two were separated from the fifty. Moses at the Red Sea, and his spiritual son Joshua at this very place, had opened the way for deliverance and fullness for the nation. The same was true for Elijah and Elisha, the forerunner and the finisher. Jordan means "to go down" into the place of baptism where we are to be immersed into the death and character of God. "Therefore we were buried with Him through baptism into His death, that just as Christ was raised from the dead by the glory of the Father, even so we should walk in newness of life" (Romans 6:4). As the fifty who did not cross the Jordan that day stood watching, Elijah and Elisha disappeared in the distance—two men dead to self, walking into newness of life. One was about to fulfill his destiny, while the other was about to be anointed for his.

Yes, Elisha passed over, went further, went beyond the others in his walk with God. That is why he was ordained by God to take Elijah's place as the major prophet of Israel. They left the fifty on the other shore. It was only *after* they had gone beyond, gone further and deeper, when they were alone, that Elijah stopped and looked at his precious son and said, "Ask! What may I do for you?" (2 Kings 2:9). I believe this is the question that every believer who wants to go further with God needs to answer for himself. Paul's answer was "that I might know Him, and the power of His resurrection, and the fellowship of His sufferings" (Philippians 3:10). There is an old revival hymn that carries these words, "Fill me with Thy hallowed presence, Come, O come, and fill me now." "Elishas" want more of Him.

THE DOUBLE PORTION

Elisha looked up at Elijah and said, "Please let a double portion of your spirit be upon me" (2 Kings 2:9). Elisha was desperate for more of God, for more of His Holy Spirit. He wanted more of the Spirit he had witnessed upon the mighty man of God he loved and served. He wanted more! This young man who had left all to follow God wanted the father's blessing for a double portion. In the Torah, the double portion was only given to the firstborn son. The oldest son received it through the father's blessing. Jacob deceived Isaac in order to get the blessing of the firstborn after Esau sold it to him. Elisha knew that Elijah was the spiritual covering for Israel and now he was about to take Elijah's place. Elijah must have told him of his commissioning in the cave at Horev to anoint Elisha as prophet in his place. Now the young prophet needed this new anointing.

His time had come. His apprenticeship was over. We are commanded to "earnestly desire the best gifts" (1 Corinthians 12:31), and to "desire spiritual gifts, but especially that you may prophesy" (14:1). Elisha, the prophet-in-process, was doing just that. His request for a double portion has been misunderstood by many translators, commentators, and ministers. Some say he did twice as many miracles, and much greater ones than Elijah. Others have written that Elijah had a "legal spirit," and Elisha had an "evangelical spirit" that was twice as great. Some dispensationalists have claimed that Elijah represents judgment and Elisha grace. In response to such assertions C.F. Keil has correctly pointed out: "There is no such meaning implied in the words, nor can it be inferred from the answer of Elijah" (*Commentary on the Old Testament*, C.F. Keil, Vol.III, p. 293).

Rather, Elisha's request was based upon the teaching of God's word. He was asking for the double portion which every Hebrew firstborn son was to receive as his portion of his father's inheritance. (See Deuteronomy 21:17.) Elisha had walked away from his earthly inheritance the day he met Elijah seven years earlier some miles up the Jordan. He had served his mentor faithfully. Like young Solomon, Elisha asked for no worldly advantage, but for the spiritual power to discharge the awesome office he was about to embrace. To fill the shoes of Elijah, given the temporal and spiritual conditions of the nation, he was going to need a massive anointing, and he knew it. Elisha has been accused of pride and ambition, wanting to out do Elijah. I don't agree. I think he, was saying, like John the Baptist, would centuries later near the same place, "He [God] must increase, but I must decrease" (John 3:30). I believe Elisha felt inadequate for his holy assignment and knew, like Paul, that our sufficiency is from God. He was about to inherit the responsibility of representing Jehovah and of being a spiritual covering for the nation. Not only that, he was about to begin serving as a spiritual father for hundreds of "the sons of the prophets" and their families, perhaps seven thousand. What daunting responsibilities! Elisha was requesting the portion of the father's substance that rightfully belonged to the eldest son. Upon his father's death, the firstborn would also inherit the responsibility of leadership for the family, as well as a double portion of the property. Here Elisha was asking to be openly acknowledged as Elijah's firstborn spiritual son. His adoption by the older prophet had been signified when Elijah had cast his prophet's mantle upon his young follower on the very parcel of land that would have been Elisha's earthy inheritance, which he then gave up to follow Elijah.

As we have seen, "the spirit of Elijah"—that is, his heart, his character—was one of obedience, humility, intimacy with God, compassion and concern for the lost, and courage to confront evil. He also had the "Father's heart" for the "sons of the prophets." His travailing and persistent prayer had raised the dead and opened the heavens. This is what Elisha was crying out for. God was about to answer him, as He always responds to a humble heart:

> For thus says the High and Lofty One
> Who inhabits eternity, whose name is Holy. "I dwell in a high and holy place,
> With him who has a contrite and humble spirit To revive the spirit of the humble,
> And to revive the heart of the contrite ones. (Isaiah 57:14-15)

One of the names for the One who inhabits eternity is simply "Holy" or *Kadosh* in Hebrew. It means that which is perfectly clean and pure, separated from everything profane and defiling. God is entirely holy in His nature, motives, thoughts, words, and deeds, so that His name is "Holy"—*Kadosh*. We are to be holy as He is holy. Elisha was asking for more of the Holy Spirit—the purity and power—which he had seen manifested through Elijah.

The double portion of the firstborn is the rightful inheritance of every child of God who has been born-again by the Holy Spirit. Jesus Christ is the "head of the body, the church, who is the beginning, the firstborn from the dead, that in all things He may have the preeminence" (Colossians1:18). He is "the faithful witness, the firstborn from the dead, and the ruler over the kings of the earth" (Revelation 1:5). If we have been bought and washed by His blood, we are joint heirs with Christ. We have received "the spirit of adoption," through the New Covenant in His blood. We need to cry out for more of His Spirit, as Elisha did. The double portion is ours by inheritance if we will appropriate it.

A HOLY DESPERATION

We are not all called to be prophets like Elijah or Elisha, but we all have gifts and callings. Many of us don't have the anointing we need because we don't pay the price of separation from the world, and to Jesus, the way these two did. Also, most of us are not desperate enough for such an anointing. Three times Elisha spoke a double oath to vow his total commitment to his master. "As the LORD lives, and as your soul lives, I will not leave you!" These words echo the Gentile Ruth's desperation for the God of Israel in her commitment to her spiritual mother Naomi. Her sister would not pay that price. Ruth's total consecration to God resulted in the blessing of her union with Boaz. She became a part of the genealogy of King David and King Jesus.

Holy desperation was the key. Elisha was desperate. Like Jacob at the Jabbok, he would not let go until he got his blessing. Elijah must have been thrilled by the young man's hunger. God will fill a hungry heart. "How much more will your heavenly Father give the Holy Spirit to those who ask Him!" (Luke 11:13).

On two occasions, one in a congregation in Israel and the other one in Singapore, I have been led by the Holy Spirit to publicly prophesy that God was going to give their ministries a "double blessing." I believed He would double their space in the near future, to make room for the coming season of harvest, because they had been caring for the needy. "Blessed is he who considers the poor … he will be blessed on the earth" (Psalm 41:1-2). The pastors of both places contacted me shortly after I was there, and said God had doubled their space.

MOUNT CARMEL MINISTRY CENTER

In 2002 the Lord spoke to us that He was going to "double" our work by giving us two more buildings on Mount Carmel adjacent to our worship center. As we stood in faith on this word from the Lord, we began to see His expanding vision for the top of Carmel. Pastor Peter Tsukahira and his wife Rita, who have been instrumental in helping found and develop the Lord's community here, received a "rhema" word concerning the former guesthouse and annex of the Stella Carmel property. The word was from Isaiah 54:2-3:

> Enlarge the place of your tent, and let them stretch out the curtains of your dwellings; do not spare; lengthen your cords, and strengthen your stakes. For you shall expand to the right and to the left, and your descendants will inherit the nations, and make desolate cities inhabited.

This Scripture is addressed to a barren woman who is being encouraged to sing. We knew that the Lord wanted us to establish here a refuge for afflicted women. We also knew that this would be a place to equip "Elishas" for Israel, as well as send workers to the nations. We already hold Schools of Ministry for believers from the nations. In addition, we want to house an on-going ministry of intercession in our Elijah Prayer Cave, dug out of the bedrock upon which our new building was built. Financing for the project has been coming from the Far East, Europe and America. We are believing God for His "double blessing." [In November 2002, we completed the purchase of the buildings and have renamed the property *Or HaCarmel*, "Light of Carmel," to reflect our calling to be "a city on a mountain, glowing in the midst for all to see" (Matthew 5:14, NLT). Peter and Rita Tsukahira now serve as the Directors of the Or HaCarmel Ministry Center. That same month we also launched a clothing distribution center in downtown Haifa, called "Elijah's Cloak." A new Arab congregation under our covering began meeting there.]

"ELISHAS"-IN-TRAINING

Elijah looked at this young man who had "poured water on his hands." (See 2 Kings 3:11.) The phrase means he had served his master faithfully. He had guarded the good reputation of his leader, always remaining loyal to him. They both had clean hands and pure hearts toward God and each other. While Elijah was hated by many in Israel, Elisha was jealous for his spiritual father's honor. Prophetic leaders are always attacked and resented. The Lord Jesus was killed by religious people because of envy. God's point men or women will be attacked, but "Elishas" will honor their spiritual fathers. There is a beautiful spiritual harmony between a true disciple and his or her mentor. They need each other. Jesus expressed this inter-generational unity this way: "A disciple is not above his teacher, but everyone who is perfectly trained will be like his teacher" (Luke 6:40).

We are very blessed to have a group of faithful spiritual sons and daughters here on Mount Carmel. For some time I had a mentoring group of a dozen young men who are hungry for God. Karen and I participated in a national conference at the end of 2002 around the theme: "Spiritual Fathers and Sons, Mothers and Daughters—Equipping the Next Generation in Israel."

SEERS

Elijah responded to Elisha's request for a double portion: "You have asked a hard thing. Nevertheless, if you see me when I am taken from you, it shall be so for you; but if not, it shall not be so" (2 Kings 2:10).

Did Elijah mean by a "hard thing," a "costly" thing? The prophet knew the terrible price he had paid to follow hard after his Lord, and to finish his race. Prophets are "seers," seeing into the realms of the spirit, where they may discern sources and motives, not just effects. For his new commission, Elisha would need to have a "single eye" for God. Jesus said that "the lamp of the body is the eye. Therefore, when your eye is good [clear, pure, healthy], your whole body is full of light" (Luke 11:33). The eye is the lens of the soul and reflects the desires, direction and total orientation of a believer's life. Prophets see what others do not see, because they are watching God. The Lord is always saying to His prophets: "What do you see, Jeremiah? What do you see Ezekiel, Zechariah?" What do you see? It depends upon where your eye is fixed. These men weren't mystics. They walked by faith by "seeing Him who is invisible." "Faith is the substance [or reality] of things hoped for, the evidence of things not seen" (Hebrews 11:1). Faith looks beyond the promise to the Promiser. Elisha was being called up higher to become a seer because he was desperate for more spiritual sight. And God would answer the young man's heart cry with an anointing that would impact his nation.

A watchman sees what is coming in the distance. He also sees beyond confusing or disturbing circumstances—to Him who is in charge of all circumstances. A seer sees a dead boy alive. A seer in Israel today sees a valley full of dry bones coming to life to become "an exceedingly great army" (Ezekiel 37:10) for the Lord, or "life from the dead" (Romans 11:15). I don't know what God told Elijah about his imminent departure, but "faith comes by hearing, and hearing by the word of God" (Romans 10:17). Elijah had heard that he was to be "taken up" by God, and Elisha was about to see it.

A CHARIOT OF FIRE

The two men continued on, conversing. Oh, I have longed to know what they discussed! Did Elijah reminisce about his days with ravens, or a widow and a dead boy? Did Elisha want to hear once more about the theophany in the cave on Horev? Did they discuss that awesome day on Mount Carmel when the heavens opened and the fire of God consumed the sacrifice? Was the future of the schools of prophets and all the "sons of the prophets" on their hearts? What about Jezebel? Were there any last directions from the Lord? I doubt if their conversation was about practical details. I think these two spiritual giants were communicating on higher ground—deep calling to deep. The Torah contains a charge from the prophet Moses to the next generation: "The secret things belong to the Lord our God, but those things which are revealed belong to us and to our children forever, that we may do all this law" (Deuteronomy 29:29). The prophetic mantle, or revelation and obedience to what the Lord reveals, was about to be passed to the next generation.

"Then it happened, as they continued on and talked, that suddenly a chariot of fire appeared with horses of fire, and separated the two of them; and Elijah went up in a whirlwind to heaven" (2 Kings 2:11). A fiery chariot drawn by fiery horses exploded out of the heavens and hurtled toward the Earth. It drove between the one who was about to leave and the one who was staying. Then Elijah was in the chariot. A whirlwind took him and the flaming chargers back up into Heaven. In Hebrew it reads that Elisha "was watching and crying." Out of his innermost being came a shattering cry, "My father, my father, the chariot of Israel and its horsemen!" (v.12). His father was taken from him. The weeping son gazed into the heavens where Elijah had gone—Elijah was alive! Elisha had seen!

The young prophet had also seen "the chariot of Israel and its horsemen" removed from the Earth. He was crying out that Elijah and the fiery beings were the true national defense, better than all of Israel's military might. The real strength and shield of a nation is due to the consecration of the holy remnant of true believers that belong to it. The sight of the Lord Jesus' ascension also gave life and power to His disciples who remained to finish His work. Read the first chapter of the

Acts of the Apostles and see how vivid was their sense that Jesus was living! They had seen!

I believe that fiery angels were the "horsemen" who escorted Elijah to Heaven. God makes His angels "a flame of fire" (Psalm 104:4). "Seraphim" means "fiery," and "cherubim" are referred to as "the chariots of God" in Psalm 68:17. Isaiah and Ezekiel also saw the fiery warriors of the Lord of Hosts. In a day of utmost darkness God honored his loyal servant with a fiery exit. There is an eternal reward for the righteous.

THE PROPHET'S CLOAK

Elisha stood on the other side of the Jordan. His father was gone and he was alone. He tore his clothes in sorrow, and wept. Through his grief and sense of loss he must have realized that he had seen Elijah taken from him, the condition for the double portion. He didn't know what to do except to get down on his knees to pray. There, on his knees in the place of humility, he saw it. The cloak was lying on the ground! It had fallen from the prophet. Elisha reached out for it. The mantle of Elijah had fallen to him.

"WHERE IS THE LORD GOD OF ELIJAH?"

Elisha draped the hairy mantle about his shoulders. Wrapped in his new anointing he went back and stood by the bank of the Jordan. He took the mantle and struck the river, and cried out, "Where is the LORD God of Elijah?" (2 Kings 2:14). He was crying out for the power of God that had rested upon Elijah. The river divided again! The God of Elijah had granted his request! He had received the double portion! With his new anointing the young prophet crossed back into Israel. The "sons of the prophets" from Jericho saw the miracle and confirmed that, "The spirit of Elijah rests upon Elisha" (v.15). They recognized Heaven's seal and bowed down acknowledging their new leader.

The mantle rested easily upon the young prophet. It would prove to be a good fit.

"THE SPIRIT OF ELIJAH"

As we have seen, "the spirit of Elijah" consisted of at least five major characteristics. First, Elijah was *consecrated*. He had begun his dramatic ministry in God's service by declaring, "The Lord God of Israel before whom I stand," and in his miraculous ministry he had stood with God in uncompromising separation from the abounding evil all around him. He was dead to the world's systems, but alive to God through his consecrated life. Too much of the Church of Jesus Christ today walks arm in arm with the world. We are often told to be a "good mixer" if you wish to win young people, or older people for that matter. Elijahs are not "good mixers." Elijah had no fellowship with darkness. He was indeed a "stranger and pilgrim" (Hebrews 11:13) here, this "sojourner" from Gilead. The only way to be a witness to Messiah is to walk with Messiah. To walk in His Spirit is to walk "outside the camp" of the lukewarm, apostate masses who continue to halt between two opinions. "Elijahs" and "Elishas" will always bear His reproach.

Secondly, he was *compassionate*. He cared deeply for his own people, but he also went to Zarephath and loved and ministered to a heathen widow and her son. For two years they lived on bread and water. What spiritual patience Elijah demonstrated, as the fruit of the Spirit of the living God flourished in the good soil of his father heart. He was a forerunner—going before, breaking new ground—as a prototype of the "one new man" in Messiah, of Jew and Gentile joined in one body in the last days. Because of his consecration to God he heard the Master's voice. In his humility and meekness he obeyed. He and Elisha were a shining light to the nations around them.

Next, he was a man of *communion*. He is honored in the New Testament as one of the greatest men of prayer. He modeled the powerful truth that the "effective, fervent prayer of a righteous man avails much" (James 5:16). We last see Elijah in rapt communion with His glorified Lord on the Mount of Transfiguration. Some rabbis think he was an angel, but we know differently: "Elijah was a man with a nature like ours, and he prayed earnestly that it would not rain; and it did not rain on the land for three years and six months. And he prayed again, and the heaven gave rain, and the earth produced its fruit" (v.17-18). Yes, his prayers brought "showers of blessing" upon his people and land.

Fourthly, Elijah was a man of resolute *courage*. He demonstrated a rare spiritual boldness. His courage was a heavenly endowment birthed and built out of his communion with his God. It came from on high, as he was clothed in power by the Holy Spirit. His cloak was the outward emblem of the supernatural courage of the true prophet. "The wicked flee when no one pursues, but the righteous are bold as a lion" (Proverbs 28:1). In his generation he displayed an unparalleled passion for the honor of God. His reward for this zeal was the awesome release of a fearlessness, a holy boldness upon him. He could say with David: "The Lord is my light and my salvation; whom shall I fear? The Lord is the strength of my life; of whom shall I be afraid?" (Psalm 27:1). A person who truly fears God is fearless of man. Elijah denounced King Ahab and his son to their faces. Alone, he confronted an army of false prophets. His was a singular voice crying in the wilderness to his stiff-necked nation: "Prepare the way of the Lord!"

Lastly, Elijah demonstrated unwavering *commitment* to the next generation. Our heavenly Father placed a mantle of fatherhood upon the lonely prophet, as he lived with a fatherless boy in a foreign land. His prayer to raise that boy from the dead is a foreshadowing of an end-time remnant of men who will willingly accept the cloak of fatherhood.

The enduring legacy of Elijah is not so much the fire from Heaven that fell on the altar on Carmel, but rather the fruit of his father-son relationship with Elisha. The two of them raised up schools of prophets, training, and discipling thousands of their people all over Samaria, Galilee, and Mount Carmel, teaching them to be "doers" of the Word. This is the heritage we so desperately need to move in today.

At great personal sacrifice, and under threat of death and persecution, Elijah left a powerful deposit of revival for Elisha and his generation to walk in. This spiritual father poured himself into his children. Such holy activity, though hidden and far less spectacular than the miracles wrought by God through him, was of far greater and lasting importance. The effect produced by witnessing supernatural wonders soon wears off. But truth received into a soul abides forever. Those discipled by Elijah and Elisha abide in eternity with them now. Ahab and his ungodly progeny are in another place.

Thousands also thrilled to the miracles of Jesus. Nonetheless the lasting fruit of His earthly ministry which revolutionized the world was the three years He spent mentoring His faltering apostles-in-training. The same is true of Elijah or of any person mightily used of God. Prophets are preachers, but also fathers. You shall know them by their fruit. Our success will be measured by our successors.

> Behold I send you Elijah the prophet
> Before the coming of the great and dreadful day of the LORD.
> And he will turn the hearts of the fathers to the children, And the hearts of the children to their fathers (Malachi 4:5-6).

ELIJAH'S CLOAK LAYS AT THE JORDAN.
WHO WILL PAY THE PRICE TO KNEEL AND PICK IT UP?

O GOD OF ABRAHAM, ISAAC AND ISRAEL,
RELEASE THE LEGACY OF ELIJAH!
RAISE UP SPIRITUAL FATHERS WHO WILL
TRAIN AN ELISHA GENERATION NOW!

12

Sons of the Prophets
and Psalmists

When Elisha crossed the Jordan and returned to Israel, he was a man with a commission from God. He was sent and empowered by the Holy Spirit to build upon the foundation Elijah had laid in northern Israel. Elisha was now the overseer of a very large flock of God's children. He immediately began to revisit the schools of the prophets where Elijah had recently held his "farewell meetings."

REACHING "GENERATION X"

Elisha retraced his steps from Jericho to Bethel. On the way, he was accosted by a large gang of youths who began mocking God's prophet. They maliciously made fun of the news which was circulating that Elijah had been taken up to Heaven alive. Blaspheming and expressing contempt toward the God of Elijah, whom Elisha now represented, is a dangerous business. Elisha pronounced one of the covenant curses upon these young idolaters, as he "declared them vile in the name of Jehovah" (2 Kings 2:24). Then two female bears came out of the woods and mauled forty-two of the mob of youths.

These young people had already been torn in two directions. They had been exposed to the immoral pagan center of calf worship nearby. On the other hand there was also a school of prophets at Bethel filled with young people who loved the true God. They had made the wrong choice, and God will not be mocked. These lost young ones at Bethel foreshadow today's "generation x," who claim they don't believe in anything but self and instant gratification. Many of the girls dress like prostitutes, and the young men love it. Ten-year-olds in Israel now emulate the teens in their dress, their music, even in using their drug of choice, "ecstasy."

Once I was having my haircut by Daniel, our Arab barber. He is a nominal Christian from Nazareth, and Karen and I often witness to him about the Lord while he cuts our hair. I couldn't see the TV set which was on over my head and the sound was off. Behind me sat a Muslim mother and her little boy, about eight years old. I could watch them in the mirror. The little boy was restless and bored while the mother looked through a magazine. The boy started watching the TV set and after a few minutes he started punching in the air and banging his fists on his legs. Then his body began gyrating seductively as he stood up focused on the TV set. He was becoming what he was watching. The mother didn't seem to notice.

The Lord wants to rescue these kids from the idolatry which our generation has heaped upon them. In Israel today we see the beginnings of a vibrant youth movement in the body of Messiah. Youth conferences now draw Jewish and Arab youth by the hundreds. We are praying for an "Elisha" generation to be raised up in the land, and are believing for a move of God upon "the sons of the prophets" again.

HARVEST TIME

In his commissioning in the cave at Horev, the Lord told Elijah to anoint Elisha ("my God saves") as the prophet to replace him.

His charge was also to find seven thousand others whose hearts were still open to Jehovah, and who had not sunk into the idolatry and debauchery of Baal worship. In simple terms, God told Elijah it was "harvest time" in Israel. The Lord was answering the plea of the prophet that his people would know that Jehovah was God, and that He would turn their hearts back to Him. It was happening. The *kairos* moment of opportunity had arrived. We are in a similar place in Israel today.

When I was ordained a minister of the gospel, the Lord gave me a life verse: "You did not choose Me, but I chose you and appointed you that you should go and bear fruit, and that your fruit should remain, that whatever you ask the Father in My name He may give you" (John 15:16). This is the call on every man or woman commissioned by God. It was the call upon Elijah and Elisha, and in their trying circumstances it would prove to be no easy task.

PROPHETIC COMMUNITIES

Although he seems to have used Mount Carmel as his home base (see 2 Kings 2:25, 4:25), Elisha was also an itinerant underground preacher. He traveled a circuit through Samaria, Galilee, and Carmel. Sometimes he would stay in someone's home, where they could hold secret meetings, or meet outdoors in some secluded place. Elijah had begun training others in the Word of God. Small, ongoing meetings were the natural result. After several years, thriving communities had been established in Jericho, Bethel, Gilgal, Mount Carmel, and other places. The prophetic ministry had an intergenerational focus as the "father" Elijah had poured himself into his "son" Elisha and other "sons of the prophets." God was indeed turning "the hearts of the fathers to the children, and the hearts of the children to their fathers" (Malachi 4:6).

These groups of prophets were given to "sitting at the feet of the master" as they studied God's holy Word. They developed a lifestyle of prayer and fasting, and continued to share their faith with those who were interested. Elijah had grounded them in the love of God and the love of their neighbors. He shared about his life of intimacy with God. His experiences of prevailing prayer and miraculous provision must have made their hearts burn within them. This man's prayers had raised the dead and called down fire from Heaven.

Elijah had become a legendary figure. He was probably a Nazirite, like Samuel and John the Baptist, taking a sacred vow of consecration to the Lord, with abstinence from alcohol, cutting one's hair, and other forms of piety. (See Numbers 6:1-13, Luke 1:15-17.) Elijah and Elisha lived a life of consistent spiritual discipline in order to be fit for the spiritual war in which they were engaged. Elijah seemed to appear wherever the battle of the Lord was to be fought. Most of the people eventually believed that he just vanished in the desert. But Elisha had seen and was a witness to the truth that God had taken him. Around communal campfires on the mountains of Israel "Abba" Elijah had shared the deep secrets of God with his "children." How Elisha longed to be like him. And now it was Elisha's time. He was chosen of God to walk in the double portion. He, too, would make disciples, confront and advise kings, and raise the dead.

EMPTY VESSELS—NOT A FEW

We have been left an instructive account of an event which sheds light on how the "sons of the prophets" were multiplied in Elisha's generation. One of the "sons of the prophets" had died. (The historian Josephus says it was the prophet Obadiah.) His widow went to Elisha in desperation. She was in debt, and the creditor was coming to take her two boys to be his slaves until the debt was paid. Elisha asked her,

"Tell me, what do you have in the house?" She responded, "Your maidservant has nothing in the house but a jar of oil" (2 Kings 4:2). Elisha told her to go and "borrow vessels from everywhere, from all your neighbors—empty vessels; do not gather just a few. And when you have come in, you shall shut the door behind you and your sons; then pour it into all those vessels and set aside the full ones" (v. 3-4). Her two sons went to their neighbors and began to borrow empty vessels from them. The two boys went all over the area making several trips because they couldn't carry all the vessels, bowls, and pitchers they were borrowing. Soon vessels of different sizes, shapes and colors were all over the widow's house. (I think of this sometimes when I look at all the variety of clay pottery on sale by Druze merchants on Mount Carmel.)

The widow and her sons obeyed the instructions of Elisha and closed their door. Then she took her only jar of oil and poured it out into one of the empty vessels. To her surprise the jar of oil she had emptied was still full. She took a second vessel. The same thing happened. The widow and her sons realized that God was performing a miracle. He was multiplying the oil! Soon her whole house was full of vessels which had been empty, but were now filled with oil. She said to her son, "'Bring me another vessel.' And he said to her, 'There is not another vessel.' So the oil ceased" (v. 6). It was only the lack of vessels that stopped the flow of oil. She told Elisha what had happened, and he said, "Go sell the oil and pay your debt; and you and your sons live on the rest" (v.7).

The widow's house containing vessels filled with oil is a picture of the way the Lord multiplied His body in Elisha's days, and how He wants to do it today. Multiplication, or revival, always begins with a desperate believer. The widow admitted her need and acknowledged that she had nothing. From this posture of humility she cried out for help. God heard her heart's cry and answered her plea through His prophet. She obeyed God's word to her, filling her house with every empty vessel she could find. Shut in with God and her boys, she then poured out all she had. All the vessels were filled and set aside—consecrated to God. If you pour yourself into others God will refill you.

Only when we empty ourselves, does God begin to multiply the oil. He never runs out of oil, He just runs out of empty vessels. Through one desperate widow (an empty vessel) God saved her family and touched her neighborhood. There are empty vessels out there-not a few. But God won't fill a vessel that is not empty, because it's already too full of self. "All of Jesus, None of Me," is a favorite song of mine written by a pastor friend.

SCHOOLS OF PROPHETS

The center or hub of the growing prophetic ministry in the time of Elisha was to be found in the schools of prophets. The Bible has left us some fascinating evidence about the structure and "curriculum" of those schools. First, like the prophet Samuel's prophetic groups many years earlier, these groups of "sons of the prophets" tended to live communally, separated from the social life around them. (See 2 Kings 2:3-5, 4:38-44.) Elijah, and later Elisha, as the "father," would appoint a "master" as the leader of each group (6:1-7). These men lived simply, foraged for food, and were sometimes given gifts of food and clothing from other devout Israelites or family members (4:42). The young prophets-in-training wore a short shoulder cape of coarse hair as a distinctive mark of their rejection of the materialistic world. Their goal was to be men of the Spirit (See Zechariah 13:4.) John the Baptist, who came in "the spirit and power of Elijah," was a spiritual descendent of the "sons of the prophets." "Now John, himself, was clothed in camel's hair, with a leather belt around his waist; and his food was locusts and wild honey" (Matthew 3:4).

DEATH IN THE POT

During a time of famine in the land, Elisha was visiting the prophetic congregation at Gilgal, where we are given an illuminating glimpse of the communal life of the prophets: "Now the sons of the prophets were sitting before him; and he said to his servant, 'Put on the large pot, and boil some stew for the sons of the prophets'" (2 Kings 4:38). As Elisha fellowshipped with the students, the servant gathered some gourds from a wild vine. He sliced them and put them into the pot of stew, "though they did not know what they were" (v. 39). After the stew was cooked and they were eating it, they began to cry out, "Man of God, there is death in the pot!" (v. 40). Elisha told them to bring him some flour which he then put into the pot. Then he said, "'Serve it to the people that they may eat.' And there was nothing harmful ["evil"] in the pot" (v. 41). One wrong ingredient had spoiled the stew or soup. The Hebrew text makes it clear that the wild gourds the servant had put in the soup were poison.

In our residential work with drug addicts and alcoholics, we have learned (sometimes the hard way) that one wrong staff member can poison the whole ministry. In such a communal work people's lives can literally be at stake. One person's attitude or character can so contaminate the atmosphere in a place of ministry that people won't even want to go near it. I have seen this happen more than once. If the "wild gourd" will not receive ministry and be willing to change he or she will need to be removed.

The flour which Elisha put in the pot represents Jesus, the "bread of life." Leaders need to pour His healing flour into poisoned stews.

In selecting workers for our ministry we have found that after having received positive references about a person, conducted interviews, and believing we have "prayed through," most of the time we have chosen the right person. But in the refining fire of the Lord's work, a person's true character will always rise to the surface. A well-known minister I know, who has served the Lord for fifty years, told me that personnel had always been his biggest problem. "Because they do not change, therefore they do not fear God" (Psalm 55:19).

THE RAVEN'S BASKET

We do thank God for the many faithful servants He has sent or raised up on Mount Carmel. In January 2002, we had a pizza party for the volunteers and staff of our Raven's Basket ministry. Our living room was filled with twenty men and women who regularly take food baskets to over eighty families on Mount Carmel. There were Jews, Arabs, Russian-speaking immigrants, and Gentiles enjoying each other's fellowship. Andrew Lessey, the leader of this ministry, has faithfully served the Lord here for years. That night, one of our volunteers, a new Lebanese believer who had been tortured for a year and a half in a Syrian prison in Beirut, told us how the Lord was healing him of his experiences by the love of Jesus expressed through his new brothers and sisters in the Lord. (At a recent altar call he said the Lord had healed him from years of migraine headaches and nightmares.) This diverse group gave testimonies of how the Lord was changing them as they ministered to the needs of the Jews and Arabs of our city. There was no poison in the pizza that night!

While Elisha was still with the disciples at Gilgal, a man brought twenty barley loaves made from new grain and gave them to the prophet. He was probably a believer who was not taking his offerings to the false priests at nearby Bethel. This was one of the ways the schools of prophets were supported. God multiplied this "bread of the firstfruits" and fed one hundred prophets-in-the-making with it. And there was even some left over, according to the word of the Lord through Elisha (v. 44). God was multiplying the provision of this ministry because of the beautiful harmony we can sense as we read these scenes. Everyone seemed to be in their right place. Then there was miraculous provision in the time of famine.

The night of the pizza party we prayed the Lord would bless and multiply the Raven's Basket ministry. After the people left that evening, a deaconess called us and said we had just received in the mail that day a large gift for the Lord's ministries here. It was from a friend we had not seen in years. Earlier that night, we had also read the vision for the Raven's Basket ministry:

> "I was hungry and you gave Me food; I was thirsty and you gave Me drink."... Then the righteous will answer Him, saying, "Lord, when did we see You hungry and feed You?"... And the King will answer and say to you, "... inasmuch as you did it to one of the least of these My brethren, you did it to Me." (Matthew 25:35-40)

THE NEW WINE IS IN THE CLUSTER

As we have pursued the Lord concerning His works on Carmel, He has led us to form a leadership team or "cluster." We received this word from the Lord: "As the new wine is in the cluster, and one says, 'Do not destroy it, for a blessing is in it'" (Isaiah 65:8). On Mount Carmel clusters of ripe grapes are carefully crushed in winepresses, producing a pure, virgin new wine with no fermentation. (Fermentation represents sin.) We, too, have been through seasons of "corporate crushing." We long to see a release and restoration of the five-fold New Covenant leadership offices of apostle, prophet, evangelist, pastor and teacher. We believe that God appoints a "leader of the leaders," commonly called "the senior pastor." He is a man set in place by God, but he is also accountable to the other leaders. Those of us in the leadership cluster try to "submit to one another in the fear of the Lord." At times we speak into each other's lives, and when needed, confess our sins to each other. Because the Lord designed each of us with very different gifts, all of which are needed to fully equip His body, it has not always been easy. Out of God's winepress the new wine of His character, grace and anointing flows.

We take Acts 15 as a model for New Covenant leadership structure. In this passage, a very serious issue over the inclusion of the Gentiles in the Lord's body was presented by Peter, Barnabas and Paul, all of whom were renowned Jewish apostles and prophets. The elders of the Jerusalem "mother" congregation listened carefully to all the arguments. After a long silence, James, the acknowledged senior leader, responded by quoting the Word of God, and then making his judgment. His anointed decision has stood the test of time for almost two thousand years. This is the way God's leaders should function. New life is the result.

THE CURSE OF COMMITTEES

There are also serious pitfalls to be avoided in "team ministry." I'm referring here to what I call "the curse of committees." Committees have probably killed more ministries than any other man-made arrangement. During the years 1996-1998, when we were building our new worship center, I came to realize that you cannot have all the leaders in on every decision. So, I would meet weekly with the architect, the engineer, the building superintendent, and the foreman, all of whom were believers. I would also try to keep the other pastors informed of important developments. For any big financial decisions we consulted and prayed together. Then I made the decision.

One instance in particular stands out as an example of the "committee curse." We needed to make a decision on the chairs we would purchase for the new sanctuary. Once, at a chair factory, seven of us started looking at chairs and sitting in them. I heard opinions on color, style, durability, and other chair characteristics. I felt like I was in a Marx Brothers' movie. Frankly, I didn't like any of those chairs and thought we were in the wrong place. I told Karen, "Never again."

I started praying more about chairs. Not long after that I was driving through the industrial section of Haifa with Gerald, our building superintendent, when we saw a furniture store and decided to check out the chairs. As the salesman showed us the first chair, we knew immediately it was the right one. The price was also right. Karen came later and chose the color. Those five hundred chairs were delivered to our new building a day early—the only early delivery on a two-and-a-half-year building project! My committee days were over. I was delivered.

Some believers think that everyone has to agree on everything before you can move. Should Moses have called a committee meeting at the Red Sea? This kind of soulish mind-set is anathema to the prophetic and God's ways. God's point man should be leading the way, seeking, seeing, and showing the vision. The goal should be that all fulfill their leadership callings of apostle, prophet, evangelist, pastor, and teacher. We all need to be in the same ship, rowing together.

The "one man band" senior pastor is also not biblical. God's point men need to be held accountable for their life, their marriage, and ministry. But when the decision to "move out" has been made, the whole cluster needs to be supportive and loyal. If the senior leader is prophetic, any prophecy he gives should be judged by the other leaders. The leader of the leaders, in turn, should have a passion to help the other leaders into God's place and destiny for their lives and ministries. When everyone is in his right place with God and each other, the new wine of revival flows. "When the righteous are in authority, the people rejoice" (Proverbs 29:2).

The prophet Elisha was such a leader. He had been a supervisor on a large farm. He knew how to plow a field with everyone positioned in his or her proper furrow. That is where the fullness is released. When a leader moves into someone else's furrow, he will end up responsible before God for creating a mess in the field of God's congregation. Such a person will miss his own maximum fruitfulness, as well as hindering the work God is doing through others. The Apostle Paul referred to this important principle as knowing "the limits of our sphere" (2 Corinthians 10:13). "God has set the members, each one of them, in the body just as He pleased" (1 Corinthians 12:18). When that happens the gates of hell shall not prevail against His church (Matthew 16:18).

As Carmel Assembly moves toward greater indigenization, the Lord has chosen Daniel Sayag to be our first native-born Israeli pastor. At our last meeting in 2001, we laid hands on Reuven Ross and his wife Yanit and released them from pastoring with us to pursue their call as national and international teachers, covered and sent by us. For Pastor Peter Tsukahira and his wife Rita, a shift in their ministry came as they took up their position as Directors of the Or HaCarmel Ministry Center. Change can be difficult, but we need to recognize and move with God in His seasons.

SCHOOLS OF PSALMISTS

Not only was there anointed teaching and discipling taking place in the prophetic schools of Elisha's day, but worship also held a central place in the spiritual life of the community. In one sense, a revival was being birthed similar to the prophetic movement begun by Samuel in the time of David, a century earlier. As in the days of the Philistine crisis, a charismatic ministry of the psalmists was being released. The prophets wrote and sang songs given to them by God. In Samuel's time, groups of prophets went to strategic places to prophesy and praise Jehovah. "You shall come to the hill of God, where the Philistine garrison is. And it will happen where you have come there to the city, that you will meet a group of prophets coming down from the high place with a stringed instrument, a tambourine, a flute, and a harp before them; and they will be prophesying" (1 Samuel 10:5). This band of prophets and psalmists had praised and prophesied right where the Philistines were encamped! The prophetic singers were claiming that high place for Jehovah.

The Scriptures offer us a description of the spiritual power of these communal groups of prophets. At a time when young David had fled from Saul to seek the protection of his spiritual father Samuel, "Abba" Samuel was presiding over his band of psalmists. King Saul sent men to capture David, but on their way they ran into Samuel and his prophetic worship team. "And when they saw the group of prophets prophesying, and Samuel standing as leader over them, the Spirit of God came upon the messengers of Saul, and they also prophesied" (1 Samuel 19:20). Imagine the scene. A group of Saul's soldiers came to capture David. Samuel's band of worshippers were praising and prophesying. The soldiers were stopped in their tracks by the Holy Spirit, and ended up joining the worship team in praising God! Then they went back and told Saul. He sent two more groups. It happened three times! Saul kept sending more men and the prophets just kept praising and prophesying in the name of the Lord. Satan, who is a fallen worship leader, is allergic to pure praise. God was guarding David, His anointed—a man after His own heart—who would become the "sweet psalmist of Israel," while Satan was trying to destroy the seed of Abraham from the tribe of Judah through whom the Messiah would come. The power of prophetic praise prevented the plans of the enemy!

THE WARRIOR SPIRIT

Lastly, the "sons of the prophets" were zealous spiritual warriors. They usually followed the armies of Israel into the field. There at the strategic place and at the right moment they would receive words from the Lord to encourage or give direction to the king. These spiritual warriors knew they were engaged in battles for the fulfillment of the purposes and people of God. Elijah and Elisha were both called "the chariots of Israel and its horsemen!" Each one of them was worth legions.

THE POWER OF WORSHIP

When David became king, singers and musicians became an important part of his ministry, before there was a temple in Jerusalem. The act of worship had saved David's life on more than one occasion. He had tasted the power of the anointing of the Holy Spirit when he played his harp before envious Saul, and had witnessed the king's deliverance from evil spirits. The musicians and singers who led worship in David's meetings after he became king in Jerusalem were leaders who prophesied through song. They were actually part of his famous army.

> Moreover David and the captains of the army separated for service some of the sons of Asaph ... who should prophesy with harps, stringed instruments and cymbals ... under the direction of Asaph, who prophesied according to the order of the king ... [they] prophesied with a harp to give thanks and to praise the LORD.... So the number of them, with their brethren who were instructed in the songs of the Lord, all who were skillful, was two hundred and eighty-eight. (1 Chronicles 25: 1-3, 7)

The explosion of praise and worship under King David would culminate with four thousand anointed musicians, singers and psalmists, worshipping Jehovah in Jerusalem. Surely the demons were shaking! David and his musicians even invented new musical instruments. They were breaking new ground as they ushered in a brief "golden age" of worship in Israel. "Four thousand praised the Lord with musical instruments, 'which I made,' said David, 'for giving praise'" (1Chronicles 23:5). Prophetic psalmists are pioneers taking us a way we have never been before. We desperately need an outpouring of prophetic praise, and it is beginning to happen again on Mount Carmel.

The Psalms of David, Asaph and his sons, and other anointed composer-singers were handed down from generation to generation among the faithful remnant in Israel. Elisha must have heard about the awesome worship in the time of David and Solomon, when the glory of the Lord filled the temple. The new schools of prophets and psalmists moved into a grand legacy that had begun with Samuel and David.

NATIONAL EXHAUSTION

In the days of Elisha the release of prophetic psalmists in the schools of the prophets began to have a national impact again. After the death of Ahab's first son, Jehoram, the second son of Ahab and Jezebel, sat on the throne of Israel. This young man made a gesture toward God by putting away a phallic pillar (totem) to Baal, but he and the nation continued in the animistic calf worship initiated by Jeroboam. Jezebel still reigned as Queen Mother with her entourage.

Jehoram asked King Jehoshaphat and the King of Edom to join him in a war against Moab, who had stopped paying tribute to Israel. Three kings and their armies marched through the desert in a roundabout route for seven days. Then they realized they were in a valley with no water for their soldiers or their animals, which they used for food and transport. The situation was hopeless, as they were trapped in the desert with no water, facing an enemy army.

I see a distinct parallel with Israel today. We are in a state of national exhaustion. After six wars and the never-ending siege of terrorism, our people are filled with hopelessness. So are the Palestinians. Our government is going around in circles, just like Jehoram was. One prime minister tries to give away much of the covenant land, including part of Jerusalem, and the offer is rejected. The next prime minister is tougher on the "land for peace" delusion. Terrorists blow up over twenty-nine people at a Passover Seder, and our army responds by uprooting the terrorist infrastructure in Palestinian towns and terrorism stops for a few days. Then the army pulls back and again suicide bombers murder innocent civilians. So, the army goes back into the territories again. The world condemns us, and we pull out. We are running around in circles.

"IS THERE NO PROPHET OF THE LORD?"

Jehoram actually blamed Jehovah for the hopeless situation which the apostate king himself had created. But once again Jehoshaphat asked, "Is there no prophet of the LORD [Jehovah] here, that we may inquire of the LORD by him?" (2 Kings 3:11). Jehoshaphat had obviously learned his lesson when he went up to Ramot Gilead with Jehoram's father and Ahab had died for disobeying God. Jehoram did not answer Jehoshaphat, but one of the king's servants did. Was this anonymous servant one of the Lord's seven thousand? This man knew that Elisha had followed the army to the war. The king didn't know it, but his servant did. It was he who answered King Jehoshaphat: "Elisha the son of Shaphat is here, who poured water on the hands of Elijah" (3:11). The reputation of Elisha was one of loyalty, service and obedience to his master, Elijah. His reputation preceded him-he was known as a man with clean hands. Jehoshaphat who had also heard of this godly anointed man, who walked in the Elijah legacy, quickly responded, "The word of the Lord is with him" (v. 12). Showing his respect for the man of God, Jehoshaphat led the other two kings to Elisha.

"BRING ME A MUSICIAN"

The three kings went to meet the prophet. The man of God looked at Ahab's son and said, "Go to the prophets of your father and mother" (v.13). The "spirit of Elijah" was certainly resting upon his successor. He told King Jehoram he would not have even looked at him, except that he had respect for King Jehoshaphat. As the three kings stood before the prophet, Elisha said a very strange thing. "But now bring me a musician" (2 Kings 3:15). There on a battlefield in the desert in front of the three kings and their armies, the prophet inquired of the Lord in prophetic worship. To "inquire" means to "seek," "search," "worship." As the soldiers looked on, Elisha was kneeling at the footstool of the Lord of Hosts ("armies"). The musician kept playing as the psalmist and the prophet worshipped together. Elisha was caught up into the throne room of God from where all blessings flow.

Pure worship permeated a battlefield in the desert in the midst of an impossible situation. "The hour is coming, and now is, when true worshippers will worship the Father in spirit and truth; for the Father is seeking such as these" (John 4:23). The Father had found a true worshipper, and in His mercy He answered the prophet's plea. The "song of the Lord" was being released. As the musician continued to play, "the hand of the Lord" came upon Elisha. God's spokesman received a clear directive from Jehovah: "Thus says the LORD: 'Make this valley full of ditches.'... 'You shall not see wind, nor shall you see rain; yet that valley shall be filled with water ... And this is a simple ["easy"] matter in the sight of the LORD" (2 Kings 3:15,18). As the kings and soldiers pondered this word, almost as an afterthought, the prophet added: "He will also deliver the Moabites into your hands."

A VALLEY FULL OF DITCHES

The thirsty army began digging ditches, or small trenches, all over the dry, barren valley floor. I wonder if there was any complaining, as the exhausted troops dug into the hard desert floor where they knew there was no water. Night was coming on. Was there a cave nearby for the prophet? Or did he simply lie under a juniper tree and gaze at the stars as he fell asleep? His work was done.

(From the desert not far from where this incident happened I have watched the sun come up over the mountains of Moab, south of the Dead Sea. The desert floor and the mountains change hues from shades of yellows to orange, and pinks turn to crimson reds.)

As the army awakened the next morning, at the very time the daily morning sacrifice was being offered in the temple of Jerusalem, something happened in the desert. "Suddenly ... the land was filled with water" (v.20). In absolute quiet, with no sound, wind or rain, through invisible sources, the ditches in the valley overflowed with water. As the sun came up on a new day, soldiers saw the miracle. They began to shout to their comrades and run to the ditches. They had been saved! There was water everywhere. They drank their fill and then gratefully watered their animals. But God wasn't finished.

In the distance, the Moabite army saw the sun shining on the water. It appeared as pools of blood. The optical illusion made them think the armies in the valley were killing each other, so they attacked. The refreshed army of Israel rose up to meet them, surprising the Moabites who then fled back to their own land. The Lord had fulfilled His word, and delivered the Moabites into the hand of Israel.

AT THE TIME OF THE MORNING OFFERING

The miracle took place at the time of the morning offering in the temple in Jerusalem. Every morning and evening the priests slaughtered an unblemished lamb, which they offered to God with cakes made of grain and oil, along with a wine offering. All of these offerings, of course, point to our perfect sacrifice, the Lamb of God, who bore our griefs and carried our sorrows and sins. The crushed grain represents His body broken for our transgressions. The wine offering was poured out even as He poured out His soul unto death. There is healing through His poured out blood, and the oil of His Holy Spirit.

That "valley full of ditches" is a picture of our battered Messiah going lower into the pit of death for the salvation of the world. Valleys are pictures of humility. "Every valley shall be exalted" (Isaiah 40:4). Jesus went even below the valley of men to lift us up. We, too, need to go lower, and deeper into the ditches in the valleys—into the fellowship of His sufferings. That is the place Elisha was that day, and where the fountains of His peace are to be found. We need to be "valleys full of ditches," and open our lives for God's love to be poured into us. Roots of character find underground springs of God's grace and anointing in the deep place in the valleys. "He sends the springs into the valleys, they flow among the hills" (Psalm 104:10).

We need to be conduits filled with living water, to give away to the weak, needy, and thirsty of our land. When Elisha worshipped the Lord, God came. If we are desperate for more of Him, the living water in the valley will be found. We need the underground springs and the rain of Heaven to fill our dry and thirsty land.

SATANIC SUICIDE BOMBERS

The king of Moab was so enraged when he was driven from the land of Israel, "he took his eldest son who would have reigned in his place, and offered him as a burnt offering" (2 Kings 3:27). Muslim terrorists and parents so hate Israel that today they condone the suicide of their own children. Jack Kelley wrote in *USA Today* (October 30, 2001):

> When visiting Hamas ["violence"] schools in Gaza ... I saw and heard an 11-year-old boy speak to his class: "I will make my body a bomb that will blast the flesh of the Zionists, sons of pigs and monkeys.... I will tear their bodies into little pieces and cause them more pain than they will ever know." His classmates shouted, "Allah is great!" And his teacher shouted, "May the virgins give you pleasure."

A sixteen-year-old Hamas youth leader in Gaza told Kelley, "Most boys can't stop thinking about virgins." Saddam Hussein sends $25,000 to the family of each suicide bomber. Saudi Arabia also sends them money.

What is our response to such demonized murderous hatred? We do what Elisha did. It was when he was worshipping God in the midst of the war that God spoke. They then obeyed His word and God acted. That is the prophetic principle. He speaks—we obey—He acts. "And this is a simple matter in the sight of the LORD," (2 Kings 3:18). We are called to be the "sons of the prophets." As the Lord brings in His harvest He will raise up small groups all over Mount Carmel and throughout Israel. We are training worship leaders, psalmists, and worshippers to lead these groups. Even as Hamas and other Islamic organizations disciple their children to become "human bombs," we need to raise up disciples to the Lord Jesus to love and intercede for our enemies.

Our desire is that our meetings will be "prophetic," meaning that what we do will not just be pre-programmed singing, preaching, and praying. We need a dialogue with the Holy Spirit. We cry out that He will come down and speak to us about the "now" and the future.

These "schools of prophets" in the days of Samuel and Elijah and Elisha held back the enemy for decades—through prophetic praise, pre-emptive prayer, and the proclamation of God's word. May we do the same.

THE BATTLE IS NOT YOURS, BUT GOD'S

The prophetic anointing upon Elisha spread even to Jerusalem and saved the city. King Jehoshaphat of Judah was on the battlefield, looking at Elisha when the prophet of God said, "Bring me a musician." The Spirit of God prophesied through Elisha and the nation was delivered. Later when three enemy armies came against Jerusalem, King Jehoshaphat called a corporate fast. The Spirit of the Lord came upon a singer named Jahaziel, who prophesied that "the battle is not yours, but God's" (2 Chronicles 20:14-15). Jehoshaphat sent the singers out ahead of the army. I wonder how the choir felt about that? But the king, like a Spirit-led pastor should obey the prophetic word of the Lord. He had learned this from Elisha. The worshippers who praised the Lord in "the beauty of holiness ... went out before the army" (v. 21). They sang one simple chorus that we sing often here on Carmel: "Praise the Lord, for His mercy endures forever" (v. 21). "Now when they began to sing and to praise, the Lord set ambushes" (v. 22). Jerusalem and God's people and purposes were preserved through prophetic praise. The Elijah legacy had been imparted through Elisha to the king of Judah, and Jerusalem was saved!

THE SONG OF THE LORD

Once an elderly pastor from abroad came up to Joy Griffiths, our keyboardist, flutist, and anointed psalmist. He asked her what she was doing during a certain part of a meeting, when she had played the flute as we all listened. Joy answered, "I was playing what I was hearing from God." "Oh, I see," the puzzled pastor replied. She explained that she listens to God, and He sometimes gives her the song of the Lord. The retired minister asked the young psalmist, "Can I also learn to do that?" Praise God, he wanted more.

Eight years ago, Joy came from Britain to work with us. She says her assignment was "to help David and Karen." She has certainly done that and much more. She is a gifted composer, singer, and musician, playing the piano, flute, and cello. She, Karen, and others began to collaborate on new songs. In the last several years we have experienced an amazing release of prophetic, intercessory praise and worship in Hebrew and English. Some of this new sound from Carmel has not only impacted Israel, but has literally reached the uttermost parts of the Earth, through Karen's three CDs recorded here, *Shout from the Mountain, Yeshua,* and *Sar Shalom.*

The worship here has touched many Israelis. Sometimes they just cry and don't know why. An Arab sister brought her Jewish music teacher to a meeting. She cried through the entire worship time. An Israeli recording engineer in Tel Aviv said he had chills as he listened to the final song on *Yeshua.* Another engineer told his friends, "These people sing love songs to God!" We explain to them that they are experiencing the presence of the Holy One. Karen has received testimonies of healings from people in the nations who have entered into this flow of worship from Mount Carmel. One person was going to commit suicide. She happened to see the *Yeshua* CD on a shelf in a bookstore and purchased it. As she played it in her car, she was touched by God and she changed her mind and chose life.

PIERCING THE DARKNESS WITH PROPHETIC PRAISE

The following is an excerpt from an article Karen wrote for a magazine that reaches much of the Far East. Entitled

Piercing the Darkness with Prophetic Praise, it explains clearly what the Lord has been doing in our midst through worship on Mount Carmel:

> In my earliest days as a Jewish believer in Jesus, the unspeakable joy of knowing God's love swept over my life. New songs flooded my heart and I was consumed with singing about my love affair with Jesus. Alongside these wonderful, exhilarating feelings, I was awakened as never before to the deep pain and comfortless grief of my own Jewish people. Centuries of anti-semitism perpetrated by so-called "Christians" in the name of Christ created thick walls of resistance in Jewish people to even hearing the name of Jesus. Most Jews today remain blind to their own Jewish Messiah and stand outside the gates of His healing love, unable to enter into His goodness. After the atrocities of the Holocaust, many Jews arrived in Israel with their essential belief in God shattered.
>
> As the worship leader of our congregation, I became keenly aware that the Lord had given us a strategic assignment on this high place. His word came to me strongly from Isaiah 42:11-13: "Shout from the top of the mountains, let them give glory to the Lord.... The LORD shall go forth like a warrior, like a man or war, He will prevail against his enemies." He was clearly calling us to take an offensive stand, as Elijah did, to declare triumphantly the victory of the Lord Yeshua (Jesus), Adonai Tzevaot (Lord of armies) over the powers of darkness. We were learning that our city of Haifa, built all across the slopes of Mount Carmel, had the highest concentration of Satanism and New Age cults in Israel. Many were deceived by the modern-day prophets of Baal and the spirit of Jezebel was clearly still entrenched here.

I understood from these verses in Isaiah that the role of worship would be central to the battle set before us, that as we would stand in faith, giving glory to the Lord, immovable in the face of the enemy, He himself would fight the battle and prevail. Our part was to "position ourselves, stand still, and see the salvation of the LORD" (2 Chronicles 20:17). Our worship was to be characterized by a prophetic "shout of victory," seeing and proclaiming that victory by faith, not by sight-just as the singers went out before the army in the time of Jehoshaphat saying, " 'Praise the Lord, for His mercy endures forever!' Now when they began to sing and to praise, the Lord set ambushes" (20:21-22).

We began fervently seeking the Lord to release to us the songs that would equip us to "shout unto God with a voice of triumph" (Psalm 47:1). We prayed for the Lord to open our spirits to hear the "sound of Heaven" over Mount Carmel—the rhythms, the melodies, and the textures that would launch the mighty weapons of the Word of God into the heavenlies, "to the intent that ... the manifold wisdom of God might be made known by the church to the principalities and powers in the heavenly places" (Ephesians 3:10). We were being called to pierce the darkness with the light of truth, knowing that our struggle was "not against flesh and blood but against the spiritual hosts of wickedness" (Ephesians 6:12).

One after another, new songs were released to us, songs with a fresh sound, carrying powerful prophetic Scriptures that the Lord was speaking to us. From week to week the living Word of God, the Lord of Hosts, was leading us forward in His triumphal procession (2 Corinthians 2:14).

In Chapter 6 of Ephesians which deals with the subject of spiritual warfare, we are told "having done all, to stand." All of us in the body of Messiah have been called as worshippers to take this stand in the face of the enemy, in this fundamental fight of faith. "This is the victory that has overcome the world—our faith" (1 John 5:4). The primary battle in which we are engaged is a battle for our faith. Worship is an act of faith that becomes an act of warfare. We must be a prophetic people who "see" the Lord high and lifted up (Isaiah 6:1), who "see" Him going before us, with the chariots of God thousands upon thousands. (See Psalm 68:7-17.) Asaph, the Levitical choir director, was described as a "seer" (2 Chronicles 29:30). We must be able to say, "I know in Whom I have believed." It is a powerful prophetic statement to say in the face of the horrors of suicide bombings faced almost daily in Israel, "Give thanks to the Lord for He is good and His mercy endures forever."

In addition to being a weapon of spiritual warfare to change the atmosphere over our cities, corporate worship can lead us into deep times of intercession and travail for the people of our land. Many times as we enter the throne room of God in the midst of high praises we suddenly find ourselves touching the very burdens of His heart. We begin to cry out for the Lord to save His people, to have mercy, to remove the hindrances. "Go through, go through the gates, take out the stones, prepare the way for the people" (Isaiah 62:10). These times of corporate intercessory worship led by the Spirit of God clear the way for the lost to find their way to salvation.

Over the past several years, we have seen a new openness in Israelis to the name of Yeshua, as the centuries-old reproach to His name is beginning to fall away. In the summer of 2001, as the terror attacks were increasing all over Israel, the Lord directed us to move our intercessory worship meetings outdoors to a public promenade with a spectacular view of Haifa. Every Monday evening we stood boldly lifting up the name of Yeshua in worship and praying for protection over our city. As the Spirit of the Lord descended on our gatherings, many Israelis were drawn to stop and listen. Several were deeply touched by His presence and later began attending our meetings. One by one we see them being drawn up to the top of the mount thirsting for living waters.

As we, in the body of Messiah fulfill our role as a "royal priesthood, proclaiming the praises of Him who called us out of darkness into His marvelous light" (1 Peter 2:9), the Lord intends that we will become His dwelling place (Ephesians 2:21). Psalm 22:3 says, "God is enthroned [dwells] in the praises of His people." Where God's presence is there is healing, salvation, and deliverance. When the King of Glory comes in, He does what no man can do, touching hearts and bringing a true revelation of himself.

Yes, God is raising up "sons of the prophets" and psalmists on the mountains of Israel again. As we cry out like Elisha, "Where is the Lord God of Elijah?", He is beginning to answer and turn the hearts of our people to the Holy One of Israel.

THE LEGACY OF ELIJAH AND ELISHA IS BEING
RELEASED AGAIN.

13

ELIJAH'S FINAL PROPHECIES— CONFRONTING JEZEBEL

In the days of Elijah and Elisha, Israel was continually under siege from neighboring Arab nations. In 2 Kings 6:8, we read, "Now the king of Syria was making war against Israel." (Each time the Syrian king formed his battle plans, the Lord would tell Elisha of the Syrian strategy. The prophet warned the king of Israel "not just once or twice," and Israel effectively countered the covert, hostile moves of Syria. "Therefore the heart of the king of Syria was greatly troubled by this thing" (v. 11). Fear and suspicion reigned in the Syrian army, as the king understandably became paranoid, believing that a traitor and spy was in his midst. Finally, an unnamed Syrian servant told his king the truth about the perplexing situation: "Elisha, the prophet who is in Israel, tells the king of Israel the words that you speak in your bedroom" (v.12). I believe this anonymous servant is a type who represents countless Muslims today who are open and interested in the God of Israel, Jesus.

The king of Syria sent a huge army into Galilee in order to kill God's prophet. "Therefore he sent horses and chariots and a great army there, and they came by night and surrounded the city" (v.14). The Syrian army invaded Israel as they crossed the Golan and the Jordan and marched west through the Jezreel Valley (where many scholars believe the battle of Armageddon will be fought). They passed not far from Muhrakah on Carmel, where Elijah had defeated the prophets of Baal and they surrounded the dwelling of the prophet on a hilltop village called Dothan, which means, "two wells," or "double feast." This is the place where Joseph was sold by his brothers for twenty shekels of silver to the Ishmaelites, the forefathers of the Arab people (Genesis 37:17). The hill of Dothan can be seen today several miles west of Jenin, the terrorist stronghold invaded by Israel in April 2002.

The next morning when Elisha's servant "arose early and went out, there was an enemy army, surrounding the city with horses and chariots. And his servant said to him, 'Alas, my master! What shall we do?'" (2 Kings 6:15). The prophet had been trained by Elijah to be a seer, a man of prayer who sees circumstances from God's perspective. He gave this answer to his disciple: "Do not fear, for those who are with us are more than those who are with them" (v. 16). Given our circumstances in Israel today, this is the word we need to embrace. Only through prevailing prayer will we receive such revelation and comfort. Had Elisha's prayers activated the angelic armies of Heaven?

CHARIOTS OF FIRE

Elisha then prayed three simple prayers which dramatically changed the situation not only for himself and his servant, but also for his people at a time of great peril. First, he called on the Lord, and said, "Lord, I pray, open his eyes that he may see" (v.17). We need to intercede that our eyes, the eyes of the believers, will be opened to see our situation the way God does. The Lord responded to his prophet's petition, and the young man (the next generation) saw into the heavenlies: "And behold, the mountain was full of horses and chariots of fire all around Elisha" (v.17). The Lord of Hosts was protecting His prophet and His covenant people, of whom Elisha was the representative. Elisha had seen Elijah's departure in a single fiery chariot. Now he was surrounded by many chariots of fire. Elijah and Elisha had also raised up an army of prophetic prayer warriors all over Israel, whose prayers were holding back the powers of darkness.

Next, Elisha prayed that the Lord would strike the Syrian army with blindness, and again God answered the prophet's on target prayer. We, too, can cry out for the Lord to blind and confuse the enemies who stand against God's purposes. The Syrian army was supernaturally led away from its evil purposes, because of one man's prayers. Elisha was walking in the Elijah legacy of the double portion at a place called "two wells."

Then the man of God lifted up a third prayer, and said, "Lord, open the eyes of these men, that they may see" (v. 20). Once again, the prophet's petition was granted. The Israelites even gave the bewildered Syrians a great feast, and sent them back to their own country. This amazing episode concludes with these words: "So the bands of Syrian raiders came no more into the land of Israel" (v. 23). Jesus teaches us to love our enemies, and to "do good to those who hate you" (Luke 6:27).

CLEANSING THE LEPROSY OF NAAMAN

There is another revealing episode recorded in the Elijah-Elisha legacy that points to revival among the Arab people. The story of Naaman, the Syrian, and his encounter with the Jewish prophet Elisha, is a prophetic parable for us today.

Naaman was the commander-in-chief of the Syrian army. We are told that he was "great and honorable" and "a mighty man of valor, but a leper" (2 Kings 5:1). Leprosy in the Bible is often a picture of sin. Moses' sister, Miriam, was punished with leprosy because of her pride and envy.

A young Jewish slave who served Naaman's Syrian wife told her mistress that there was a prophet in Samaria (now "the West Bank"), who could heal Naaman of his disease. This young lady was one of the seven thousand faithful to the God of Israel. The king of Syria then sent his commander-in-chief to Israel with a large and impressive entourage and expensive gifts. The renowned Syrian general arrived in his chariot at the dwelling of Elisha. The prophet "sent a messenger to him, saying 'Go and wash in the Jordan seven times and your flesh shall be restored to you and you shall be clean'" (v.10). The prideful Syrian was furious and left in a rage, claiming that the rivers of Damascus were "better than all the waters of Israel" (v.12).

Some servants of the general reasoned with their master ("my father") to obey the prophet and "wash and be clean" (v.13). These servants are a prophetic picture of countless Arab people now in bondage, but who are actually open to the word of the Lord. The Arab servants had received God's word through the Jewish prophet. Naaman finally listened to his servants and obeyed Elisha's word. As he came up out of the Jordan the seventh time, "his flesh was restored like the flesh of a little child, and he was clean" (v.14). The reborn Syrian now walked in newness of life, as he humbly returned to thank the Jewish prophet. There he testified before all his soldiers and servants, "Indeed, now I know there is no God in all the earth, except in Israel" (v.15).

Naaman and his servants took their new revelation and relationship with Jehovah back to Syria. They had met Him while outside their homeland. Today the Lord is also saving many Muslims from the Middle East while they are away from their own countries. In His timing, they will go back to their nations with the gospel. Several hundred Afghani refugees have recently come to the Lord. I know many Arabs who have met the Lord in Europe or America.

I have always seen Naaman's story as a metaphor which foretells the coming humbling of Arab nations. I have witnessed rugged Lebanese soldiers weep like babies when they met Jesus. One tough young man who was tortured in a Syrian prison, today exudes meekness and the love of the Lord. His wife witnesses to Orthodox Jewish women. Jesus used Naaman the Syrian, as one of His two examples in His first recorded message in the synagogue in Nazareth. (See Luke 4:27.) Elijah ministered to a heathen widow, while Elisha reached out to a Syrian general. The Elijah legacy is a model for anointed outreach to the Muslim nations in this final hour of global harvest.

THREE UNFULFILLED PROPHECIES

There were three major prophecies given by the Lord to Elijah which were yet to be fulfilled. In the cave at Horev, God had told Elijah that Hazael would become king of Syria, and Jehu king of Israel (1 Kings 19:15-16). And finally in Naboth's vineyard, Elijah had proclaimed the doom of Jezebel, "Dogs shall eat Jezebel by the wall of Jezreel" (21:23). Elisha now became the Lord's instrument to bring about the fulfillment of these prophecies. I believe that these three events also have prophetic significance and major applications for the Lord's body in Israel and the nations in the last days.

The Holy Spirit prompted Elisha to go to Damascus where King Ben-Hadad was seriously ill. The Syrian king hoped that Elisha would heal him, even as Commander Naaman had been healed at the word of the prophet.

Ben-Hadad sent forty camel loads of gifts of the famed riches of Damascus to Elisha. The historian Josephus understood this to be an ostentatious Middle Eastern caravan, which was paraded through the streets of Damascus. Elisha evidently was not impressed by the show. In those days, God's prophets were not preaching a false Western "prosperity" gospel! Elijah and Elisha did not use their miracle working ministries for personal gain. They didn't "name and claim" camels or Cadillacs. Rather, Elisha was on a mission with a sobering word from his God.

The expensive gifts from the king of Syria were brought to Elisha by the king's attendant, Hazael ("God sees"). This was the same Hazael about whom the Lord had spoken to Elijah in the cave years before (1 Kings 19:15). Elijah had obviously shared with his spiritual son what had happened in the cave.

THE MAN OF GOD WEPT

Elisha told Hazael to tell his master, Ben-Hadad, that he would recover from his sickness. Then the prophet added, "However the LORD has shown me that he will really die" (2 Kings 8:10). The seer had seen into the heart of Hazael. Elisha kept staring at Hazael until the Syrian became ashamed. Then, "the man of God wept" (v. 11). When Hazael asked Elisha why he was weeping, the prophetic word of God was released from the depths of his being as he answered, "Because I know the evil that you will do to the children of Israel: their strongholds you will set on fire, and their young men you will kill with the sword; and you will dash their children, and rip open their women with child" (v.12). He concluded his prophecy with these words: "The Lord has shown me that you will become king over Syria" (v.13). The next day, Hazael assassinated the king of Syria by smothering him in his bed, "and Hazael reigned in his place" (v.15).

Elisha's prophecy of Syrian attacks upon Israel is also a picture of our own era. Syria joined other Arab armies to attack Israel in 1948, 1967, and 1973, and sponsors Hizbullah terrorists who fire rockets and missiles across Israel's northern border today.

JUDGMENT UPON ISRAEL THEN AND NOW

I continue to believe that the "great strong wind" that "tore into the mountains and broke the rocks in pieces before the Lord," and the earthquake and fire that Elijah witnessed on Mount Horev (1 Kings 19:11-12) were prophetic signs of His coming judgment upon apostate Israel. Revival which brought a great harvest had come, but God's righteous judgment upon the persistent national idolatry was also coming. It was coming then and is also coming now. True prophets, like Elisha, receive and fearlessly declare the full counsel of God.

A murderer and usurper was now on the throne of Syria. Joram, the evil son of Ahab and Jezebel, ruled in Israel. Ahab's daughter Athaliah had married Jehoram, the son of Jehospaphat, who reigned in Jerusalem in Judah. Three evil leaders had come to power. The cup of iniquity was full. Even as Elijah and Elisha were raising seven thousand spiritual children, Ahab and Jezebel had also spawned an evil progeny. The stage was set for Elijah's final prophecies to come to pass. God was about to avenge the blood of his martyred prophets on the house of Ahab and Jezebel.

THE JEHU ANOINTING

Joram, the son of Ahab, now made war against Hazael, the king of Syria. Like his father before him, Israel's king was seriously wounded on the Golan, and returned to Jezreel to recuperate. Elisha then told one of his disciples of "the sons of the prophets" to take a flask of oil and anoint Commander Jehu king over Israel. As Elisha's disciple poured the oil on Jehu's head, God's messenger gave the following prophecy:

> Thus says the Lord God of Israel: "I have anointed you king over the people of the Lord, over Israel. You shall strike down the house of Ahab your master, that I may avenge the blood of My servants the prophets,

and the blood of all the servants of the Lord, at the hand of Jezebel. For the whole house of Ahab shall perish ... the dogs shall eat Jezebel on the plot of ground at Jezreel, and there shall be none to bury her." (2 Kings 9:6-10)

Jehu, God's newly appointed king, took a company of men and rode in his chariot to Jezreel where the wounded King Joram remained. Ahab's son rode out in his chariot to meet Jehu "on the property of Naboth the Jezreelite" (v. 21). God was watching over his word to Elijah to perform it. "Now it happened, when Joram saw Jehu, that he said, 'Is it peace, Jehu?' So he answered, 'What peace, as long as the harlotries of your mother Jezebel and her witchcraft are so many?'" (v. 22). Joram tried to flee, but Jehu shot him in the back with an arrow that "came out at his heart" (v. 20). Then they threw the dead body of Ahab's son into the field of Naboth.

"THROW DOWN JEZEBEL"

Finally, God's word about Jezebel was to be fulfilled. The "queen mother" heard that Jehu had come to Jezreel. The aging harlot-witch put on her make-up, her royal robes and crown in preparation to meet the man who had just killed her son. She looked out of an upper window of her palace as Jehu rode into the courtyard. Jehu looked up at her and cried out, "Who is on my side? Who?" as "two or three eunuchs looked out at him" (v. 32). God's prophetic time clock had wound down for Jezebel. Jehu shouted, "Throw her down." The eunuchs obeyed, and threw her out the window, "and some of her blood spattered on the wall and on the horses; and he trampled her underfoot" (v. 33).

After Jehu went inside to have a meal, he thought about the dead woman in the courtyard and told some of his men to bury her. "Go now, see to this accursed woman, and bury her, for she was a king's daughter." But when they went to bury her corpse all they could find of her was "the skull, the feet and the palms of her hands" (v. 34-35). Dogs had consumed the rest of her body. When they reported this to Jehu, he realized what had happened and told his men:

> This is the word of the Lord, which He spoke to His servant Elijah the Tishbite, saying, "On the plot of ground at Jezreel dogs shall eat the flesh of Jezebel; and the corpse of Jezebel shall be refuse on the surface of the field, in the plot at Jezreel, so that they shall not say, 'Here lies Jezebel.'" (2 Kings 9:36-37)

Jehu ("Jehovah is He") was the instrument God had chosen to finally cleanse the land from the curse of Jezebel and Ahab. God had anointed a king who would confront Jezebel. Jehu purged all that remained of the house of Ahab in Jezreel (including seventy sons), and all Ahab's "great men and his close acquaintances and his priests, until he left none remaining" (2 Kings 10:11). Jehu then publicly proclaimed that the destruction of Ahab's house was God's doing: "Know now that nothing shall fall to the earth of the word of the Lord which the Lord spoke concerning the house of Ahab; for the Lord has done what He spoke by His servant of Elijah" (v. 10). The terrible sins of the father had been visited upon the ungodly offspring of Ahab and Jezebel.

THE JEZEBEL SPIRIT

With the death of Jezebel, the literal fulfillments of the prophecies of Elijah had come to pass. But, as we have seen, each prophecy is often a type or foreshadowing pointing toward intermediate and final fulfillments. Biblical prophecy involves not only completed prediction, but also continuing pattern. In this light, I believe that the character of Queen

Jezebel is a prototype which has major continuing significance and application for the body of Messiah, especially in the last days. It is also revealing that the harlot-sorceress dynasty was the last stronghold to fall through the power of the ministry of Elijah.

Through my study of the Scriptures, our personal experiences on Mount Carmel, and by observation of the Body of Christ internationally, I have come to believe that the spirit that controlled Jezebel is a demon of seduction and destruction operating in the world today, and is sometimes active among God's people.

Not long after Queen Jezebel's ghastly death, the prophet Hosea described the northern kingdom as a land contaminated with "the spirit of harlotry." Hosea lamented over the idolatry, ritual prostitution, and rampant sexual immorality practiced on the mountains of Israel. Ahab and Jezebel had helped to usher in and propagate this demonic plague. Hosea accurately described the destructive consequences:

> For the spirit of harlotry has caused them to stray, and they have played the harlot against their God.... Therefore their daughters commit harlotry, and your brides commit adultery ... the men themselves go apart with harlots, and offer sacrifices with a ritual harlot. (Hosea 4:12-14)

The spirit of harlotry released through the union of Jezebel and Ahab had contaminated their own family, and permeated the very fabric of the society of God's people. Fathers, mothers, brides and children had come under its influence or control. This unclean spirit is diametrically opposed to "the spirit and power of Elijah," which turns "the hearts of the fathers to the children" (Luke 1:17). These two opposing forces are always on collision course.

"HER HARLOTRIES AND SORCERIES ARE SO MANY"

The spirit of Jezebel is certainly apparent in Israel today. The aggressive sensuality of a significant portion of the Israeli society is worse than in the days of Elijah. Fornication among Israeli youth is accepted by most secular Jewish parents. One mother berated Karen for not allowing our teenage boys to go to all-night clubs on weekends. Many Israeli parents allow their teenage children to stay out all night, because they know that all of them (boys and girls) will serve in the army after high school. The thinking seems to be, "Let them party now, the army will discipline them later."

One of the disastrous results of this rampant promiscuity is the fact that Israel has one of the highest abortion rates in the world. There are approximately sixty thousand abortions per year, nearly one for every two live births. Since 1948, there have been 1.5 million abortions, the same number of children as were murdered in the Holocaust. We now face an "abortion holocaust." As many as three hundred Israeli infants are slaughtered each week in the hospitals and clinics in the Mount Carmel area. The Israeli army provides two free abortions to female soldiers during their two-year service. In the Soviet Union, abortion was practiced in epidemic proportions. Many Russian-speaking immigrants have had multiple abortions, and require deep, compassionate ministry as a result. In our Or HaCarmel women's shelter we have been able to house unwed pregnant women who desire to keep their babies. The child sacrifice so hated by God in the days of Jezebel is even worse today. (See Jeremiah 19:3-5.)

Mount Carmel is also known for its many cults. On this mountain one can find everything from transcendental meditation, to "physical immortality." A resident of a New Age artists' village not far from our new worship center told us that "the spirits" were calling their followers back to

Mount Carmel for the last days. This lady's sculptures were blatantly pornographic. The priests of Baal and Asherah are still with us.

THE CHARACTERISTICS OF JEZEBEL

The original Jezebel was the daughter of a pagan king who had murdered his own brother in order to take his crown. He was also the high priest of Sidon. Jezebel would have been raised as a devotee of the goddess Asherah (or "Ashtoreth") "the abomination of the Sidonians" (2 Kings 23:13). Ashtoreth was the sexual partner of Baal, and the goddess of fertility, sex, and debauchery in Canaanite belief and practice. Child sacrifice, prostitution of young girls, and homosexuality were ritually practiced at her shrines on the high places.

Jezebel married the king of Israel and usurped authority over the people of God. Ahab became a partaker and practitioner of the spirit of harlotry through the process described in the New Testament, "Or do you not know that he who is joined to a harlot is one body with her? For 'the two,' He says, 'shall become one flesh'" (1 Corinthians 6:16).

Jezebel lusted after authority and control. To attain her ends she married King Ahab, and then systematically murdered the prophets of God. Destruction through seduction was her method. She installed herself as the patroness and leader of hundreds of false prophets. As Queen of Israel she built a temple to her false gods and led thousands of God's people into idolatry, apostasy, sexual immorality, and perversion.

Jezebel was alternately seductive and intimidating. Even Elijah ran from her. I believe that the ruler demon that controlled her still stalks God's point men because it wants to usurp their place. Jezebel hates the authority of God.

The Jezebel spirit is a spirit of anti-Christ. This demonic force is what the Apostle Paul described as a "ruler of the darkness of this age" (Ephesians 6:12). It's greatest lust is to be in control. But Jesus triumphed over these "rulers" on the Cross (Colossians 3:15). Ultimately, the battle with Jezebel is the Lord's battle.

JEZEBEL IN THE CHURCH

Jesus sternly warned His powerful church at Thyatira of a woman He called "Jezebel." Our Lord's description sounds like a character profile of King Ahab's wife. Jesus, "the Son of God, who has eyes like a flame of fire," charged His church:

> I have a few things against you, because you allow that woman Jezebel, who calls herself a prophetess, to teach and seduce My servants to commit sexual immorality ... I gave her time to repent of her sexual immorality, and she did not repent. Indeed I will cast her into a sick bed, and those who commit adultery with her into great tribulation, unless they repent of their deeds. I will kill her children with death, and all the churches shall know that I am He who searches the minds and hearts. And I will give to each one of you according to your works. (Revelation 2:20-23)

Jezebel is such a threat to God's Church that Jesus promises to deal ruthlessly with her.

Jesus then identifies the source of this idolatry and harlotry encamped in His Church as "the depths of Satan" (v.24). The demonic spirit of Jezebel was loose in the Church of Jesus Christ. These are most solemn words, especially for those called to be under shepherds of the Lord's flock. We are commanded not to tolerate Jezebel because she is bent on destroying God's people and purposes.

The prototype Jezebel, the Sidonian sorceress who married into the royal house of Israel, represents demonic spiritual authority that challenges and seduces God's people in order to abort God's purposes. In Jesus' letter to the church at Thyatira we see the re-emergence of this spiritual power in the midst of the New Testament Church. Jesus identified the main traits and symptoms of this demonic spirit, which include: idolatry and witchcraft, sexual immorality, false prophecy, sickness, envy and hatred of God-given authority, and lust for control—all leading to physical or spiritual death, or both.

In both the Old and New Testaments, Jezebel exhibited all of the works of the flesh: "Adultery, fornication, uncleanness, lewdness, idolatry, sorcery, hatred, contentions, jealousies, outbursts of wrath, selfish ambitions, dissensions, heresies, envy, murder, drunkenness, revelries, and the like" (Galatians 5:19-20). This spirit manifests itself through people. If we continually indulge in one of these besetting sins, we may open ourselves to the spirit of Jezebel. This demon is searching for a place to set up shop, and we are commanded not to "give place to the devil" (Ephesians 4:27). If we continue to practice the works of the flesh we "will not inherit the kingdom of God" (Galatians 5:2 1). This is the ultimate goal of Jezebel— destruction. We need to repent and renounce the works of the flesh, and put them under the blood of Jesus. A person growing in the fruit of the Spirit, which is Christ-like character, is protected from Jezebel.

DON'T TOLERATE JEZEBEL

During our years on Mount Carmel, we have endured some painful encounters with this demonic spirit. We have also come to realize that sometimes we are only dealing with wounded or willful people, where flesh and soul are mainly involved. Even then, the battle can be prolonged and painful because, "Rebellion is as the sin of witchcraft; and stubbornness is as iniquity and idolatry" (1 Samuel 15:23).

James described the process of demonic infiltration when he solemnly warned the Church against the sins of envy and self-seeking: "This wisdom does not come from above, but is earthy, sensual ["soulish"], demonic. For where envy and self-seeking exist, confusion and every evil thing are there" (James 3:15-16). The Jezebel infection begins in the flesh. If unchecked, it will root itself in a person's soul.

Self-seeking ("getting ahead") is a much admired trait in modern society. The opposite characteristic is the "spirit of Elijah"—"He must increase, but I must decrease" (John 3:30). The humility and meekness of Jesus are the antidotes to personal ambition. Jesus was crucified because of envy. Satan was jealous of God and attempted to overthrow Him. A third of the angels of Heaven have followed him to their doom.

Jealousy, or covetousness, is the root of the lust for control. Jezebel disinherited Naboth by taking his God-given land and then murdering him. Whatever disguise Jezebel may assume, underneath she is always self-seeking and self-absorbed. A person infected with this spirit will often talk about themselves, and will usually have a hidden agenda.

Jezebels are always "religious" and often appear to be the most spiritual of a group. She or he may be the first to cry, or travail, claiming a burden from God. Such people may claim to be "special" vessels of God, and exhibit spiritual elitism. When exposed and unmasked, false spirituality and an independent "lone ranger" spirit of rebellion will be revealed.

When Karen and I were called to plant new works on Mount Carmel, we were unaware that we had become two of her targets. This was new territory for us. Even before we left New York City in 1989, as we were preparing to go to Israel, we had a major encounter with the spirit of Jezebel. Two seemingly harmless sisters-in-the-Lord joined our Israel prayer group. Soon one of them started giving false words to Karen. We took it to the Lord and He showed us that envy was the root. We dealt with the situation by confronting the facts with this sister and her husband. Years later she begged forgiveness. The other woman attempted to steal someone else's ministry while that person was sick. Selfish ambition was at work, and it was exposed.

Once, in the sanctuary of our church in New York I happened to look at these two women, and in an open vision they turned into two large pythons before my eyes! The Lord in His mercy had shown us the demonic activity of this spirit working through believers who were coming against God's purposes—believers who had given way to its influence and were partnering with it.

After Paul and his team planted the first European church at Philippi, a slave girl tried to join the fledgling congregation. Paul discerned demonic activity and cast a spirit of divination out of her. "Divination" in Greek is "python"—a large snake that squeezes and suffocates its prey. Pastor Paul confronted the Jezebel spirit, and the Church was delivered from demonic infiltration. (See Acts 16:16-18.)

I have come to learn, through sometimes painful experience, that spirits of control and intimidation can only be broken through persistent prayer. Like King Jehu, we must "throw down Jezebel." "The weapons of our warfare … are mighty in God for pulling down strongholds … and every high thing that exalts itself against the knowledge of God" (2 Corinthians 10:4-5). The Lord has given us the weapons if we will use them. (Two excellent books on this subject are John Bevere's, *Breaking Intimidation,* and *Unmasking the Jezebel Spirit,* by John Paul Jackson.)

WAVES OF "JEZEBELS"

Our first year in Israel beginning in the summer of 1989 was a comparative spiritual "honeymoon" because we weren't in any kind of recognized authority. But when we began to pioneer the first Messianic rehabilitation center for Jews and Arabs, and to plant a congregation at the same time, the "Jezebels" seemed to come in waves.

This spirit often works through women, but not always. Some of the women we have had to confront were over-compensating for weak husbands who had abrogated their priestly functions as godly leaders, as Ahab had done. The husbands had given up and were of little help. One woman had obviously married a weak man on purpose. Other single women, who were carrying deep wounds from men or authority figures in their past, had opened themselves to this anti-authority spirit. In some cases, sexual sins, such as fornication and homosexuality, had to be addressed. One couple later left Israel and were divorced. A common trait was that nearly all of these women considered themselves "prophetic." It's difficult to argue when someone claims, "But God told me!" Each of these individuals had a murky track record from the past and had not been biblically sent to Israel. Some had serious illnesses.

In our early days on Carmel, I made the mistake of laying hands on and praying for a woman who had come to work with us. She had asked me to pray for her illness. Immediately afterwards I was attacked by severe abdominal pain and had to be rushed to the hospital the next morning. The doctors never diagnosed why I was so violently ill. But Karen and I realized that the spirit of Jezebel was still operating on Carmel, this time through a lady who hardly ever allowed her docile husband to speak. Shortly after, the young leader of another ministry came to me about the disruption and confusion this same couple had brought into his work. He was at his wit's end. We challenged the spirit in seasons of prayer, and the couple finally left the country. Later on they converted to Judaism, returned to Israel, and wanted to rejoin our congregation. This spirit is tenacious. We firmly but graciously said, "No." We pray that they will repent.

We have also seen people with these characteristics manifest multiple personalities. Sometimes I would say to Karen, "Which one were you dealing with today?" A person with two voices is usually a channel for a demonic spirit. As we have tried to help women who have some of these problems, we have come to understand some of the root causes for such destructive and self-destructive behavior. There almost always has been a history of painful relationships with a man or men. The root usually involves one or more of three problems: (1) no man; (2) a weak man; or (3) a domineering man. The root may have lodged in the person's soul through a painful relationship with a father (or no father), husband, ex-husband, or lover. The solution begins with walking in genuine repentance and forgiveness. If the woman will not realize, repent, renounce, and forgive the authority figure who wounded her, she will open herself to demonic activity.

"JEZEBEL" RELEASES CONFUSION

Because we serve a God of order, the demonic will always try to release confusion, in the attempt to bring division among God's leaders and His people. I have seen ministries destroyed by this demon. I know of a major international ministry that was split in half by this spirit. One of the leaders believed that his co-worker was under the influence of a Jezebel. It was actually another person who was the source of the confusion and division. Discerning the truth, the senior leader, God's point man, confronted the person and her followers. They left the ministry along with many others, some of whom backslid. The pain was almost unbearable for the senior leader. But God was with him and brought them through. Today the ministry is healthy and flourishing, and bearing fruit as never before. God is a gardener, who prunes His vineyard.

A person who exhibits some of these symptoms will often have a critical spirit and may claim to "see more" than the pastor. When not entrusted with decision-making authority, he or she finds it very easy to second-guess God's leaders. This stratagem has been called the "Absalom syndrome," after

Absalom who tried to steal the hearts of the men of Israel from his father David. (See 2 Samuel 15:6.) The critical person is quick to see or imagine the faults of others, but rarely acknowledges their own flaws. If a person with these character traits is in a position of authority, those who are under them or associate with them will most likely be hurt. Such an individual must be removed from authority for the sake of God's people. One person can contaminate a ministry environment so much that others will dread co-laboring with them. One rotten apple will spoil a bushel of apples if not removed.

Some of these controlling people can be very gifted. Others are flatterers of those in authority. Some tend to be legalistic, performing good works by the "letter of the law," and then making sure other people know about it.

Such individuals may be saved, but are often miserable. Jesus warned us that if believers partner with this spirit, He would cast them "into a sick bed," and "great tribulation" (Revelation 2:22). I have seen the tears and heard the heart cries and anguish of such tormented people. Some of them refuse to repent and be healed. But others who have repented and renounced their sin have been wonderfully set free and are being used by the Lord today to build His Kingdom.

CHARACTERISTICS OF
JEZEBEL'S FOLLOWERS

Jesus warned us that a person with a Jezebel spirit will "prophesy," teach, and seduce or fool others to follow her or him. Here are some characteristics we have observed in those who are drawn to a person with this spirit:

(1) Jezebel's followers can simply be naive, or what the Bible calls "foolish" or "simple." Throughout the Book of Proverbs foolishness is the opposite of wisdom. "He who walks with wise men will be

wise, but the companion of fools will be destroyed"
(Proverbs 13:20).

(2) A wounded person longing for emotional
dependence is a prey for Jezebel. Co-dependence will
result if the relationship matures. The follower will go
to her "mentor" or "prayer partner," not God. Jezebels
make disciples to themselves, not to God.

(3) Those ruled by fear may be attracted to a
person with a Jezebel spirit. Fear of man and fear of
decision-making are traits of some of her followers.
The individual with a Jezebel spirit seems spiritually
powerful and can be very intimidating to a fearful
person.

Jesus said that those who become her followers will
be miserable, and will experience "great tribulation, unless
they repent of their deeds" (Revelation 2:22). "Tribulation"
means to be pressed or crushed like grapes or olives in a press.
The result of bonding with a Jezebel spirit will be pressure,
oppression, stress, anguish, adversity, unexplained illness, and
affliction. This is a warning from Jesus. That is why this is
such a serious matter for His Church which He bought with
His blood.

We know of those who have been emotionally and
physically healed after repenting and renouncing an unholy
alliance with a person with a strong Jezebel spirit.

Jezebel is on the prowl for the naive and foolish, those who
have a need to be emotionally co-dependent, and those who
operate out of a spirit of fear. However, her ultimate target
is God's chosen leaders. This spirit hates prophets and godly
pastors.

In *Unmasking the Jezebel Spirit*, John Paul Jackson makes
this observation: "Every church that embraces a prophetic
ministry will have to contend with the Jezebel spirit because
this demonic spirit mimics the prophetic gifts and callings of

God" (p. 117). The counterfeit always follows the genuine. Jezebel will always oppose God's prophets. She did in Elijah's day and she does today.

"GIVE ME THE HEAD OF JOHN THE BAPTIST"

The demonic spirit that inspired Herodias to murder John the Baptist was the spirit of Jezebel. Herod had an Ahab spirit, and John came in "the spirit and power of Elijah." Herod was living in Galilee in public adultery with Herodias, his brother's wife. She was also Herod's niece! "Jezebel" means "unhusbanded." The prophet John confronted the king in his adulterous and incestuous relationship and Herod put the prophet in prison. When Herod was drunk on his birthday Herodias used her own daughter Salome as bait to trap her weak, lust-driven, Ahab-like lover. He placated her demands, unable to say no. Herodias/Jezebel got what she wanted—the grisly death of the prophet who threatened her rise to power. (See Matthew 14:1-12.) Jezebel wants the head of God's leaders on a platter. Pastors beware. We've been warned by Jesus.

SHUTTING THE DOOR ON JEZEBEL

Over the years, I have come to realize that if God's house is in His order, He will guard His Church. He charges us not to tolerate Jezebel. If the leaders are appointed by God, and are in the right place with Him, their wives, and their fellow-leaders, the false authority of the spirit of Jezebel will find no access. Jezebel attacked Elijah and John the Baptist when they were alone.

The restoration of the Lord's design of the five-fold ministry is a safeguard of accountability and covering for leaders who may be stalked by Jezebel. One of her greatest pleasures is to gloat over a fallen man of God. Ahab whimpered in his bed, while Jezebel mocked him and plotted to murder Naboth and take his land and inheritance. I know of famous men of God who have been followed by "groupies" attempting to seduce them. Powerful men are targets for this "ruler" spirit. We know anointed men of God who have fallen into adultery. They had been deceived and were leading a double-life. They were also not accountable to other leaders. One such man has been marvelously restored to his wife and children. The husband and wife now have a powerful marriage ministry. "The spirit of Jezebel" lusts to bring the devastation of divorce into God's church, even as the "spirit of harlotry" in the time of Hosea destroyed families in Israel. Jezebel wrecks families—Elijah restores them.

REWARDS FOR OVERCOMERS

Jesus said that He will remove His presence ("lampstand") from any congregation that tolerates Jezebel. Some leaders do not carry out their God-given mandate because of indifference, personal friendships, or fear of people, and confrontation. Others settle for false peace and harmony. Compromise and cowardice breed confusion. Such a church may have a lot of activity, or programs, but the life of Christ will not be there. Either Jezebel must go, or Jesus will go. The leaders are commanded by Jesus to confront Jezebel. Displaced or unsanctified "mercy" is not an option. Sloppy agape is a recipe for disaster.

Jesus promised us that overcoming Jezebel will bring a powerful release of divine power for advancing the Kingdom of God. To the church at Thyatira, Jesus made this marvelous promise: "And he who overcomes and keeps my works to the end, to him I will give power over the nations" (Revelation 2:26). The victorious believer will share in Messiah's victory over evil and evildoers. The Son of God promises overcomers a corporate spiritual authority over rulers of darkness. These saints will also rule with Jesus in eternity. Such promises are worth fighting for now!

THE MORNING STAR

Jesus concludes His message to the church at Thyatira with another exceedingly great and precious promise. To the overcomer (who does not tolerate Jezebel) He says, "I will give him the morning star" (2:28). Jesus is the "Morning Star." He is "the Sun of Righteousness" (Malachi 4:2) who heralds a new day. However, "the morning star" was a position originally given to Satan. "How you have fallen from heaven, O star of the morning, son of the dawn!" (Isaiah 14:12, NASB). Lucifer lost his place of authority at his fall, as Jesus acknowledged, "I saw Satan fall like lightning from heaven" (Luke 10:18). Jesus took back this place of spiritual authority on the Cross, where "having disarmed principalities and powers, He made a public spectacle of them, triumphing over them" (Colossians 2:15). Therefore, Jesus says: "I am the Root and Offspring of David, the Bright and Morning Star" (Revelation22:16). When Jezebel is gone, it is a new day.

While I was writing this section on Jezebel we were also battling in the spirit with a Jezebel situation. At that strategic moment a prophetic intercessor-psalmist gave me this word which she had received in song:

> I am the word that speaks creation I am the morning star
> I am beginning, I am forever I am the fire!
> And I will answer you, I will do wonders I promise you I am here
> When the morning comes you'll see my glory
> And the darkness will disappear.[1]

THE ELIJAH LEGACY INCLUDES THE MORNING STAR.

---

1 "I Will Answer You" written by Joy Greig ©2003 Galilee of the Nations

-14-

THE RISE AND FALL OF ISLAM

In the seventh and eighth centuries AD, Muslim hordes swept out of what is today Saudi Arabia and overran the Middle East. The spirit of Islam came upon the nations that surround Israel today. We have seen how the Lord used the prophetic ministries of Elijah and Elisha to confront and defeat the powers of darkness in and surrounding Israel in their generation.

As terrible as the darkness was in Elijah's day, today the situation facing Israel is much worse. Approximately three hundred million Muslims surround six million Jews. Israel is less than ten miles wide at one point. You can drive across it in ten minutes!

A fierce war in the spiritual realm is being waged against Israel and God's end-time purposes. The spirit of Islam has descended like a cloud of locusts upon the Middle East.

The forerunner and finisher ministries of Elijah and Elisha offer a powerful prophetic foreshadowing and example for us to follow at this *kairos* moment. These two prophets understood the enemy clearly. The Church today needs revelation concerning the nature of Islam. We need to know our enemy if we are to be aligned with the Lord in His *last-days* conflict with Islam. The roots of the conflict between

Islam, Israel, the Church, and the West can be traced back to the time of Abraham.

On September 11, 2001, the demonic spirit of Islam was exposed to all the world for those who have eyes to see. We, who live and serve the Lord in Israel, experience this most ancient of hatreds on an almost daily basis. Since the rebirth of the nation of Israel in 1948, when five Arab armies attempted to destroy the infant state, thousands of Arabs and Jews have died in the ongoing deadly conflict. Israel has fought seven wars in her sixty-one years of existence. But the current situation surrounding Israel is just the latest manifestation of an ancient hatred that goes all the way back to the time of Abraham.

HAGAR AND ISHMAEL

Over four thousand years of hostilities between Arabs and Jews began because of the sin of unbelief. Sarah and Abraham did not wait for the fulfillment of God's prophetic promise. Here is the genesis of the world's longest running family feud:

> Then Sarai, Abram's wife, took Hagar her maid, the Egyptian, and gave her to her husband Abram to be his wife, after Abram had dwelt ten years in the land of Canaan. (Genesis 16:3)

When Hagar, the Egyptian maid, became pregnant she began to "despise" her mistress, Sarai. Abram's wife dealt "harshly" with her pregnant maid and Hagar "fled from her presence. Now the Angel of the LORD found her by the spring of water in the wilderness" (v.16:7). The Lord had mercy on Hagar and Abraham's child whom she carried. God gave the distraught Hagar this prophecy:

Behold, you are with child, and you shall bear a son. You shall call his name Ishmael ["God hears"], because the LORD has heard your affliction. He shall be a wild man; his hand shall be against every man, and every man's hand against him. And he shall dwell in the presence of all his brethren. (Genesis 16:11-12)

Hagar called the name of the LORD who spoke to her, "You-Are-The-God-Who-Sees," for she said, "Have I also seen Him who sees me?" (v.13). I believe the Lord Jesus appeared and prophesied to her in a theophany. Hagar obeyed the Lord and she bore a son, who was returned to Abraham. The child was to be "a wild man," violent and aggressive against all. God named him Ishmael and also prophesied that he would dwell near his brothers.

GOD'S PROMISES TO ISHMAEL— THE ARAB PEOPLE

The Arab people claim descent from Ishmael, Hagar's son. Thirteen years after the birth of Ishmael, when Abraham was ninety-nine, God told the patriarch that Sarah would bear him a son. Abraham loved his teenage boy, Ishmael, and cried out to God about him:

"Oh, that Ishmael might live before You!" Then God said, "No, Sarah your wife shall bear you a son, and you shall call his name Isaac; I will establish My covenant with him for an everlasting covenant, and with his descendants after him." (Genesis 17:18-19)

God also answered Abraham's prayer for Ishmael:

"And as for Ishmael, I have heard you. Behold, I have blessed him, and will make him fruitful, and will multiply him exceedingly. He shall beget twelve princes, and I will make him a great nation. But My covenant I will establish with Isaac." (Genesis 17: 20-21)

GOD'S COVENANT FOR THE LAND AND THE MESSIAH THROUGH ISAAC

This has been the crux of the controversy between the Arab and Jewish people for nearly four thousand years. God's covenant promises for the land of Canaan and the coming Messiah are through Isaac. God also promised that Ishmael would be blessed by exceeding fruitfulness, and he would be a great nation. A glance at a map of the Middle East will clearly show this prophecy has been fulfilled.

When Isaac ("laughter"), the miracle child of the covenant, was born, relatives and friends of Abraham and Sarah celebrated with a great feast. All rejoice for the patriarch, his wife, and child, except Hagar and Ishmael, who were "scoffing" ["mocking"]" (Genesis 21:9). Sarah told her husband to put the "bondwoman" and her son out of the house. Abraham was deeply distressed because of his love for Ishmael, but the Lord told him to obey his wife.

The aging patriarch sent Hagar and his son Ishmael away. The agonizing wound of rejection cut Hagar and Ishmael deeply. Ishmael and his mother wandered in the Wilderness of Beersheba ("seven wells"). There in the desert the mother and son drank their last water. Hagar put Ishmael under a shrub to guard him from the sun. In her loneliness and misery, "she said to herself, 'Let me not see the death of the boy.' So she sat opposite him, and lifted her voice and wept" (v.16). I have always felt this is a deeply moving picture of the Arab people, weeping in the desert over the wound of rejection inflicted upon them by Father Abraham. God still hears that cry today, even as He heard Ishmael then: "And God heard the voice of the lad" (v.17). (This is a play on words of Ishmael's name.)

He also answered the tears of the mother of the Arab people. "Fear not, for God has heard the voice of the lad where he is. Arise, lift up the lad and hold him with your hand, for I will make him a great nation" (v.17-18). "The God Who Sees" then "opened her eyes and she saw a well of water.... So god was with the lad" (v.19-20).

Ishmael began to live in the desert where he took an Egyptian wife. Many children were born to him, and his sons roamed the desert often in conflict with others. Indeed, twelve Arabian princes were his legacy. (See Genesis 25:12–17, NKJV.)

When Abraham died, Isaac and Ishmael, the two half-brothers, buried their father in Hebron, in the cave of Machpelah, which the patriarch had purchased. (To this day the battle between Arabs and Jews still rages in this place. Twelve Israelis were murdered there in December 2002.) Hebron is the inheritance of Caleb (Joshua 14:13), and where the elders of Israel anointed David as king (2 Samuel 5:4).

"TWO NATIONS ARE IN YOUR WOMB"

The family of Abraham was about to enter its second generation of sibling strife. Even as Isaac's wife, Rebekah, gave birth, the twin boys struggled together in her womb. The LORD told her, "Two nations are in your womb, Two peoples are separated from your body; One people shall be stronger than the other, and the older shall serve the younger" (Genesis 25:23). Esau the older of the twins became a skillful hunter and was his father's favorite.

But "Rebekah loved Jacob." Esau who was called "Edom" ("red") sold his birthright, the double portion of the eldest son, to Jacob. Thus Esau despised his birthright" (v. 34). Later when Esau realized that Jacob had received the father's blessing of the firstborn, "He cried with an exceedingly great and bitter cry ... and said to his father, 'Have you only one blessing, my father? Bless me—me also, O my father!' And Esau lifted his voice and wept" (Genesis 27:34-38). Isaac then prophesied over Esau: "By your sword you shall live, and you shall serve your brother; and it shall come to pass, when you become restless that you shall break his yoke from your neck" (v. 40).

Ishmael hated Isaac, and now in the next generation, "Esau hated Jacob." The oldest son sold his father's blessing for a bowl of lentils and then declared, "I will kill my brother Jacob" (v. 41).

ESAU MARRIED INTO ISHMAEL'S FAMILY

Cunning Jacob fled from his vindictive twin brother. Esau—now in open rebellion against his father—"saw that the daughters of Canaan did not please his father Isaac, so Esau went to Ishmael and took Mahalath ["disease"] the daughter of Ishmael, Abraham's son ... to be his wife" (Genesis 28:8-9). (She was his third wife.)

Esau knowingly married into the line of Ishmael and the Canaanites, a people cursed by Noah. (See Genesis 9:22–25.) While Esau was joining himself to the house of Ishmael and the idol-worshipping Canaanites, Jacob had an encounter with the God of his fathers in a dream. The LORD renewed His covenant and told Jacob, "the land on which you lie I will give to you and your descendants ... and in your seed all the families of the earth shall be blessed" (28:13-14). Jacob woke up and was terrified. "How awesome is this place! This is none other than the house of God, and this is the gate of heaven!" (v.17). God's holy covenant promises are to the seed of Abraham, Isaac, and Jacob—not to Ishmael and Esau. The conferring of the covenant was God's sovereign choice. Jacob, "the supplanter," was asleep. God's initiating grace renewed and released His covenant promises to the third generation.

In order to biblically understand the conflict that rages over Israel in the Middle East we must trace its roots. At the death of Isaac, the second patriarch, his two boys were also there. "His sons Esau and Jacob buried him" (Genesis 35:29). Esau and Jacob were twin brothers. Ishmael and Isaac were half-brothers with the same father—Abraham. Arabs and Jews today are their descendants.

"ESAU IS EDOM"

The entire chapter of Genesis 36 is devoted to the genealogy of Esau. It begins with this statement: "Now this is the genealogy of Esau, who is Edom" (v. 11). It is most important for those of us who hope to understand God's purposes to realize that "Esau" is "Edom." We are told this important fact three times in this chapter. Esau, the one who would "live by the sword," took more wives from the daughters of Canaan, including Hittite and Hivite women. Later, Esau moved his wives, children, and grandchildren to Mount Seir, which in Scripture becomes synonymous with Esau and the Edomites. The word "seir" means "rough male goat," "devil," or "satyr." A satyr was a half-goat, half-male demon. Satyrs in pagan religions were synonymous with lechery and rape. Esau and Ishmael had become one large family or tribe. In the recorded genealogies of Esau-Edom and Ishmael (the Arab people) we find names of individuals and tribes who later would become murderous enemies of God's covenant people. Israel is the name God gave to Esau's twin brother, Jacob. Some of these mortal enemies of Israel include: Kedar, Teman, Omar and Amalek. As Ishmael and Esau and their descendants were spawning a massive pagan progeny, Jacob fathered twelve sons, who became the patriarchs of the twelve tribes of Israel.

This is the biblical background which has fostered such deep enmity between three hundred million Arabs (the descendants of Ishmael and Esau), now surrounding seven million Jews (descendents of Isaac and Jacob), now living in a narrow strip of the land given them from God by His holy covenant. When we see "Edom" or "Seir" in the Psalms, Prophets or New Testament, they are references to the offspring of Esau and Ishmael, sworn enemies of the Jewish people.

AMALEKITES

The wandering desert tribe of Amalek ambushed Israel shortly after the nation came out of Egypt (Exodus 17:3, NKJV). The founder of the tribe was a grandson of Esau. Amalek means "warlike." As Joshua battled the Amalekites in the valley, Moses' prayers on the mountain brought victory. Because the Amalekites attacked the sick, elderly, the stragglers, and the women, God put a curse upon them:

> "I will utterly blot out the remembrance of Amalek from under heaven!" And Moses built an altar and called its name, The Lord Is My Banner; for he said, "Because the LORD has sworn: the LORD will have war with Amalek from generation to generation." (Exodus 17:14–16)

King Saul was removed as Israel's first king because he disobeyed God and did not utterly destroy the Amalekites. Saul spared Agag, king of the Amalekites, but the prophet Samuel "hacked Agag in pieces before the LORD in Gilgal" (1 Samuel 15:33). Haman in the Book of Esther was an Amalekite. Herod the Great, at the time of Jesus, was an Edomite usurper of the throne of David. He is remembered for the massacre of innocent Jewish children, the murder of several of his sons, and his appalling death. Haman and Herod both tried to destroy the Jews and the Lord's Messiah. They came from the line of Ishmael-Esau-Edom.

THE RISE OF ISLAM

In the eighth century AD, Muslim armies came from the Arabian peninsula (Saudi Arabia today) and conquered the Middle East, northern Africa, Spain, Turkey, and the Balkans. Their armies were finally stopped in France and Austria. The schisms, corruption, and heresies of the Roman and Greek Orthodox churches had opened the way for the ascendancy of this demonic religion. Any objective history book will show that Islam is a religion birthed and bathed in blood. Mohammed received visions and words from "spirits," which became incorporated into the Koran, a book dedicated to the subjection of the world to a false god, called "Allah." The word "Islam" means "submission." The Mohammedan hordes slaughtered, raped and pillaged millions in the seventh and eighth centuries. Mohammed's own harem of "wives" included an eleven-year-old girl. Islam is the only world religion with a written, clearly articulated agenda of forceful world conquest. Jihad ("holy war") against all infidels (non-Muslims) is one of Islam's fundamental beliefs. The Koran places all the people of the world into two groups: "The House of Peace" ("Islam") or the "House of War" (everybody else). You either accept Islam or you are a target for destruction. Muslim militants simply take the commands of the Koran seriously. The Koran also teaches that Jesus did not die on the Cross. Rather it claims that an "imposter" was crucified, meaning that Jesus was not raised from the dead, and is not the Son of God.

ISLAM AND THE SPIRIT OF ANTI-CHRIST

"Who is a liar but he who denies that Jesus is the Christ? He is antichrist who denies the Father and the Son" (1 John 2:22). "Anti" is a Greek preposition that has two meanings: "against," and "in place of." The ultimate purpose of the "spirit of anti-Christ" is to put a false Messiah in the place of the true Messiah—Jesus the Jew, the Prince of Peace. Not only is the spirit of anti-Christ against Jesus, it seeks to replace Him with an imposter. Allah, the moon god (note the Islamic flag) of Mesopotamia, has no son. This god is not the God of the Bible.

Mohammed claimed to be a prophet who received "messages" from the angel Gabriel, who had announced the incarnation of Jesus to a Jewish virgin named Miriam (Mary). Mohammed contended that Islam was the true fulfillment of both the Old and New Testaments and had replaced them. According to Mohammed, the Gospels were a perversion of the truth which he was restoring. He rejected Christianity and thought the Jewish people would become his followers. When they in turn rejected him and his new anti-Christ religion, the Muslims turned against the Jews as well and became their persecutors.

Islam bears unmistakable marks of the "spirit of anti-Christ." Not only does it deny the divinity and atoning death of Jesus, it also attempts to replace Him and the Bible with the teachings of Mohammed and the Koran as the final revelation of God. We are in a war for the truth, with the "spirit of anti-Christ." (For more information on Islam, I recommend George Grant's *The Blood of the Moon;* and *The Closed Circle,* by David Pryce-Jones.)

MOHAMMED VERSUS JESUS

Shortly after September 11, 2001, the international television and print media began a massive campaign attempting to whitewash Islam. Of course, they say that Christianity is just as bad. They are correct with regard to the atrocities which were committed by so-called "Christians" in the Crusades, Inquisition, and pogroms. But they miss the root of the matter. Jerusalem-based AP reporter, David Dolan, clarifies this important point:

Modern Muslim apologists note that incessant conflicts also racked "Christian" Europe.... Yet there is a fundamental difference between Christianity and Islam, and it is the key to understanding why we are precariously perched on the edge of a precipice.... European leaders and warriors were hardly imitating the Jewish Prince of Peace or His first century disciples when they violently lashed out against each other. But warring Muslim leaders ... have precisely reflected the bloodstained actions of their revered Prophet and earliest followers.... No contemporary Muslim ... can deny Muhammad was a quintessential jihad warrior ... most justify his violent actions as sanctioned by Allah, as recorded in the Koran. His powerful example of what one does to religious opponents who stand in the way of the spread of Islam is the main reason why men like Saddam Hussein and Osama bin Laden have found myriads of Islamic defenders for their violent actions today, even sometimes those directed against fellow Muslims ("Holy Violence," David Dolan, Crisis Update, 3 October 2001).

Dolan is right. Mohammed shed the blood of thousands. Jesus allowed His own blood to be shed for our salvation.

SATAN'S MASTERPIECE

Islam is one of Satan's masterpieces. It is built upon lies, half-truths, and terror, all of which continue today in Indonesia, Pakistan, Iran, Syria, Lebanon, Saudi Arabia, Sudan, Nigeria, the Palestinian Authority, and Gaza. After the Gulf War, Saddam Hussein's oldest son, Uday, oversaw the systematic mass murder of over one hundred thousand Iraqi Muslims. (Some reports even say three hundred thousand.) They had been held in one of Iraq's notorious prisons (information taken from *The Jerusalem Report*, p. 28-29, January 28, 2002). Hafez Assad, the father of Syria's present dictator, liquidated forty thousand of his own Muslim people.

Mohammed became the self-proclaimed prophet-priest of a false religion, which worships a false god called "Allah." His followers were and are characterized by male domination, power, and violence. The Koran teaches that the appropriation and distribution of all female captives is a virtue. Women have few rights under Islam. Afghanistan is a prime example, but is only one of many. In some places Muslim women are "circumcised" with scissors or knives, so they are unable to have pleasure during sex. This is even true in so-called "moderate" Muslim dictatorships, like Egypt. Men may also have up to four wives. "Martyrs" for the cause of Islam are told they go to Heaven where seventy virgins supposedly await them, and that seventy family members will also go to Heaven, if the martyr blows himself up with some Jews. Today over one billion people are held in subjection to totalitarian Islamic regimes. Women and children have few rights in countries where power is held by wealthy tyrants and murderers who harbor and encourage global terrorism. There has never been a real democracy in a Muslim nation. An "Islamic republic" is a contradiction in terms.

We are in a war to the death with the spirit behind Islam. What was unleashed on September 11, 2001, for all the world to watch as it happened was a horrific demonstration of the murderous spirit of Islam. It was a worldwide warning.

Jesus described Satan as a "murderer from the beginning ... he is a liar and the father of lies" (John 8:44). Israel was chosen by God to give the world His Word (the Bible), and His Messiah, His Son, to redeem the world. Jesus is coming back to Jewish Jerusalem (See Zechariah 14:4 and Acts 1:11.) when the Jews will finally have received their Messiah. (Romans 11:26-27). Today many are already turning to Him. There are approximately 10,000 Messianic Jews In Israel.

Pharaoh, Haman, Herod, Hitler, Hizballah, and now Hamas ("violence" in Hebrew) have all tried to destroy Israel and God's redemptive plan. (Why did the Palestinian Muslims support Hitler in World War II and Saddam Hussein in the Gulf War?) The murderous spirit behind Islam hates Israel because the Jews have been restored to their ancient homeland, which God gave them through an everlasting covenant. The goal of Islam is to annihilate Israel.

But God is watching over His Word to perform it. Those who attack Israel, "the apple of God's eye," "His anointed ones," will be contending with Jehovah Tsevaot, "the Lord God of armies." (See Psalm 105:7–15.)

THE SPIRIT OF ISLAM UPON
THE SEED OF ISHMAEL

When the Islamic hordes invaded and subjugated the Middle East, the spirit of Islam ("anti-Christ") came upon the descendants of Ishmael and Esau-Edom. We have seen that Ishmael and Esau were rejected by Abraham and Isaac. For millennia the wound of rejection has manifested itself through envy, rebellion, revenge and murder. We are in the continuing war between the half-brother's Ishmael and Isaac. Mohammed was also rejected by Judaism and Christianity. Rejection demands revenge or acceptance.

> The casting out of Ishmael has been productive of bitter fruit, surviving in the religion of Mohammed.... Little did Sarah know, when she persuaded Abraham to take Hagar, that she was originating a rivalry which has run in the keenest strife through the ages, and which oceans of blood have not stopped. The Muslim Arabs claim descent from Ishmael." (*All the Men of the Bible* p. 160.)

THE BATTLE FOR JERUSALEM

The Dome of the Rock shrine to Allah was built upon the Temple Mount above the ruins of the First and Second Temples. I have only entered the shrine once, and then I was "prayed up" and was with a team of intercessors. Inside there is an exposed rock, where a sign in several languages proclaims the lie that upon that rock Abraham offered up his son Ishmael. Over one billion deluded people believe this lie. Other Arabic inscriptions proclaim: "Allah is the only God, and has no son. Mohammed is his prophet."

Israel has given authority over the Temple Mount area to Islam. Israeli media have recently disclosed that Muslims are covertly destroying any remains of the First and Second Temples. In fact, a large bulge has recently appeared for all to see on the face of the Western Wall. "The Wailing Wall"— the holiest place in Judaism—is the remaining section of the retaining wall of the Second Temple. Muslims claim that there were no Jewish temples in Jerusalem, and that the Jews are liars who have no right there. Jerusalem is not even mentioned in the Koran. However, Jerusalem is written over three hundred times in the Bible. For over eighteen hundred years, devout Jews have prayed toward Jerusalem three times a day. At every Jewish wedding the couple declares that they will not forget Jerusalem as they break a glass.

THE COVENANT OF DEATH AGAINST ISRAEL

In Psalm 83, we have a clear prophetic picture of the situation in Israel today. The enemies of God state: " 'Come, and let us cut them off from being a nation, that the name of Israel be remembered no more!' For they have consulted ["plotted"] together with one consent ["heart"]; they form a confederacy ["cut a covenant"] against You" (v. 4-5).

And who are these conspirators against Jehovah and the nation of Israel? "The tents of Edom and the Ishmaelites ... Amalek; Philistia [Gaza]" (v. 6-7). There is a clear listing of all the Muslim nations surrounding Israel today. And here is what these Muslim nations are saying: "Let us take for ourselves the pastures of God for a possession" (v. 12). The PLO has never rescinded its covenant calling for the destruction of Israel. Iran, Iraq, and Syria have publicly called for the liquidation of Israel. Hamas has also covenanted to destroy her. Tiny little Israel is an island of embarrassment and "desecration" in the Islamic sea of pride and dominion in the Middle East. By its very existence in "Mohammed's land" Israel brings shame on the honor of Islam. On April 3, 2002, Yasser Arafat lied on the Al-Jazeera TV network, that "the Palestinian people have been rooted in this land before the time of Abraham." In Arabic he proclaimed the way to victory is through suicide bombings of innocent Israelis. We need to understand that mass murderers are not martyrs.

WHO IS OCCUPYING WHOM?

The Arabs claim that the land of Israel was theirs and was taken away from them by the Jews is a lie with no historical basis. According to Joan Peters in her carefully documented book, *From Time Immemorial*, perhaps 90% of the Arabs migrated here beginning in the late nineteenth century, after Diaspora Jews began returning to their homeland as pioneers.

Israel became a nation two thousand years before the rise of Islam and long before there existed any Arab nation. Israel has been the national homeland of the Jewish people since biblical times. It was subsequently "occupied" more than fifteen times, by nations such as Egypt, Assyria, Babylon, Persia, Greece, Rome and the Ottoman Muslim Turks (1517-1917). They were followed by the British, who, under the Mandate of the League of Nations (later the U.N.) ruled in order to renew a homeland for the Jewish people. Jews have had a continuous presence in Israel for over 3,300 years.

The PLO propaganda machine has mastered the "Big Lie" technique. They have attempted to rewrite history, and by continuous repetition on television, radio, books, and newspapers, their lies have come to be believed by a mass general audience who do not know the true history of this disputed land. Arabs are not descendants of the Philistines (who came from Crete). Rather the Arabs came from the Arabian peninsula, now called Saudi Arabia, and are descendants of Ishmael. Because of massive oil deposits in Arab countries—Europe, Russia, Scandinavia, Britain, and the U.S., acting out of self-interest, are silent or consenting to the gross Arab distortions of history. The real question is: "Who is occupying whose land?" The Word of God has the answer.

THE "LAND FOR PEACE" LIE

Israel is God's land which He chose to give the Jewish people, the descendants of Abraham, Isaac, and Jacob, in an everlasting covenant.

> He is the LORD our God; His judgments are in all the earth. He remembers His covenant forever; the word which He commanded, for a thousand generations, The covenant which He made with Abraham, and His oath to Isaac, and confirmed it to Jacob for a statute, to Israel as an everlasting covenant, Saying, "To you I will give the land of Canaan as the allotment of your inheritance." When they were few in number, indeed very few, and strangers in it. When they went from one nation to another. From one kingdom to another people, He permitted no one to do them wrong; Yes, He rebuked kings for their sakes,

saying: "Do not touch My anointed ones, and do My prophets no harm." (Psalm 105: 7–15)

The judgment of God awaits those nations who attempt to change the borders of God's covenant land of Israel.

THEY SHALL NOT DEVOUR ISRAEL

In September 1993, when the secret Oslo peace accords were made public, Karen and I were in Finland. As I sought the Lord about the consequences of Israel selling her birthright, the Holy Spirit quickened this verse to me: "The Syrians before and the Philistines behind; and they shall devour Israel with an open mouth" (Isaiah 9:12). This is what has been happening since the Oslo peace accords were signed. Open mouths are still trying to devour Israel. They will not succeed.

THE APPLE OF GOD'S EYE

In these last days, the nations who attempt to force Israel into territorial compromise will have a controversy with the Lord of Hosts. The word of the Lord is clear: "He who touches you [Israel] touches the apple ["pupil"] of His eye" (Zechariah 2:8). God will deal severely with these nations: "For surely I will shake My hand against them, and they shall become spoil for their servants. Then you will know the Lord of hosts has sent Me" (v. 9). God spoke through the prophet Joel concerning the judgment which will surely come upon those nations who divide His land:

> For behold, in those days and at that time,
> When I bring back the captives of Judah and Jerusalem,
> I will also gather all nations,
> And bring them down to the Valley of Jehoshaphat;
> And I will enter into judgment with them there

On account of My people, My heritage Israel,
Whom they have scattered among the nations;
They have also divided up My land. (Joel 3:1-2)

Egypt, Assyria, Babylon, Greece, Rome, Germany, Britain
and the Soviet Union have all experienced the wrath of God
because of their treatment of Israel.

We have earnestly prayed that President Bush, and now
President Obama, will align himself with the Word of God and
not with worldly counselors and coalitions. David Wilkerson
prophesied with this warning in January 2002:

> Let me say it again: Diligently pray that President
> Bush will be given the spirit and godly zeal of Josiah,
> the king of Israel who turned a godless society back
> to God. If President Bush touches Israel—if he allows
> the Palestinians to have a portion of Jerusalem as their
> capital—we are doomed.

A U.S. Senator gave that message to President Bush.

THE FALL OF ISLAM

Before Jesus returns, Islam will fall and the Lord will sweep
millions of former Muslims into His kingdom. It is beginning to
happen in Kosovo, Indonesia, Mozambique, Uganda, Nigeria
and Afghanistan. The Lord is beginning to shake the empire
of Islam. When I was teaching young leaders in Kosovo in
the summer of 1999, all of them were ex-Muslims. The young
church that has emerged there since the war consists almost
entirely of former Muslims. Since September 11, over two
thousand Afghanis have come to the Lord. There is massive
revival in the midst of terrible persecution in Indonesia, as
well as northern Mozambique. Fifty thousand Muslims have
come to the Lord in Algeria. In Isaiah, chapter 63, God says

that He will judge Edom (Islam) and there will be a mighty move of salvation:

> Who is this who comes from Edom,
> With dyed garments from Bozrah,
> This One who is glorious in His apparel,
> Traveling in the greatness of His strength? —
> "I who speak in righteousness, mighty to save."
> (Isaiah 63:1)

I believe the Bible clearly prophesies the fall of Islam. This Scripture predicts that the collapse will be violent and bloody, but multitudes will be saved. The Lord will tread the winepress of His wrath alone, "For the day of vengeance is in My heart, and the year of the redeemed has come" (v. 4). God promises that Islam's strength will be "brought down" (v. 5). We need to pray for the Lord to hasten this day.

Jeremiah chapter 49 is another prophetic passage concerning the fall of Islam. Speaking against Edom, the Lord of Hosts ("armies") says that He "will bring the calamity of Esau upon him" (v. 8). In this violent conflict with Islam, He says there will be many "fatherless children, I will preserve them alive; and let your widows trust in Me" (v. 11). This is already happening in Mozambique, Afghanistan and Indonesia.

TAKE UP THE ELIJAH CLOAK

I believe the Spirit is calling and commissioning an army of missionaries to take up the cloak of the Elijah legacy, and go to the widows and orphans—the Hagars and the Ishmaels—of the Islamic world. Iraq may be next. God is moving mightily in all the former Soviet Republics that are now Muslim nations. In March 2002, an Iraqi believer stood in our meeting and asked forgiveness for what his nation has done to Israel. He had a message to Israeli Arabs and Palestinians to embrace God's purposes for Israel. Amazingly, he had been led to the Lord by an Iranian believer in Sweden, where a revival has broken out among Iranian immigrants.

BLOOD FOR BLOOD

Perhaps the most specific prophecy about God's judgment upon Islam is the entire 35th chapter of Ezekiel. The Lord tells the prophet to prophesy against Mount Seir. We have seen that "seir" represents a demonic root of Edomite paganism. When the demonized anti-Christ religion of Islam overran the Middle East, the spirit of Islam also came upon the descendants of Ishmael and Esau-Edom. I have even seen this spirit manifest itself in blatant anti-Semitism through Christian missionaries who have been working with Muslims. God told Ezekiel to prophesy that He—"Adonai Jehovah"—would stretch out His hand against Edom and make them desolate. But out of the judgment and destruction would come a mighty revival: "Then you shall know that I am the LORD" (v. 4). This is happening today in Indonesia, Kazakhstan, and Algeria. We are to prophesy and pray for this to be accomplished throughout the Muslim world.

The Lord then states why and what He will do to Islam.

> Because you have had an ancient ["everlasting"] hatred, and have shed the blood of the children of Israel by the power of the sword at the time of her calamity, when her iniquity came to an end, "therefore, as I live," says the Lord GOD, "I will prepare you for blood, and blood shall pursue you; since you have not hated blood ["bloodshed"], therefore blood will pursue you." (Ezekiel 35:5-6)

The principality behind Islam (is it Satan himself?) hates Israel. The Edomites joined the Babylonians in the destruction of Jerusalem. Today Islam intends to destroy Israel so the Messiah won't come back to Jewish Jerusalem. The Lord of Hosts promises a horrific and bloody confrontation—"blood shall pursue you,"— since Islam was birthed and is bathed in bloodshed. God promises justice and retribution.

The Lord continues in His prophecy, saying that because Islam intends to possess the land of Israel and has said:

> "We will possess them," although the LORD was there, "therefore, as I live," says the Lord GOD, "I will do according to your anger and according to your envy which you showed in your hatred against them; and I will make Myself known among them when I judge you. Then you shall know that I am the LORD." (Ezekiel 35: 10–12)

Millions of Muslims will come to know He is Jehovah, not Allah. God will finally judge the envy, hatred, and violence of Islam against the true Church and against Israel. The Church and Israel will realize that God did it. So will the remnant of Islam. What a scenario we face in the near future—Jews, nominal Christians, and Muslims coming to the Lord in the millions.

GOD HAS A CONTROVERSY AGAINST ISLAM

God has a controversy with Islam because they have blasphemed Him. They have boasted against God and Israel. The Lord concludes His awesome prophecy by saying, "Thus says the Lord GOD ["Adonai Jehovah"]: 'The whole earth will rejoice when I make you desolate ... then they shall know that I am the LORD'" (v. 14-15). The whole world witnessed the demonic bloodbath of September 11, 2001, and the whole world will also witness the fall of Islam.

Today, Iran is racing to develop deliverable nuclear warheads, and has vowed to wipe Israel off the map. Civilization is in a race against time as terrorist organizations and tyrants are driven to acquire more biological and nuclear arsenals, warheads and delivery systems. It was revealed in February 2002, that Iran had given ten thousand missiles to the Hizballah terrorist organization in Lebanon, who are just twenty-five miles from Haifa. In July 2006, Hizballah rained down over 3,000 missiles on Galilee and Haifa. We had to move all of our students and staff out of House of Victory. News sources now report that Hizballah has stockpiled close to 80,000 rockets and missiles, some capable of hitting Tel Aviv. Iran has warned and threatened Israel not to consider attacking its nuclear power plants, which Russia is building for them. Israel destroyed Iraq's nuclear power in 1981. Thank God! Iran promises to "retaliate in ways unimaginable to any Israeli politician" (*The Jerusalem Post*, Feb. 5, 2002).

In January 2002, in a daring raid in the Red Sea, Israeli commandos captured the "Karine A" ship. Fifty tons of explosives and weapons were on board. The ship was financed by Iran and was on its way to Gaza. In January 2009, the Israeli air force destroyed a huge shipment of arms from Iran, as it was being transported through Sudan on the way to Hamas in Gaza.

ISLAM'S HARVEST OF HATE

On March 10, 2002, a major Saudi Arabian state-controlled newspaper published a two-part series stating the lies that "the Jewish people must obtain human blood so that their clerics can prepare holiday pastries.... The Jews' spilling blood to prepare pastry for their holidays is a well-established fact ... all throughout history." Rich detail was offered about how Jews supposedly ritually slaughter Christian and Muslim children ten years old or younger for Passover. A similar series of articles appeared in a major state-controlled Egyptian newspaper last year. In Muslim states, including the Palestinian Authority, all news media are controlled by the governments. In April 2009, Hamas TV showed a "Passover" video depicting Muslim actors dressed as Orthodox Jews discussing killing Muslim children and using their blood to make matzah for Passover. Such articles, books and television shows are simply reappearances of the ancient anti-Semitic blood libel that began in "Christian" Britain and was popularized in Europe during past times of terrible persecution of the Jews. Another example is *The Matzah of Zion*, a popular Syrian book claiming that Jews use Christian and Muslim blood to make matzah for Passover. A televised version of this book is shown on Arabic TV in the Middle East.

As these articles were running in a Saudi Arabian state-controlled newspaper, the Saudi Arabian government offered their new much-publicized "peace plan" for Israel and the Palestinians. Did the Western world forget that fifteen of the nineteen Muslim terrorists aboard the doomed American airliners on September 1, 2001, were from Saudi Arabia, as is Osama bin Laden? Can Israel possibly believe the sincerity of a corrupt Arab dictatorship that has shown nothing but hatred toward Israel for over half a century? In Saudi Arabia anyone found accepting another religion is beheaded. Recently, President Obama bowed to the Muslim King of Saudi Arabia. Did he meet any of the king's harem of multiple wives? Islamic hatred for Israel and the "Christian" West found its perfect expression on that clear September morning of September 1, 2001. Six months later the "Passover massacre" of twenty-nine, mostly elderly, Jews celebrating the Passover Seder meal at a seaside hotel not far from us, became another expression of such hate. In the month of March 2002, one hundred twenty-five Israelis died in terrorist attacks and suicide bombings.

INCITEMENT—"TO STIR UP TO ACTION"

In Israel we live under the dark cloud of the Palestinian Authority's raw incitement to hatred and murder. For instance, the Palestinian people heard these words from a government-appointed spokesman on live official PA television:

> The Jews ... they must be butchered and killed, as Allah the almighty said: "Fight them. Allah will torture them at your hands."... Have no mercy on the Jews, no matter where they are, in any country. Fight them, wherever you are. Wherever you meet them, kill them. (quoted in *The Washington Post*, March 31, 2002).

We are facing an entire generation of Palestinians indoctrinated and schooled in hatred of the Jews. An Arabic translation of *Mein Kampf* (Hitler's manifesto) is now a bestseller in the "territories." The poisonous incitement of the Palestinian media against Israel has been birthed, funded, written, taught, and consistently broadcast by the Palestinian Authority. This murderous hatred has exploded precisely in the era in which Israel has agreed to major concessions of territory, the establishment of the Palestinian Authority, and to thousands of Palestinian police actually given arms by Israel. The "land for peace" delusion has become the reality of "land for war."

After vilifying Israel for years through every channel at their disposal, Palestinian state-controlled media have glorified "martyrdom operations," as Muslim mothers and fathers have appeared proudly on TV after sending their sons and daughters to their death so they can kill as many Jews as possible. The Palestinian campaign of lies and hatred has birthed an orgy of unprecedented murder-suicide. During the Passover holiday, as the Christian world celebrated Easter Sunday, March 31, 2002, a Muslim suicide bomber blew himself up along with fourteen Jews and Israeli Arabs in a Haifa restaurant managed by Israeli Arabs. An Arab pastor friend of ours was driving by the restaurant when it blew up. He sent his family home and then helped put out the flames on burning bodies, as a girl screamed from her car, "My Daddy is in there!" Her father had gone in to pick up some salads. Later the pastor walked home covered with Jewish and Arab blood. The next day the highest-ranking Egyptian Muslim cleric declared that female suicide bombers are sanctioned by the Koran.

"MILLIONS OF MARTYRS MARCHING TO JERUSALEM"

On March 29, 2002, two days before this "Passover Massacre," Yasser Arafat told the Arab network of Al-Jazeera TV: "To Jerusalem we march—martyrs by the millions." He repeated his mantra five times.

Middle Eastern incitement of hatred and murder from Cairo, Teheran, and Damascus is consistently proclaimed in schools, mosques, universities and the media. Assad, the "Fox of Damascus" cried: "Syria must unite the Arab world against the infidels—the West and the Jews." His son publicly told the Pope that Israelis are "Nazis." The "Butcher of Baghdad," Saddam Hussein, took an ancient oath to restore the glories of Babylon and "to wash my hands and feet in the blood of the infidels for the glory of Babylon forever." And the ayatollahs of Teheran also vow to destroy the Jews and the "Great Satan" of America.

A MODERN HISTORY OF HATE

Here are some milestones in the recent history of the age-old conflict being waged in Israel today. The Balfour Declaration of 1917 declared that Palestine was to be a homeland for the Jewish people. In 1922, the British gave three-fourths of Mandatory Palestine to the Arabs and named it Jordan. Seven years later the ancient Jewish community in Hebron was massacred by Arabs. During World War II the grand mufti of Jerusalem, Haj Amin al-Husseini, met with Hitler in an attempt to solve the "problem of the Jewish element in Palestine ... by the same method that the question is now being settled in the Axis countries." They collaborated in developing the "final solution" of annihilating the Jews. The Arab world rejected the U.N. partition plan of 1947, that would have created a Jewish and a Palestinian State. In 1948, five Arab armies invaded the newly established State of Israel. Holocaust historians estimate that at least one million Jews perished because Britain refused to let them return to Mandatory Palestine. (For more information, see *Prophecy Today*, July-August, 2002.)

From 1948 until 1967, all Israelis were prevented from praying in Jordanian-controlled Jerusalem. Three Arab armies launched a "battle of annihilation" against Israel in 1967. Six days later, Israel controlled Jerusalem for the first time in centuries. Now all faiths are allowed to worship there.

In 1972, the PLO slaughtered Israel's Olympic delegation in Munich, Germany. Later that year Egypt and Syria launched a surprise attack on Yom Kippur. Mr. Arafat supported Saddam Hussein during the Gulf War. After signing the Oslo accords, Chairman Arafat consistently called (in Arabic) on the Muslim world to wage "jihad to eliminate the State of Israel." Arafat told President Clinton at Camp David that there never has been a Jewish Temple in Jerusalem, as PA-controlled television featured children singing in Arabic, "When I wander in Jerusalem, I will be a suicide bomber." Several days later the renewed terrorist attacks of the *intifada* ("Arab uprising") began on Rosh Hashanah 2000, the Jewish New Year.

"A SEASON OF THE SUDDEN"

God will have the last word. Islam will be humbled, and millions of captives will be set free.

> Therefore thus says the Lord God: "I will also stretch out My hand against Edom ... and make it desolate. I will lay My vengeance on Edom by the hand of my people Israel, that they may do in Edom according to My anger, and according to My fury; and they shall know My vengeance," says the Lord GOD. (Ezekiel 25:13-14)

Israel will not wait to be destroyed by Iran. In the Six-Day War when Arab armies prepared to attack her, Israel destroyed the Egyptian air force before it could get off the ground. If Israel's very survival is threatened again she will strike Iran's nuclear facilities. In the Gulf War, we had a three-minute warning of incoming Iraqi scuds. In 2006, Hizballah rockets hit Haifa on Mount Carmel sixty seconds after they were launched. Today, the warnings are measured in seconds. We are in a "season of the sudden."

MUSLIM HARVEST

In the midst of God's coming judgment upon Islam, there are also wonderful prophecies of the ingathering of a mighty harvest of Muslim souls. The entire vision of Obadiah is a picture of God's judgment upon Edom. However, the prophet's vision concludes with this marvelous promise: "Then saviors ["those who have been saved"] shall come to Mount Zion to judge the mountains of Esau, and the kingdom shall be the Lord's" (Obadiah 21). I see *jihad* warriors transformed into radicals for Jesus, and leading their own people to salvation. The Lord is saving a remnant outside their native countries and many will return home to evangelize their own Muslim people.

THE TABERNACLE OF DAVID

The end-time "Elijah Company" will be used "to restore all things," as Jesus prophesied. One of the things that will be restored is "the tabernacle of David, which has fallen down" (Amos 9:11; Acts 15:16). The tent (or booth) of David was where the king communed with the Lord. David sat ("remained") before the Lord in the tent where the ark of His Presence stood (2 Samuel 7:18). Those walking in the legacy of Elijah will be consistently saturated with the presence of God. The restored tabernacle of David also represents the descendants of David, his spiritual offspring who are warriors and worshippers, like the psalmist king. Amos prophesied that God was going to raise up the ruined tabernacle, and beautify it and complete it as in "the days of old" (Amos 9:11).

Who will be the partakers of this restored intimacy with the Lord and the magnificent multi-ethnic worship released there? The biblical Jewish roots will be restored to the Church and Jews and Arabs will be worshipping Jesus together—as they are beginning to do here on Mount Carmel and in other places in Israel and along the Isaiah 19 "highway." Not only will Arabs and Jews be in God's "house of prayer for all nations" (Isaiah 56:7), but they will be joined by "all the Gentiles who are called by My name" (Amos 9:12). This is where we are heading. And who will accomplish this mighty end-time work? It will be Jehovah "who does this thing" (v. 12).

I have been blessed to taste of the restored tabernacle of David with brothers and sisters from the Palestinian Authority, Syria, Lebanon, Turkey, Saudi Arabia, Bahrain, the Arab Emirates, Kuwait, Sudan, Nigeria, Kosovo, Malaysia, and Indonesia. I have also worshiped with my Egyptian brothers in Cairo. No demonic power will stop the fulfillment of the Elijah legacy of the "one new man in Christ."

At the Jerusalem Council in Acts 15, the Jewish prophets Paul and Barnabas described how the Holy Spirit had been poured out upon the Gentiles. James ("Jacob") proclaimed that the prophesied restoration of the tabernacle of David had begun, "So that the rest of mankind may seek the LORD" (v. 17). The salvation of the house of Israel and the remnant out of Islam is an eternal longing in the heart of God. Isaac and Ishmael will be one in the Father's house. "Known to God from eternity are His works" (v. 18).

"SHALOM AND "SALAAM"

In June 2002, Karen and I ministered at the annual conference of the Pentecostal Church of Finland. Thirty thousand people attended from all over Finland. The theme was "Isaac and Ishmael"—reaching out to Jews and Muslims. At one meeting Karen was asked to sing in Hebrew, while a brother from Egypt was to sing in Arabic. However, the Egyptian was not able to obtain a visa to leave his country. When Karen was asked if she could sing another song in his place she told the organizers that she could sing something in Arabic.

At the meeting, which was held in two huge tents, Karen felt impressed by the Lord to sing the Arabic worship song, "Salaam" ("Peace"). The words are those spoken by Jesus, as recorded in John 14:27: "Peace I leave with you, My peace I give to you; not as the world gives do I give to you."

After Karen finished singing she sat down. A former Muslim from Israel came to the pulpit to share about his TV ministry to Muslims in Europe. With tears in his eyes he said, "I was so moved when the Jewish sister from Israel sang 'Salaam.' My friend from Egypt who could not come today was supposed to sing in Arabic. He is the one who wrote

'Salaam.'" (Karen did not know this when she chose to sing that particular song.

Then the ex-Muslim asked Karen to come up and stand with him in prayer for Jesus to reveal himself to Muslims and Jews. There was a large rugged wooden Cross next to the pulpit. Karen and the Arab man from Israel ("Isaac and Ishmael") stood together under the Cross and prayed over the throng of people. We were witnessing a "first fruits" fulfillment of Ephesians 2:14-15:

> For He Himself is our peace, who has made both one [Jew and non-Jew], and has broken down the middle wall of separation, having abolished in His flesh the enmity … so as to create in Himself one new man from the two, thus making peace.

THE TRUE CHURCH WILL BE IN THE FOREFRONT OF THIS
MIGHTY RESTORATION OF THE "ONE NEW MAN,"
AS WE ANSWER THE CALL TO PICK UP THE CLOAK OF ELIJAH
AND ACCEPT OUR END-TIME MANDATE AS FORERUNNERS
AND FINISHERS.

TRIBULATION AND TRIUMPH

The Scriptures describe future events in Israel and the Middle East. In this final chapter, I would like to conclude with my understanding of several major prophecies yet to be fulfilled. I believe that Israel will become a blessing in the midst of the Earth, even as deep darkness and global anti-Semitism increase. The body of Messiah in Israel and the nations will go through times of persecution. There will be an outpouring of the Holy Spirit on Mount Carmel and Galilee, even as northern Israel is attacked by a coalition of enemy forces in the Gog and Magog war.

A BLESSING IN THE MIDST OF THE EARTH

For fifteen years pastors from Israel and the Middle East have met annually to pray together. The vision for these meetings has been Isaiah 19:24-25:

> In that day Israel will be one of three with Egypt and Assyria—a blessing in the midst of the land [Earth], whom the LORD of hosts shall bless, saying, "Blessed is Egypt My people, and Assyria the work of My hands, and Israel My inheritance."

These gatherings are held in Turkey, Jordan, or on the island of Cyprus. I have been privileged to fellowship with brothers and sisters from Israel, Lebanon, Syria, Jordan, Egypt, Iraq, Sudan, Yemen, and Kuwait. Now, a younger "Joshua Generation" participate.

Once in a gathering in Cyprus, a pastor from Egypt shared with us the moving account of what happened to him when he was an Egyptian soldier in the Six-Day War of 1967. He told us that after the Egyptian army crossed the Suez Canal and invaded the Sinai Peninsula, a spirit of fear and confusion came upon them. There was a fierce battle with Israeli forces and many Egyptians fled. Over 25,000 Egyptian soldiers were killed.

He wandered alone in the desert trying to get back to Egypt. One night, he saw a light and started walking toward it. This light began to come toward him. There in the desert he had a dramatic encounter with Jesus.

After the war, he became a pastor, but refused to read the Old Testament because of his bitterness toward Israel. In 1973, when Egypt attacked Israel in the Yom Kippur War, he was called up to serve in the army again. At the conclusion of the war God spoke to him about Israel. The Lord told him that if he didn't love "My people Israel, you don't love Me." The pastor said he asked God to forgive him, and to his amazement received a great love for the Jewish people. From that time on he began to study the whole Bible. Now he is a leader of a Bible school and teaches his Egyptian students that God still has a covenant with the Jews and the land of Israel is their inheritance.

When the pastor concluded his moving testimony, a Jewish pastor from Jerusalem rose and walked over and hugged his Egyptian brother. Then the Messianic Jew said, "Brother, I also was on that battlefield in 1973 in the Israeli army."

Then a believing Druze sheik from Galilee stood up and joined the Egyptian and the Israeli. He looked at both of them and said, "I also was in the Israeli army and was on the same battlefield." They all embraced each other. Several years later, the Egyptian pastor gave his testimony to members of the Israeli Knesset in Jerusalem, and the story was on the front page of the Jerusalem Post.

"ONE NEW MAN"

We were observing the reality of the "one new man" in Christ reconciled to God and each other "in one body through the cross, thereby putting to death the enmity" (Ephesians 2:16).

These three former soldiers are a living demonstration of "the unity of the faith" (4:13) into which we are to "grow up." Jesus is coming back for His bride, composed of Jew and Gentile in one body. His deepest longings involve bringing His bride to completion.

AMBASSADORS FOR CHRIST

The fullness of the purposes of God will only be fulfilled when Israel embraces Yeshua, and the bride of Messiah is composed of Jews and Gentiles who are reconciled to each other and become the Israel of God. There is a pure, bridal anointing of new wine for the last days body of the "one new man."

In Cyprus we were witnessing a "first fruits" testimony of the Lord's ministry of reconciliation. "Now then, we are ambassadors for Christ, as though God were pleading through us: we implore you on Christ's behalf, be reconciled to God. For He made Him who knew no sin to be sin for us, that we might become the righteousness of God in Him" (2 Corinthians 5:20-21).

In the midst of the terrible darkness of the Middle East, there is a light in the desert. There is a great glory coming. "For it is God who commanded light to shine out of darkness, who has shone in our hearts to give the light of the knowledge of the glory of God in the face of Jesus Christ" (2 Corinthians 4:6).

Three soldiers who had fought in battle had been reconciled to God and each other. We took the Lord's Supper together as one body. We were tasting the new wine of the kingdom of God—a foretaste of His glory—a blessing in the midst of the Earth.

TWO OLIVE TREES

In the fourth chapter of the book of Zechariah, the prophet is awakened by an angel, and sees a vision of a solid gold lamp stand with two olive trees by it. Zechariah questions the angel about the two olive trees: "What are these, my lord?" (v. 4). The angel responds that a great mountain shall be removed and that the capstone of the temple will be brought forth with shouts of "Grace, grace to it" (v. 7). He also says that these events will occur not through human power: "Not by might nor by power, but by My Spirit, says the LORD of Hosts" (v. 6).

Two more times the prophet asks the angel about the two olive trees. In the vision Zechariah can now clearly see that golden oil is dripping from the branches of the olive trees into the receptacles of the golden lamp stand. Finally the angel answers the prophet: "These are the two anointed ones [lit. "sons of fresh oil"], who stand beside the Lord of the whole earth" (v. 14). Then the vision ends. To the prophet, the two olive trees would have represented Zerubbabel, the prince, and Joshua, the current high priest. As new covenant believers, we are called to be a kingdom of priests.

The prophet knew that the seven-branched lamp stand (*menorah*) was the symbol of the presence of Jehovah in the tabernacle and the temple. Today the menorah is the symbol of the nation of Israel, imprinted on Israeli public buildings and currency, and displayed in synagogues and many Jewish homes. In chapter 1 of Revelation the Apostle John had a vision of seven golden lamp stands with Jesus standing in the midst of them. Jesus tells John that the lamp stands represent His church: "The seven lampstands … are the seven churches" (v. 20).

Symbols in the Bible generally mean the same thing. By applying what Bible scholars call "the law of consistency," we can determine what the two olive trees represent for us at the end of the age. Twice the New Testament describes two olive trees. The best commentary on the Old Testament is the New Testament. In Romans, chapter 11, the Apostle Paul describes Gentile believers as "a wild olive tree" (v.17). His own Jewish people are "a cultivated olive tree" (v.24), and Gentile believers have been grafted into the olive tree of Israel. I see Zechariah's vision as pointing to an end-time body of the "one new man" of Jew and Gentile. Purified golden anointing oil will be poured out through Jewish and Gentile believers. Both are needed for the Lord's testimony in the last days.

God commanded that the lamp stand in the tabernacle was to be wrought from one piece of pure gold. (See Exodus 25:31-40.) It was of "beaten work," cut by chisels and hit hard by hammers. The Church will go through suffering, affliction, and great adversity in order to become the pure golden vessel exhibiting the fullness of the Lord Jesus. Today I believe the "sons of fresh (new) oil" are anointed Jews and Gentiles in one body. The Lord will have both in His Church. Those congregations who do not embrace God's purposes and heart for Israel will miss the fullness of this last days anointing. The "two witnesses" in Revelation 11 are also described as "two olive trees … standing before the God of the earth" (v. 4). Do they not represent Jews and Gentiles witnessing with great power at the end of the age?

As the nations turn against Israel, where will the Church stand? It is clear where Jesus stands.

REVIVAL IN THE MIDDLE EAST

A great spiritual awakening is taking place in the Middle East all along the Isaiah 19 "highway" (Isaiah 19:23-25). It is a highway of blessings and reconciliation between the descendants of Isaac and Ishmael, Jewish and Arab believers. It is also a vertical highway of praise, prayer, and proclamation. Hundreds of thousands have come to the Lord along this highway in a huge end-time harvest.

EGYPT

In Egypt, there has been an outpouring of the Holy Spirit among members of the ancient Coptic Church and other nominal Christians. The Copts trace their roots back to the Jewish Apostle Mark, who brought the gospel to Egypt. There have been large spontaneous meetings in various places in Cairo and other cities. Huge meetings in enormous caves have even been broadcast on satellite TV. The revival seems to be growing and spreading. Much of it is underground.

LEBANON

There are approximately ten thousand born-again followers of Messiah in Lebanon. We have a reliable report that over a thousand Lebanese MBBs (Muslim Background Believers) prayed to receive Jesus during the 2006 Hizballah war with Israel. A Lebanese friend of ours has personally led over one hundred Hizballah terrorists to Jesus. In March 2009, he testified to our congregation that he had a leg blown off when he stepped on a terrorist mine. After receiving a prosthetic leg, he returned to Lebanon to preach to his enemies.

TURKEY

Fifteen years ago, there were only about three hundred known believers in Turkey. Now there are approximately three thousand. There has been persecution and several believers have been martyred.

IRAQ

During the Saddam Hussein reign of terror, there were approximately five hundred known born-again believers in Iraq. Today, there are twenty new evangelical churches in Baghdad alone. Iraqis are also coming to the Lord by the hundreds in Europe and Sweden. There is a genuine revival among the Kurds in northern Iraq. Satellite Christian TV, which was illegal during Saddam's era, is now widely available in Iraq.

SYRIA, JORDAN, AND SAUDI ARABIA

Many Muslims are meeting Jesus in dreams and visions. In the last decade, the number of believers in Syria has grown from one thousand to approximately four thousand. Jordan now has about five thousand born-again Christians. Reliable sources believe there are over one hundred thousand secret MBBs in Saudi Arabia, although there is also severe persecution.

IRAN

Satellite TV is making a huge impact in Iran, even though it is still illegal. Informal sources tell us that there are about one million secret believers. More Muslims have come to the Lord in the last few years than in the last fourteen centuries! A Shiite cleric was outraged to hear that fifty Muslim girls per day are accepting Jesus.

Reliable sources report an incident in which two missionaries were driving over the border into Iran with a car full of Bibles in Parsi, the Iranian language. Their car broke down by the side of the road, and an elder of the village came out to meet them, asking, "Where are the books?" It turned out that the whole village had dreams of Jesus the night before, and Jesus told them that someone would bring them books the next day!

One Iranian Muslim woman watched the "Jesus" film on satellite TV. At the conclusion of the film, the TV presenter read Revelation 3:20: "Behold, I stand at the door and knock. If anyone hears My voice and opens the door, I will come in to him and dine with him, and he with Me" The woman went to her door, opened it and saw Jesus there! He came into her home and she received Him into her life.

We hear reports of thousands of Muslims coming to the Lord through dreams and visions, watching satellite TV, and listening to internet radio and TV broadcasts. Revival has begun in the Middle East.

(In another Muslim nation in Southeast Asia, Indonesia, churches are also growing rapidly. Karen and I have been blessed to minister in a church there of thirty thousand believers, mostly MBBs.)

PERSECUTION AND MARTYRDOM

Along with the great harvest of souls among Muslims, there is also terrible persecution. Believers have been martyred in Gaza, Turkey, Iran, Iraq, Saudi Arabia, Sudan, and Indonesia. Persecution and torture are commonplace in some of these Islamic nations.

THE RISING TIDE OF ANTI-SEMITISM

As the battle for Muslim souls rages, the enemy is waging a furious counter-attack. A flood of anti-Israel lies and propaganda is spewed continuously to a billion people through Arabic and Islamic media, schools, and mosques. The rapid advances in technology have made it much easier to disseminate misinformation. Satellite dishes, television, and the Internet are being used to inflame the Muslim world against Israel. For instance, consider this quote from Thomas L. Friedman in *The New York Times*, May 12, 2002, writing from Indonesia:

> At its best, the Internet can educate more people faster than any media tool we've ever had. At its worst, it can make people dumber faster than any media tool we've ever had. The lie that 4,000 Jews were warned not to go into the World Trade Center on September 11 was spread entirely over the Internet and is now thoroughly believed in the Muslim world. Because the Internet has an aura of "technology" surrounding it, the uneducated believe information from it even more. They don't realize that the Internet, at its ugliest, is just an open sewer: an electronic conduit for untreated, unfiltered information.

Mr. Friedman also reported about the Arab News Network (ANN), which is seen all over the Middle East. What he viewed, and what the Middle East watches on a daily basis, was non-stop footage of Israelis beating, dragging, and shooting Palestinians. There was no context or words, just pictures and military music designed to inflame the passions of Muslims against Israel.

This deluge of venomous hatred of Jews, Holocaust denial material, and incitement against the Jewish people is now widely available in books, magazines and DVDs in Europe. It will become much worse.

THE ALLIANCE OF ISLAMIC FASCISM AND "POST-CHRISTIAN" EUROPE

The extent of Islamic hatred toward Israel is shocking, but not surprising, given the demonic roots of this false religion. But the reappearance of ancient anti-Semitism and the growth of the current unholy alliance between Islamic fascism and the moral relativism, pacifism and appeasement of European governments is much more disturbing. Arab nations, along with Scandinavia, Europe and Britain now boycott Israeli products in an attempt to cripple the economy of Israel. Jews are afraid to walk the streets of Paris, and are warned not to vacation in France. Anti-Semitic cartoons reminiscent of the time of Mussolini appear in Italian newspapers. The new Germany places an embargo on military components for Israel's army in an attempt to punish Israel for its defensive actions against the swarms of Muslim homicide bombers who murder Jewish civilians.

When was the last time Germany embargoed products from the "Islamic Republic" (a contradiction in terms) of Iran, whose leaders openly dedicate themselves to the liquidation of Israel, as they develop long-range ballistic missiles and deny the Holocaust?

Synagogues are torched, ransacked, and plundered and Jewish cemeteries defaced in Western Europe, while British diplomats tell anti-Semitic jokes about Israel at cocktail parties. The news media is simply bringing out what is really in the heart of Europe.

Should Israel really listen to sanctimonious lecturing from France and Belgium and other countries that cooperated with Nazi Germany by bringing their Jewish citizens to railway cattle cars for delivery to death camps in Poland and Germany? Should Israel listen to pompous platitudes from politicians from Britain, the nation that turned away thousands of Jews from Mandatory Palestine and thereby consigned them to their death? Should Israel learn morality from "post-Christian" Europe and Scandinavia?

These nations are playing with fire—the fire of Jehovah's jealousy for His people.

I believe the same spirit of fear that was upon the European nations in the time of Nazi Germany is still there, but this time these apostate nations are afraid of Islam. This unholy alliance with evil is reminiscent of Shakespeare's words: "Politics makes strange bedfellows." Once again, Israel will be the "scapegoat" in what is being called "the new anti-Semitism."

We have seen that Islam is on a collision course with Israel and the true Church. Islam also embodies a major contradiction with the European "New World Order" of humanism and the New Age. A New Age animal rights activist recently murdered an anti-Islamic politician in Holland. Islamic fundamentalism is approaching a violent showdown with European pluralism. Europe itself is a prime target for the weapons of murderous Islamic terrorists. The "civilized paganism" of Europe is ripe for a great shaking.

TIMES OF PERSECUTION

The greatest revival in history is taking place in China today. Untold millions have come to faith in Jesus. In December 2001, the Chinese government sanctioned and launched another wave of attacks on the Chinese house church movement. Humble Chinese believers are being brutally persecuted, imprisoned, tortured, and martyred. The situation is equally appalling in North Korea. In the past decade, Islamic jihad has caused the death of at least one million Christians in southern Sudan. Thousands have been sold as slaves. Thousands of Christians have been martyred by Muslims in Indonesia.

The body of Messiah in Israel is also coming under persecution, not from Muslim militants, but from ultra-Orthodox Jews. For seventeen centuries, Orthodox Jews have read and believed the blasphemous legends about Jesus in the Talmud and other Jewish religious literature. Our Messiah is often referred to as "the Transgressor," "the hanged One," or "the accursed One," as well as the illegitimate bastard son of an unmarried immoral woman. An Israeli we were witnessing to told us that Jesus was not a Jew because he was illegitimate.

The works of Jesus have also been ascribed to witchcraft and Beelzebub, or Satan, and the gospels referred to as "the sinful and mischievous writing." Rabbinic hatred of His followers, especially Jewish believers, has labeled Messianic Jews as "apostates" and "worse than heathen." For centuries Orthodox Jewish liturgy has been recited daily, which curses the "Nazarenes" together with all apostates (Messianic Jews). One such prayer is that they be "suddenly destroyed, without hope, and be blotted from the Book of Life!"

Centuries ago, Jesus' precious name, in Hebrew "Yeshua" ("He will save"), was changed to "Yeshu," an acronym taken from the words which mean, "Let Him, His name and memory be blotted out forever." Today, in Israel, He is still referred to as "Yeshu." I know of no finer source to quote on this painful subject than scholar David Baron, who was raised as an Orthodox Jew. After his life-changing encounter with Jesus, he became one of our greatest theologians and prophets in the early years of the twentieth century. He states:

> No person in the history of the Jews has provoked such deep-seated abhorrence as He who came only to bless them, and who even on the Cross prayed, "Father, forgive them, for they know not what they do." When on Earth, at the end of His three and a half years of ministry among them they finally rejected Him, their hatred was intense and mysterious. "Away with this man; release unto us Barabbas … crucify Him, crucify Him!" was their cry. And all through the centuries no name has provoked such intense abhorrence among

the Jews as the name of Jesus. (David Baron, *Types, Psalms, and Prophecies*)

MISREPRESENTING JESUS

Jewish repulsion towards Jesus and His followers can also be traced back to the terrible sufferings the Jewish people have endured at the hands of "Christians." A gross misrepresentation of the true Jesus, the Jewish Messiah, has been presented to the Jewish people through virulent and deadly Christian anti-Semitism, beginning as early as the third century A.D. (One of the best documented histories of this topic is Dr. Michael Brown's, *Our Hands Are Stained With Blood*.)

Isaiah prophesied that Jesus would be the One "whom man despises" and "whom the nation abhors" (Isaiah 49:7). This prophecy clearly describes the attitude of men in general who show contempt for Him and reject His gospel by living as if there never was a Messiah who died for our sins. But Jesus is also "[He] whom the nation [Israel] abhors." This prophecy uttered centuries before His first coming is so particular and specific, it sounds like a terse account of Jewish history written after the events it describes. Although Orthodox Jews only make up approximately 15% of the total Jewish population in Israel, the city of Jerusalem is rapidly becoming an ultra-Orthodox Jewish city. Over 85% of the Jewish school children in Jerusalem now attend religious schools. The Orthodox believe Jerusalem belongs to them. As a result, many secular Jerusalemites have been moving to Tel Aviv.

PERSECUTION IN ISRAEL

One teenager who was distributing invitations to receive the "Yeshua" video was viciously attacked by an enraged Orthodox Jew. The boy was stabbed six times and survived only by the grace of God. The Jerusalem police did little to apprehend the assailant. In May 2002, about one hundred ultra-Orthodox Jews forced their way into the International Convention Center in Jerusalem during a Christian conference. *The Jerusalem Post*, May 14, 2002, reported: "'The mob stormed the platform and threw a stink bomb into the audience,' said conference organizers, who also claimed sound equipment was stolen. Police said they are investigating." Several people were slightly injured.

Recently, the teenage son of a Messianic leader found a Purim gift basket on their front porch. When he opened it, the package exploded. He was very seriously injured, but miraculously survived. Ultra-Orthodox Jews are suspected, but the police have done little to find and arrest the would-be murderers.

Also, recently occurring was an incident of New Testament Scriptures being publically burned by Orthodox Jews.

I believe that the body of Messiah in Israel will enter into times of much greater persecution, as Jesus predicted. "Now a brother will deliver up brother to death, and a father his child; and children will rise up against parents and cause them to be put to death. And you will be hated by all for My name's sake. But he who endures to the end will be saved. When they persecute you in this city, flee to another. For assuredly, I say to you, you will not have gone through the cities of Israel before the Son of Man comes" (Matthew 10:21-23). Both persecution and revival are coming to the cities of Israel.

REVIVAL IN GALILEE AND CARMEL

In the century after Elisha's death, the Assyrians over-ran northern Israel. "Galilee of the Nations" was the first area to fall beneath the yoke of the Assyrian onslaught. Most of the Israelites were either killed or deported. Assyria was renowned for its cruelty and savagery toward its enemies. Samaria was resettled with Assyrians and Babylonians, then part of the Assyrian empire. For centuries Galilee was considered rural and backward and held in disrepute and contempt. But God in His wisdom was about to compensate for this dishonor to His people and land. The prophet Isaiah was the first to see the rays of Immanuel's light breaking through the darkness of northern Israel. "Galilee ["circuit"] of the Gentiles" (Isaiah 9:1) may also be understood as referring to the circuit of the Gentile nations, or the world at large. This phrase has broader implications than just northern Israel, and refers to something of far wider range. The Galilean ministries of Elijah, Elisha and Jesus pointed outward toward the Gentile world, even as Israel is called to be a "light to the nations." "Galilee of the Nations" is the name of a major record company that produces and distributes Messianic worship music in Israel and the nations.

The "great light" that was to shine on "those who dwelt in the land of the shadow of death" (v. 2) was the light which radiated from the resurrection of Messiah—the Man from Galilee. On the night He was betrayed Jesus told His Galilean disciples: "But after I have been raised, I will go before you to Galilee" (Matthew 26:32).

On resurrection morning at the empty tomb in Jerusalem, the Angel of the Lord told the Galilean Mary Magdalene: "He is not here; for He is risen … and indeed He is going before you unto Galilee; there you will see Him. Behold, I have told you" (Matthew 28:6-7). On that same resurrection day, the risen Savior himself told His disciples: "Do not be afraid. Go and tell My brethren to go to Galilee, and there they will see Me" (28:10). It was to these men of Galilee, on a mountain in Galilee, that the great commission was given. "The eleven disciples went away into Galilee, to the mountain which Jesus had appointed for them" (v. 16). Was it Tabor or Carmel? "And Jesus came and spoke to them, saying, 'All authority has been given to Me in heaven and on earth. Go therefore and make disciples of all the nations, baptizing them in the name of the Father and of the Son and of the Holy Spirit, teaching them to observe all things I have commanded you; and lo, I am with you always, even to the end of the age'" (v. 18-20). Jesus' first thirty years were spent in Galilee where He then began to preach and perform His first miracles. The greater part of His ministry was in the vicinity of the Sea of Galilee, and most of His disciples were simple Galileans. Elijah's last appearance was also in Galilee at the Lord's Transfiguration. The Galilean fishermen Peter, James and John saw the glorified Elijah, even as Elisha had seen his fiery exit. When the three disciples questioned Jesus about Elijah's miraculous appearance, Jesus responded that, "Indeed, Elijah is coming first and will restore all things" (Matthew 17:11). Jesus was not talking about John the Baptist who had already been martyred. Rather, I believe He was prophesying restoration of an Elijah-type company in our own day both in Israel and the nations.

The final words of Jesus as He was about to return to glory were addressed to the "men of Galilee" (v. 11), as He told them: "You shall receive power when the Holy Spirit has come upon you; and you shall be witnesses to Me in Jerusalem, and in all Judea and Samaria, and to the end of the earth" (v. 8). The Galileans were charged to take the gospel "to the ends of the earth!" This is our continuing call on Mount Carmel today. A great harvest is coming and we are to make disciples, release them in Israel, and also send them as a light to the nations.

THE COMING WAR

Most of the activity of Elijah and Elisha we have chronicled took place on "the mountains of Israel" in and around the valley of Jezreel ("God sows"). Elijah and Elisha sowed to the Spirit, and of the Spirit reaped a great harvest of souls. Ahab and Jezebel sowed to their flesh and demonic powers, and reaped a harvest of evil, corruption and death. I have come to believe that the Elijah legacy presents us with a foreshadowing of what is happening and about to happen in northern Israel today.

JENIN—A PRELUDE?

In April 2002, the whole world focused on a little town on the southern edge of the Jezreel Valley, called Jenin. Israel gave this town to the Palestinian Authority as part of the Oslo peace accords. In a fierce seven-day battle, twenty-three Israeli soldiers and about fifty Palestinian gunmen died in Jenin. Seven non-combatant Palestinians were also killed there.

In the preceding month of March, one hundred and thirty-two Israelis (mostly civilians) had been killed in twenty-four terrorist attacks. Almost two-dozen suicide bombers had come from Jenin. The invasion of Jenin by the Israeli Defense Forces, part of "Operation Defensive Shield," was an attempt to eliminate the major terrorist base in northern Israel. Would any other sovereign nation have done less?

Israel could have simply bombed the town, as America had done only months earlier in Afghanistan, where hundreds of civilians died as "collateral damage." Instead, the IDF invaded Jenin with tanks and infantry, most of whom were reservists who had been called from their jobs into active duty. The son of a pastor friend of ours was among the Israeli troops. The soldiers used loud speakers warning civilians to leave. Most non-combatants did leave.

Searching for terrorists, the Israeli forces went from house to house (most of which were booby-trapped) at great risk to themselves. Four warehouses filled with explosives were destroyed, along with more than a dozen other bomb factories. Tanks and bulldozers demolished homes which had served as nests of terrorists, and which had been purposely placed among the civilian population. Hizballah in Lebanon and Hamas in Gaza use the same strategy. After a week of fierce fighting, the major terrorist training, equipping, and sending center in northern Israel had been destroyed. Then the Israeli forces withdrew.

This was not the first battle in Jenin. In the 1930's, the town was already well-known as an Arab terrorist training camp. In the summer of 1938, a Muslim terrorist assassinated the British district commissioner. The suspected assassin was killed by British troops, and the British authorities decided that "a large portion of the town should be blown up" as punishment. In that Jenin operation , local Arabs were forced to drive "mine-sweeping taxis ahead of British vehicles where Arab terrorists were believed to have planted mines in order to reduce British casualties." Official British policy was justified because "British lives were being lost," and the British were being confronted "not with a chivalrous opponent playing the game according to the rules, but with gangsters and murderers" (taken from documents declassified by the British government in 1989). Yet Britain was one of the loudest voices condemning Israel's eight-day incursion into Jenin in 2002.

Like much of the Jezreel Valley, Jenin has a continuing history of hatred, violence, and bloodshed. For three thousand years, foreign armies have fought in this valley. And the Bible promises that a final fulfillment of God's prophetic word will yet be enacted in and around Jezreel.

GOG AND MAGOG

In chapters 38 and 39 of the Book of Ezekiel, we have been given an end-time prophecy about northern Israel. This unfulfilled prophecy describes a time when many Jewish people have been re-gathered to the mountains of Israel and "dwell safely" in un-walled towns (Ezekiel 38:8). At God's appointed time a huge army made up of a confederacy of different nations led by "Gog, the prince of Rosh" ("head"), will invade Israel from the north. The intention of this coalition will be to destroy the restored nation. The invaders will not know that the God of Israel will have brought them. "I ["Adonai Jehovah"] will turn you around, put hooks into your jaws, and lead you out, with all your army" (v. 4). The Lord says that this mighty army "will come up against My people Israel like a cloud, to cover the land. It will be in the latter days ... so that the nations may know Me, when I am hallowed in you, O Gog, before their eyes" (v. 16). (Could the "cloud" be an indication of biological or chemical warheads?) The Lord tells us His purpose. Nations will know Him when He is revealed in the midst of this awesome event.

Jehovah promises to release His fury, jealousy, and wrath upon the invading army. There will be a tremendous shaking in the land, and as Israel attempts to defend itself, God will intervene and rain down "great hailstones, fire and brimstone" (v. 22). The result will be the utter destruction of the foreign forces. God will magnify himself and will be "known in the eyes of many nations. Then they shall know that I am the LORD" (v. 23).

The Lord continues this frightening prophecy by saying He "will give Gog a burial place there in Israel, the valley of those who pass by east of the sea" (Ezekiel 39:11). This could be a reference to the Jordan Valley or to the Valley of Jezreel. Whichever valley it is will become a huge burial ground, called "the valley of Hamon Gog ["the multitude of Gog"] " (v. 11). The Lord concludes His prophecy by again proclaiming His purposes for the destruction of the enemies of Israel. "I will set My glory among the nations ["Gentiles"]; all the nations shall see My judgment which I have executed, and My hand which I have laid upon them" (v. 21).

This event will not only impact all the nations, but will usher in a great revival in Israel. "So the house of Israel shall know that I am the LORD their God from that day forward" (v. 22). As a result of the Gog and Magog war, God also promises another massive "aliyah," or re-gathering of the rest of the Jews from the Diaspora. "Now I will bring back the captives of Jacob, and have mercy on the whole house of Israel; and I will be jealous for My holy name" (v. 25). To conclude this prophecy Jehovah makes a final declaration to His people, " 'And I will not hide My face from them anymore; for I shall have poured out My Spirit on the house of Israel,' says the Lord GOD" (v. 29). Retribution and revival are coming to northern Israel.

THE YOM KIPPUR WAR

In October 1973, Israel was relatively relaxed and at peace as the nation entered its annual observance of Yom Kippur, the Day of Atonement—the holiest and quietest day of the year when all shops and restaurants are closed and no one drives. Suddenly the worst of Israel's wars for survival erupted with massive enemy attacks from the north (Syria) and the south (Egypt). Israel was taken by surprise as soldiers and reservists were rushed to the Golan Heights to meet the scores of invading Syrian tanks. Inexplicably, Syrian troops suddenly became confused when they could have easily invaded Tiberias and Galilee. Syrian tanks simply stopped on the Golan. Israel barely survived the initial attack, but recovered and drove the enemy armies back to Damascus and Cairo. Many Israelis admitted that God had intervened.

I have been told by Israelis that people in the land, at that time, began talking about "Gog and Magog." Ezekiel 38 and 39 became a topic of discussion in schools and even in Israeli media. A retired Israeli friend of mine, who fought in the Yom Kippur War and still volunteers for guard duty on Mount Gilboa, recently asked me about Gog and Magog and the Messiah. I told him that Israel will be attacked by a massive enemy coalition coming from the north. I explained to my friend that as Israel begins to defend herself God will intervene and destroy the invading army in the Jezreel Valley which runs past Mount Gilboa. He stared at me for a moment, then said, "I don't believe it. Where was God in the Holocaust? No one will help the Jews. We must defend ourselves." This is the prevailing secular sentiment today. The nation feels alone. There is much controversy concerning the prophecy of Ezekiel 38 and 39. I think we should be very careful about dogmatic positions. Ezekiel's symbolic and apocalyptic imagery could possibly point to a Middle East missile war. Attempting to date the exact time of this cataclysmic event, and to identify the names of the modern nations involved has led to widely differing views and factions. For me, a more interesting historic fact and prophetic pattern is that many of the invasions of Israel have come from the north. Babylon and Persia (Iraq and Iran today), Assyria, Greece, Rome, Crusaders, France, and Turkey (the Ottoman Empire), all came from the north.

In the war described by Ezekiel, nations from different geographic locations will attack Israel from the north. At the moment when all seems lost and Israel is about to be destroyed by this alliance of evil, the God of Israel will supernaturally intervene. The attacking confederation will be destroyed on "the mountains of Israel."

God will release the forces of nature against Gog and his allies. A great "earthquake" or shaking will devastate the foreign army. Dissension and confusion will descend upon these hostile forces (Ezekiel 38:19-21). There will evidently be some kind of atomic or nuclear missile attack, described as "great hailstones, fire, and brimstone" (v. 22) or supernatural fire from Heaven. Often in Israel's history, the enemies' weapons have backfired upon them. It will happen again as they destroy each other. For instance, a missile could fall short of its intended mark and explode in the midst of their own forces. (In the Yom Kippur War, Syrian troops actually shot down some of their own Russian MIGs with Russian surface-to-air missiles!)

Iran now has "Shihab 3" missiles capable of hitting Israel and Europe, and is developing the "Shihab 5" to bring the United States into its range as well. Russia continues to assist Iran to build its nuclear reactors. Will the nuclearization of the Middle East be halted? Will the U.S. and other Western nations keep the Middle East from turning into a forest of nuclear-tipped missiles? If not, we are entering a season of nuclear terror, and nuclear brinkmanship for the first time since the Cold War ended. (See *The Jerusalem Report*, "Before It's Too Late," July 29, 2002.)

In July 2006, the first Hizballah rocket hit Mount Carmel near one of my prayer places, just up the mountain from our House of Victory. We had to move the staff and students out of House of Victory during this Hizballah war. In September 2007, Israel bombed a Syrian nuclear reactor, which was being built by North Korea. In May 2009, Iran successfully tested a surface to surface missile capable of striking Israel, parts of Europe and American military installations in the Middle East.

A FINAL GATHERING

After Ezekiel's vivid account of the aftermath of the Gog and Magog war, he also described God's purposes in orchestrating these events. The supernatural destruction of these invading forces will not only result in a mighty harvest of souls, but will also bring a final ingathering of Jewish people back to their biblical homeland. "Therefore thus says the Lord GOD: 'Now I will bring back the captives of Jacob, and have mercy on the whole house of Israel; and I will be jealous for My holy name'" (Ezekiel 39:25). As this great exodus returns to the land God declares: "'And I will not hide My face from them anymore; for I shall have poured out My Spirit on the house of Israel,' says the Lord GOD" (v. 29).

A VILLAGE OF PRIESTS ON MOUNT CARMEL

Our congregational worship center is strategically situated on the highest point of the Mount Carmel range. Near our property was an army radar station, which was used to track incoming Iraqi missiles during the Gulf War. Whoever controls Mount Carmel will have a decided military advantage over southern Galilee and the Jezreel Valley below.

In our position on top of Mount Carmel we are called to be a "village of priests," those who minister to the Lord in worship and strategic intercession. Adjacent to the worship center, in our Or HaCarmel ("Light of Carmel") Ministry Center, disciples are being trained in the Dor Elisha ("Elisha Generation") internship program. Also housed at Or HaCarmel is our women's shelter, where we are ministering to those He sends to us, as a "city of refuge." Since 2006, we have been housing Sudanese and Eritrean refugees, mostly mothers and children. (In total, Israel has taken in 10,000 Sudanese and Eritrean refugees.)

THE ELIJAH MANDATE

Elijah's first recorded words, "As the LORD God of Israel lives, before whom I stand ... " (1 Kings 17:1), describe a man who was in right standing with Jehovah. "Stand" means that Elijah lived a lifestyle of abiding, dwelling with his Lord, who was his source, nourisher, and sustainer. The legacy he left behind challenges us to emulate his life of communion, consecration, compassion, community, courage, covenant, and total commitment to our God. His mandate to us is that we, too, like Elisha, should pick up the Elijah mantle and stand against the deepening darkness of these end times.

ELIJAH'S PRAYER

The God of Elijah is turning His attention to the restored nation of Israel. The Lord continues to answer the cry of the prophet of fire. Let us take our place as prophetic intercessors as we join our voices with Jesus, our Great High Priest, and with the heart cry of Elijah:

> LORD God of Abraham, Isaac and Israel let it be known this day that You are God in Israel.... Hear me, O LORD, hear me, that this people may know that You are the LORD God, and that You have turned their hearts back to You again. (1 Kings 18:36-37)

JESUS, WE BESEECH YOU, RELEASE THE ELIJAH LEGACY NOW.

Epilogue

Several years ago I was praying at one of my "secret places" on Mount Carmel, about two hundred meters down a path from the place where the Lord dramatically visited me in the rental car in the 1980s. I was actually standing on the roof of an abandoned British machine-gun bunker from bygone Mandate days. The concrete bunker is built into a promontory on Mount Carmel overlooking the Mediterranean. On this beautiful clear spring morning, I watched Israeli guided missile cruisers slowly patrolling the Haifa coast and port. Three military helicopters flew by, evidently returning from guarding the Lebanese border. I was struck by the contrast of the bunker, helicopters, and the warships against the legendary beauty of Carmel cloaked with multi-colored spring wildflowers and the shimmering emerald sea stretched out before me. I sensed that I was observing the calm before the storm. The still, small voice of the Lord came to me, saying,

> Be still, and know that I am God;
> I will be exalted among the nations,
> I will be exalted in the earth!
> The LORD of hosts is with us;
> The God of Jacob is our refuge.
> (Psalm 46:10-11)

SELECTED BIBLIOGRAPHY

Austin-Sparks, T.   *What is Man?*
                        Pratt Printing, Indianapolis, IN
                        The School of Christ
                        World Challenge, Lindale, TX

Baron, David   *Types, Psalms, and Prophecies*
                        Hodder & Stoughton, London, 1907

Bevere, John   *Breaking Intimidation*
                        Creation House, FL, 1998

Brown, Michael L.   *Our Hands are Stained with Blood*
                        Destiny Image, Shippensburg, PA, 1992

Croft, Jim   *The Muslim Masquerade*
                        Boca Raton, FL, 2002

Davis, David   *Valley of Trouble, Mountain of Hope*
                        Destiny Image,1999
                        (Also titled *The Road to Carmel*)

Grant, George   *The Blood of the Moon*
                        Thomas Nelson, Nashville, TN, 2001

Herschel, Abraham T.   *The Prophets*
                        Prince Press, Peabody, MA, 1999

Orr, James, (Ed.) | *International Standard Bible Encyclopedia, Vol. III.* Eerdmans, Grand Rapids, MI

Jackson, John Paul | *Unmasking the Jezebel Spirit* Streams Publishing, North Sutton, NH, 2002

Josephus, Flavius | *The Works of Josephus* Peabody, MA, Hendrickson, 1988

Keil, C.F. and Delitzsch, F. | *Commentary on the Old Testament, Vol. III.* Eerdmans

Lockyer, Herbert | *All the Men of the Bible* Zondervan, Grand Rapids, MI, 1958

Pawson, David | *When Jesus Returns* Hodder & Stoughton, London, 1995

Peters, Joan | *From Time Immemorial* Harper, NY, 1985

Pink, A. W. | *The Life of Elijah* Banner of Truth, Carlisle, PA 1956

Pryce-Jones, David | *The Closed Circle* Grafton Books, London, 1990

Redman, Matt | *The Unquenchable Worshipper* Kingsway, Eastbourne, UK, 2001

Shorrosh, Dr. Anis | *Islam Revealed* Thomas Nelson, Nashville, TN, 1988

Stern, David H.	*Jewish New Testament Commentary* JNTC, Clarksville, MD, 1992
Taylor, William M.	*Elijah the Prophet* Harper, NY, 1876
Tozer, A. W.	*The Knowledge of the Holy* Harper & Row, CA, 1961
Twain, Mark	*Innocents Abroad* London, 1881

PERIODICALS

Crisis Update October 3, 2001

The Jerusalem Post May 14, 2002

The Jerusalem Report January 28, 2002; July 29, 2002

The New York Times May 12, 2002

Prophecy Today July/August, 2002

USA Today October 30, 2001

The Washington Post March 31, 2002

ISRAEL TODAY

APPENDIX

Twenty Facts About Israel and the Middle East

by William Bennett, Jack Kemp, Jeane Kirkpatrick
May 22, 2002

The world's attention has been focused on the Middle East. We are confronted daily with scenes of carnage and destruction. Can we understand such violence? Yes, but only if we come to the situation with a solid grounding in the facts of the matter—facts that too often are forgotten, if ever they were learned. Below are twenty facts that we think are useful in understanding the current situation, how we arrived here, and how we might eventually arrive at a solution.

ROOTS OF THE CONFLICT

1. When the United Nations proposed the establishment of two states in the region—one Jewish, one Arab—the Jews accepted the proposal and declared their independence in 1948. The Jewish state constituted only 1/6 of one percent of what was known as "the Arab world." The Arab states, however, rejected the UN plan and since then have waged war against Israel repeatedly, both all-out wars and wars of terrorism and attrition. In 1948, five Arab armies invaded Israel in an effort to eradicate it. Jamal Hussenini of the Arab Higher Committee

spoke for many in vowing to soak "the soil of our beloved country with the last drop of our blood."'

2. The Palestine Liberation Organization (PLO) was founded in 1964—three years before Israel controlled the West Bank and Gaza. The PLO's declared purpose was to eliminate the State of Israel by means of armed struggle. To this day, the website of Yasser Arafat's Palestinian Authority (PA) claims that the entirety of Israel is "occupied" territory. It is impossible to square this with the PLO and PA assertions to Western audiences that the root of the conflict is Israel's occupation of the West Bank and Gaza.

3. The West Bank and Gaza (controlled by Jordan and Egypt from 1948 to 1967) came under Israeli control during the Six Day War of 1967 that started when Egypt closed the Straits of Tiran and Arab armies amassed on Israel's borders to invade and liquidate the state. It is important to note that during their 19-year rule, neither Jordan nor Egypt had made any effort to establish a Palestinian state on those lands. Just before the Arab nations launched their war of aggression against the State of Israel in 1967, Syrian Defense Minister (later President) Hafez Assad stated, "Our forces are now entirely ready to initiate the act of liberation itself, and to explode the Zionist presence in the Arab homeland. The time has come to enter into a battle of annihilation." On the brink of the 1967 war, Egyptian President Gamal Nassar declared, "Our basic objective will be the destruction of Israel."

4. Because of their animus against Jews, many leaders of the Palestinian cause have long supported our [American] enemies. The Grand Mufti of Jerusalem allied himself with Adolf Hitler during WWII. Yasser Arafat, chairman of the PLO and president of the PA, has repeatedly targeted and killed Americans. In 1973, Arafat ordered the execution of Cleo

Noel, the American ambassador to the Sudan. Arafat was very closely aligned with the Soviet Union and other enemies of the United States throughout the Cold War. In 1991, during the Gulf War, Arafat aligned himself with Saddam Hussein, whom he praised as "the defender of the Arab nation, of Muslims, and of free men everywhere."

5. Israel has, in fact, returned most of the land that it captured during the 1967 war and right after that war offered to return all of it in exchange for peace and normal relations; the offer was rejected. As a result of the 1978 Camp David accords—in which Egypt recognized the right of Israel to exist and normal relations were established between the two countries—Israel returned the Sinai desert, a territory three times the size of Israel and 91 percent of the territory Israel took control of in the 1967 war.

6. In 2000, as part of negotiations for a comprehensive and durable peace, Israel offered to turn over all but the smallest portion of the remaining territories to Yasser Arafat. But Israel was rebuffed when Arafat walked out of Camp David and launched the current Intifada.

7. Yasser Arafat has never been less than clear about his goals—at least not in Arabic. On the very day that he signed the Oslo accords in 1993—in which he promised to renounce terrorism and recognize Israel, he addressed the Palestinian people on Jordanian television and declared that he had taken the first step "in the 1974 plan." This was a thinly veiled reference to the "phased plan," according to which any territorial gain was acceptable as a means toward the ultimate goal of Israel's destruction.

8. The recently deceased Faisal al-Husseini, a leading Palestinian spokesman, made the same point in 2001 when he

declared that the West Bank and Gaza represented only "22 percent of Palestine" and that the Oslo process was a "Trojan Horse." He explained, "When we are asking all the Palestinian forces and factions to look at the Oslo Agreement and at other agreements as 'temporary' procedures, or phased goals, this means that we are ambushing the Israelis and cheating them." The goal, he continued, was "the liberation of Palestine from the river to the sea," i.e. the Jordan River to the Mediterranean Sea—all of Israel.

9. To this day, the Fatah wing of the PLO (the "moderate" wing that was founded and is controlled by Arafat himself) has as its official emblem the entire state of Israel covered by two rifles and a hand grenade—another fact that belies the claim that Arafat desires nothing more than the West Bank and Gaza.

10. While criticism of Israel is not necessarily the same as "anti-Semitism," it must be remembered that the Middle East press is, in fact, rife with anti-Semitism. More than fifteen years ago the eminent scholar Bernard Lewis could point out that: "The demonization of Jews [in Arabic literature] goes further than it had ever done in Western literature, with the exception of Germany during the period of Nazi rule." Since then, and through all the years of the "peace process," things have become much worse. Depictions of Jews in Arab and Muslim media are akin to those of Nazi Germany, and medieval blood libels—including claims that Jews use Christian and Muslim blood in preparing their holiday foods have become prominent and routine. One example is a sermon broadcast on PA television where Sheik Ahmad Halabaya stated, "They [the Jews] must be butchered and killed, as Allah the Almighty said: 'Fight them: Allah will torture them at your hands.' Have no mercy on the Jews, no matter where they are, in any

country. Fight them, wherever they are. Wherever you meet them, kill them."

11. Over three-quarters of Palestinians approve of suicide bombings—an appalling statistic but in light of the above facts, an unsurprising one.

THE STATE OF ISRAEL

12. There are 21 Arab countries in the Middle East and only one Jewish state, Israel, which is also the only democracy in the region.

13. Israel is the only country in the region that permits citizens of all faiths to worship freely and openly. Twenty percent of Israeli citizens are not Jewish.

14. While Jews are not permitted to live in many Arab countries, Arabs are granted full citizenship and have the right to vote in Israel. Arabs are also free to become members of the Israeli parliament (the Knesset). In fact, several Arabs have been democratically elected to the Knesset and have been serving there for years. Arabs living in Israel have more rights and are freer than most Arabs living in Arab countries.

15. Israel is smaller than the state of New Hampshire and is surrounded by nations hostile to her existence. Some peace proposals including the recent Saudi proposal demand withdrawal from the entire West Bank, which would leave Israel 9 miles wide at its most vulnerable point.

16. The oft-cited UN Resolution 242 (passed in the wake of the 1967 war) does not, in fact, require a complete withdrawal from the West Bank. As legal scholar Eugene Rostow put it, "Resolution 242, which as Undersecretary

of State for political affairs between 1966 and 1969 I helped produce, calls on the parties to make peace and allows Israel to administer the territories it occupied in 1967 until 'a just and lasting peace in the Middle East' is achieved. When such a peace is made, Israel is required to withdraw its armed forces 'from territories' it occupied during the Six Day War—not from 'the' territories nor from 'all' the territories, but from some of the territories."

17. Israel has, of course, conceded that the Palestinians have legitimate claims to the disputed territories and is willing to engage in negotiations on the matter. As noted above, Israeli Prime Minister Ehud Barak offered almost all of the territories to Arafat at Camp David in 2000.

18. Despite claims that the Israeli settlements in the West Bank are the obstacle to peace, Jews lived there for centuries before being massacred or driven out by invading Arab armies in 1948-49. And contrary to common misperceptions, Israeli settlements—which constitute less than two percent of the territories—almost never displace Palestinians.

19. The area of the West Bank includes some of the most important sites in Jewish history, among them Hebron, Bethlehem and Jericho. East Jerusalem, often cited as an "Arab city" or "occupied territory," is the site of Judaism's holiest monument. While under Arab rule (1948-67), this area was entirely closed to Jews. Since Israel took control, it has been open to people of all faiths.

20. Finally, let us consider the demand that certain territories in the Muslim world must be off-limits to Jews. This demand is from a piece of Hitler's proclamation that German land had to be "Judenrein" (empty of Jews). Arabs can live freely throughout Israel, and as full citizens. Why should Jews

be forbidden to live or to own land in an area like the West Bank simply because the majority of people is Arab?

In sum, a fair and balanced portrayal of the Middle East will reveal that one nation stands far above the others in its commitment to human rights and democracy as well as in its commitment to peace and mutual security. That nation is Israel.

(Used with permission of Empower America)

For more information or additional ministry materials by
David Davis

Website: www.carmel-assembly.org.il
Email: info@carmel-assembly.org.il
PO Box 7004 Haifa, 31070 Israel